Becoming a teacher
Issues in secondary teaching

Edited by
Justin Dillon and
Meg Maguire

Open University Press
Buckingham · Philadelphia

Open University Press
Celtic Court
22 Ballmoor
Buckingham
MK18 1XW

and
1900 Frost Road, Suite 101
Bristol, PA 19007, USA

First Published 1997

A catalogue record of this book is available from the British Library

ISBN   0 335 198236 (pb)   0 335 198244 (hb)

Library of Congress Cataloging-in-Publication Data
Becoming a teacher : issues in secondary teaching / edited by Justin
   Dillon and Meg Maguire.
      p.   cm.
   Includes bibliographical references and index.
   ISBN 0–335–19824–4 (cl : alk. paper). — ISBN 0–335–19823–6 (pb :
alk. paper)
   1. High school teaching—Great Britain.   2. High school teaching—
Social aspects—Great Britain.   3. Classroom management—Great
Britain.   4. Curriculum planning—Great Britain.   I. Dillon.
Justin.   II. Maguire. Meg.
LB1737.G7B43   1997
373.1102′0941—dc21   96–51587
                                                                            CIP

Typeset by Graphicraft Typesetters Ltd, Hong Kong
Printed by Great Britain by Redwood Books, Trowbridge

Becoming a teacher

Contents

Notes on contributors

All the contributors work in the School of Education, King's College London unless otherwise indicated.

Chris Abbott taught in special schools and in mainstream schools for 16 years before working as an Advisory Teacher for information technology (IT) and special education needs (SEN). He later became Director of the Inner London Educational Computing Centre and, when ILECC closed, moved to take up a research post at King's.

Stephen J. Ball is Professor of Education and has been involved in research into educational policy developments for a considerable period, publishing widely. He is the editor of the *Journal of Education Policy*.

Paul Black is Emeritus Professor of Science Education at King's. He was chair of the Government's Task Group on Assessment and Testing, Deputy Chairman of the National Curriculum Council and is an expert adviser to major educational projects in Western Europe and the USA including the OECDs main educational study on *The Curriculum Redefined*.

Jo Boaler has worked as an anti-racism and special educational needs officer for the NUT, a secondary school mathematics teacher and a researcher and lecturer. Her main interests include under-achievement in mathematics education, the application and relevance of school mathematics, equity issues and setting and mixed ability teaching.

Kelly Coate Bignell is studying for an MPhil/PhD at the Institute of Education, University of London, supported by the Economic and Social Research Council. Her thesis is on the history of Women's Studies as an academic subject area in the UK. She serves on the Executive Committee of the Women's Studies Network Association (UK).

Alan Cribb joined King's in 1990 having previously worked for the Centre for Social Ethics and Policy and the Department of Epidemiology and

Social Oncology, University of Manchester. His research interests include moral and political philosophy and applied ethics.

Justin Dillon taught in London schools for nine years including a spell as an adviser. Since joining King's he has worked in Nigeria and Indonesia and is a governor of a primary school in South London. He was Deputy Course Director for the PGCE for several years and was course organiser of the part-time PGCE from its inception.

Bob Fairbrother has taught science in a number of schools, has been an examiner and awarder for the GCSE and A level, and was a member of the SEAC/SCAA science subject committee. He has done research into problems of assessment, and has lectured widely at home and abroad.

Sharon Gewirtz has been researching education policy for nine years and has published extensively in the field. Her current research, funded by the Economic and Social Research Council, is on the shifting culture and values of English schooling in the light of recent educational reforms.

Peter Gill taught mathematics and physics in schools and colleges for 18 years before joining King's. He was responsible for the mathematics PGCE and was involved in the original National Curriculum assessment inservice work.

Christine Harrison taught for 13 years in secondary schools in and around London, before moving on to a curriculum development project and consultancy work in science education. She has research interests in assessment, science education and in-service training and is responsible for the Biology PGCE at King's.

John Head is a former secondary schoolteacher who has worked in the UK and the USA. His current research interests, as a Senior Lecturer at King's, encompass psychology applied to issues of adolescence such as identity development and gender differences.

Faith Hill has taught health education in secondary schools and has run national projects for the Health Education Authority. She has trained teachers throughout the UK and published widely in the area of health education, particularly for young people aged 16–19. She runs a Masters programme in health education and health promotion at King's.

Jane Jones taught for many years in primary and secondary schools in London and Kent and her last school post was as senior teacher responsible for profiling and assessment in a large comprehensive school in Wandsworth. Her research interests include school leadership and governance, counselling in schools and all aspects of language learning.

Sheila Macrae has taught in secondary schools in Scotland and England and in a pupil referral unit in Inner London. She now works as a Research Fellow at King's where her main interests are in the psychological and social development of adolescents.

Meg Maguire taught for many years in London including a spell as a headteacher. She is the course leader of the MA in Urban Education as well as the part-time Postgraduate Certificate in Education (PGCE). She has published on teacher education and issues of equity.

Martin Monk has worked in Belize, India, Indonesia, Lesotho and Nigeria and been a consultant to projects in the former Czechoslovakia, Egypt and Korea. His principal research interests focus on psychology, epistemology and the history of science.

Michael Quintrell was a comprehensive school teacher for 17 years (including 13 as a Head of English faculty) before working for an LEA Inspectorate in the development and evaluation of INSET. His research interests include: the promotion of speaking and listening and their assessment; class management; pastoral care; pupil grouping; and the effective use of IT by the English teacher.

Barbara Watson was a lecturer in further education and is now a full-time PhD student at King's. She is a governor of a special school and has recently worked on an ESRC project focusing on minority trainee teachers.

Deryn Watson taught geography for several years in London and has been actively involved since the mid-1970s in the research and development of computer-assisted learning materials in the Humanities and Languages. Her research interests include the impact of IT on children's learning and the role of the teacher. She is Assistant Head of the Education Department at King's College London.

Dylan Wiliam is Head of the School of Education at King's College London. He taught mathematics in London for several years and has published widely on matters relating to education, particularly in the field of educational assessment.

Chris Wright is currently Deputy Principal at the International School in Jerusalem. Until recently he was responsible for the RE PGCE at King's College. His research and writing interests include collective worship in schools and the teaching of Christianity and Buddhism.

Introduction

Justin Dillon and Meg Maguire

Becoming a Teacher is designed to be read by new teachers. By new teachers we mean students on teacher education courses as well as people in their first year of teaching. The book is a collection of chapters written, unusually, by the staff of one institution – the School of Education at King's College London. All of the authors have taught, usually in London schools, and many have worked overseas, from Indonesia to Israel. Some of the authors have experience as headteachers, as inspectors and as heads of department. Almost all of them have worked as tutors on Postgraduate Certificate in Education (PGCE) courses for many years.

Some time ago, a visit from Her Majesty's Inspectorate (HMI) encouraged us to look at the amount of reading that our own PGCE students did. For many reasons, including accessibility of libraries, the cost of books and the level of grants, the amount of reading that students did was much less than we thought appropriate. Looking around we could not find a suitable textbook that addressed the issues that we knew concerned our students as they progressed through their course. So we wrote one ourselves. It proved to be popular so, with the help of the Open University Press, we have produced a more polished version which we hope will address your needs.

This is not a tips for teachers book. Each chapter is designed to give you some background in terms of, say, historical context and to illuminate the key issues that teachers are faced with every day. Some of the chapters should enable you to make sense of what goes on in school and should help you to gain an overview of a particular topic. The authors have tried to give you evidence to support points of view – there is too much unsubstantiated opinion in education that has affected teachers and children detrimentally for too many years. This book will give you some evidence, from the literature, to back up, or maybe to challenge, your own opinions and experience.

Much of teaching relies on confidence. You need to be confident in your knowledge of your subject. Your students need to be confident in you as a teacher. You need to appear confident when you work with a class. Confidence can develop through experience and through feedback from other people. This book is designed to help you to become more confident in your understanding of what learning to teach involves. There will be much in this book that you have not thought of before – things that you disagree with or things that you feel are obvious. It is designed to be dipped into rather than read sequentially and, we hope, will point you in the direction of further reading.

How to use the book

Each chapter is designed to be read on its own, although you will find recurrent themes. If you are doing an essay on a topic such as learning or special educational needs or you feel that there are areas of education about which you know very little, then you can use the chapters here as starting points. Some of the chapters are linked in terms of content, so if you are interested in learning, you will find that the chapters on adolescence, differentiation, language and assessment are interrelated. Indeed, the complexity of education is what makes it such an interesting area to work in.

The book is divided into four major sections. We have called Part 1, A Basic Framework because it addresses the fundamental areas of concern for a new teacher: what does learning to teach mean?; teacher education and training; the current education scene; the philosophical issues underpinning education; and the law as it relates to teachers.

Part 2, Social and Political Issues provides a grounding in the broader context in which education sits. As well as looking at the historical roots of the problems facing teachers and learners, particularly in the inner-city, the section provides a vision of alternative and possible futures.

In the classroom, most of your concerns will be more immediate than those outlined above and Part 3, Teaching and Learning Issues, is a collection of interrelated articles addressing issues such as classroom management, adolescence, language and assessment. In each chapter you will find practical advice based on sound theoretical understandings as well as some key issues to consider.

Part 4, Whole Curriculum Issues, appears daunting. The responsibilities of teachers beyond that of subject specialist has grown steadily over the years. The authors of the chapters in this section provide information about roles and responsibilities in areas including health education, information technology and vocational education. A key role that almost all new teachers now find themselves in is that of form tutor; the final chapter in this part looks at some of the roles and responsibilities involved.

Finally, Stephen Ball provides an epilogue – Better Read: Theorising the Teacher! – in which he pulls together many of the issues raised in preceding chapters. This chapter is not one for beginners and we recommend that you read it last – after some months of school experience.

Endnote

In putting together this book we have tried to emphasise the three Rs: reading, reflection and research. Good teachers are able to learn from their experiences, reflecting on both positive and negative feedback. The best teachers are often those who not only learn from their experience but also learn from the experiences of others. Reading offers access to the wisdom of others as well as providing tools to interpret your own experiences. We have encouraged the authors contributing to this book to provide evidence from research to justify the points that they make. We encourage you to reflect on that evidence and on the related issues during the process of becoming a teacher.

Part 1 | A basic framework

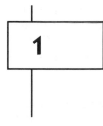

1 Developing as a new teacher

Meg Maguire and Justin Dillon

Anticipating teaching

If you are about to embark on a course of teacher training then you face what may be the most challenging period of your life. But take heart – the stimulation and the enjoyment of working with learners can be immense. Looks on faces, words of thanks, the physical excitement that only young people seem to be able to generate come frequently enough to justify the effort.

Most of your own experience of education will probably have been spent sitting down, facing the front being directed by an older person. Your teacher training will involve a rapid dislocation; some of the time you will be the teacher and some of the time you will be a learner. It is not a dichotomous situation though. It is critical that you learn while you are teaching.

What sort of teacher are you going to be? At the moment your model may be based on teachers that you have had or, possibly, based on the teachers you wished that you had had. This is common in new teachers and you will find yourself saying and doing things that your teachers said and did to you. Your first concern may well be with the behaviour of your students and there will be times, usually just before a lesson, when you look back at your decision to become a teacher and think 'why did I do that?' As you become more confident and more competent at teaching your concern will shift from behaviour to learning. The two are intrinsically linked. It is difficult for students to learn if they are not working in a well-managed environment and if they feel they are learning something worthwhile they are more likely to respond to being managed.

Learning to teach involves a range of practical skills 'and a subtle appreciation of when and how to apply them' (Claxton 1990: 16).

Whether you like it or not, how you teach and how you learn to teach are bound up with your own personality, philosophy and values.

Somewhere inside there is a set of personal standards – whether tacit or articulated, ill-informed or carefully thought out – that determine what shocks you, interests you or angers you about schools, and that serve as the benchmarks which you will use to guide and evaluate your progress as a teacher.

(Claxton 1990: 18)

Training to become a teacher can therefore be a challenging as well as a frustrating business. Your undergraduate learning experience may have focused on a formalised acquisition of content. Your seminars may well have looked at prepared papers or content-driven academic debates. While these forms of learning feature in current teacher training, and while there is a necessary emphasis on classroom techniques and skills, learning to teach is fundamentally a personal challenge which employs a wide range of teaching styles, where practical, personal and emotional attributes are just as salient as intellectual capacities. 'The PGCE is a complex and unique part of becoming a teacher' (Head *et al*. 1996: 83). A lot of ground is covered in a short time and this can result in feelings of stress and anxiety. The PGCE provides a vocational training built around a demanding and challenging induction into the teaching profession.

Many secondary trainee teachers (but not all) come into teaching as mature students, with a rich and broad experience of working in a variety of settings. Many are parents and have first-hand experience of their own children's schooling or that of close friends and family members. Sometimes in the light of these experiences, teaching can seem to be a 'common-sense' affair – all about conveying some useful and hopefully interesting aspects in a lively manner which motivates young people to succeed. For people who think this way, becoming a learner teacher can sometimes explode any 'simple' version of encouraging others to learn, it also involves a high degree of personal risk and challenge. Teaching children who are less motivated than ourselves or who do not seem like the children we know, can present practical and personal difficulties where we may 'blame' the children instead of our own inexperience. It can also make for a stimulating and rewarding work setting.

Teacher qualities

At the heart of this book is a concern with becoming a teacher. Teachers are in an extremely privileged position; educating other people's children is a critical and influential task in any society. But this job is made more complex in times of acute social, economic and political change. One way in which to approach becoming a contemporary teacher is from the trainee perspective, as above. Another way might be to ask what is involved in teaching and what might we, as a society, want to prioritise at particular moments in time? Do we want compliant pupils who can apply what they have learned? Do we want problem-solvers and flexible learners? Do we want specialists or generalists? Are there any common strands which are recognisable as key components of a good teacher? In what follows we will consider four main themes through which we hope to raise questions about the central qualities involved in being and becoming a teacher:

classroom management, the wider role of the teacher, professional and personal qualities.

Classroom management

Obviously there are some key aspects which are fundamental to good teaching. Good classroom management and organisation, the capability of teaching effectively in a mixed 'ability' classroom (and are not all classrooms mixed ability, however they are arranged?), knowledge of subject and subject application, assessment, record-keeping and all the other criteria listed by the Government are important. (These of course make up the stated criteria through which trainee teachers are assessed). But what is important to recognise is that all of these variables depend on the degree to which a teacher can maintain a positive and open climate in the classroom. The research into classroom life clearly demonstrates the manner in which teachers and school students are in constant negotiation over boundaries, relationships, curriculum content sequencing and pacing (Beynon 1985; Delamont 1990). This means that there are not simple 'codes' or 'regimes' which have a totality of application. This does not mean that trainee teachers cannot be helped with these issues either. But these are not just aspects of performance which are incrementally added to the teaching repertoire. They require a different type of learning and a different type of understanding in action.

We all know that the very best teaching depends on sensitive communication. We all know very well qualified people who really understand their subject but cannot help others into it in a 'user friendly' manner. It is not only important to be able to help our school students understand by clear and effective communication modes, it is important that teachers listen, observe and become sensitive to the children and 'where they are at' in relation to their understanding. In this context, assessment has a different meaning. It is clearly related to understanding and development. Communication is a two-way process. Teachers need to be able to listen and 'read' their students. This, too, takes time and practice to refine, and even for the most experienced of teachers, it sometimes 'goes wrong'. Dealing with adolescent people is not always straightforward or predictable. Sometimes it is the unrecognised forms of communication – non-verbal expressions or aspects of body language that need consideration (Neill 1991; Wooton 1993). At other times there is the basic issue of respect for persons, sometimes ignored when dealing with youngsters.

Student teachers frequently worry about 'control' and eagerly seek for ranges of strategies to help them with this in their school experience settings. Experienced teachers know only too well that controlling – or creating a climate to allow learning to happen – is intimately bound up with their knowledge of the children. Trainee teachers are placed in a novel situation of attempting to manipulate the atmosphere in larger grouped settings. This is an unusual skill to develop and is not the same as managing adults in a workplace setting. It takes time and personal investment in good relationships with school students and it would be unrealistic for new teachers to achieve this overnight. All this suggests that 'control' is more related to relationships than external strategies or mechanistic skills.

The wider role of the secondary school teacher

Teaching in contemporary schools involves building relationships with many different school students with a variety of backgrounds, needs, expectations, motivations and aspirations. It is not possible to help children learn effectively unless you have some knowledge and insight into their concerns. The pastoral role of a teacher is related to the widest aims of teaching. The National Curriculum places a statutory responsibility upon schools to promote 'the spiritual, moral, cultural, mental and physical development' of the school students. This means being interested in the children, getting to know them, feeling comfortable about discussing issues related to their learning and perhaps advising them in certain ways. At particular times issues related to health, sexuality, substance abuse, and so on, become salient in the classroom, and society expects schools to address and educate round these concerns. Teachers need to know what they can do, as well as what they cannot, in this context. And from this pastoral role comes an obvious extension – working with parents. In the current policy setting this aspect of the role of the teacher has significance for the maintenance of a healthy developing school (Gewirtz *et al.* 1995; Munn 1993). Communicating clearly and professionally with parents is a core attribute for effective teaching; it is recognised that parents and schools working together provide a continuity and coherence for the school student (Bastiani 1989).

Professional qualities

New teachers do need to be oriented to the fact that becoming a teacher means entering into membership of a particular community. They are members of a school staff, they are involved in a profession which needs to hold debates within itself and they have to participate in these debates. They need to 'keep up' with their subject(s) and should be encouraged to join a relevant subject association or phase-specific group. Essentially teachers need a feeling of responsibility and control (ownership if you like) over their work. They need to participate in decision making and indeed hopefully will develop over time to take a lead in this process.

Other professional qualities, which we believe are required, are related to the structural elements of the job. Teachers need to be on the 'inside' of professional concerns and issues related to their salary, pay structure and conditions of service.

Another important dimension to all this is the capacity to relate with colleagues and to work in a collaborative manner. Teachers need the confidence to challenge assumptions about their work and the way in which it proceeds. They need to be in a position where not only can they work with colleagues but they are able collectively as a staff as well as individuals, to ask fundamental questions about what they are doing. Is it worthwhile? It is this capacity which is characteristic of a professional teacher as opposed to a 'deliverer' of a curriculum devised elsewhere.

Personal qualities

Typically, trainee teachers experienced their school days as well-behaved and well-motivated students. Their role model of what it is to be a teacher may well have been constructed from this. For intending teachers who may have experienced selective schooling and may have been in top sets, the challenges of working with different types of students may be initially daunting. Children who have come to a recognition that school has little to offer them, that school only confirms in them a sense of failure and of 'being stupid' are going to be harder to reach and harder to teach (Hargreaves 1982). In some of our schools, trainee teachers may well meet many different types of children from the sort of child that they were – restless, unable to concentrate, not well motivated, perhaps with some particular learning difficulty. They will also meet students who are assertive and who demand respect and who will not be passive recipients of teachers' knowledge. Students will challenge what they perceive to be unfair or unjust in a way that might sometimes be constructed as provocative. Trainee teachers will discover that they need lots of different attitudes, different ways of being with children in the school setting. They will need to experiment with different strategies. They will need to develop a flexible and adaptive repertoire of teaching. They will need to see themselves as learners throughout their lives and see this as a challenge and an opportunity, not a threat. At the heart of these personal qualities for teachers and student teachers must be the capacity to see their professional life as one of continual growth and development. For trainee teachers what is required is a state of adaptability, an experimental attitude, a capacity to recognise that they are going through a period of 'transitional incompetence', perhaps learning to tolerate their own fallibility and accept that they can make mistakes as part of this process of becoming a teacher.

Concluding comments

The teacher is the ultimate key to educational change and school improvement. The restructuring of schools, the composition of national and provincial curricula, the development of bench-mark assessments – all these things are of little value if they do not take the teacher into account. Teachers do not merely deliver the curriculum. They develop, define it and reinterpret it too. It is what teachers think, what teachers believe and what teachers do at the level of the classroom that ultimately shapes the kind of learning that young people experience.

For some reformers, improving teaching is mainly a matter of developing better teaching methods, of improving instruction. Training teachers in new classroom management skills, in active learning, co-operative learning, one-to-one counselling and the like is the main priority. These things are important, but we are also increasingly coming to understand that developing teachers and improving their teaching involves more than giving them new tricks.

Teachers teach in the way they do, not just because of the skills they have or have not learned. The ways they teach are also grounded in their backgrounds, their biographies, in the kind of teachers they have become. Their careers – their hopes and dreams, their opportunities and aspirations, or the frustration of these things – are also important for teachers' commitment, enthusiasm and morale. So too are relationships with their colleagues, either in supportive communities, or as individuals working in isolation, with the insecurities that this sometimes brings.

> As we are coming to understand these wider aspects of teaching and teacher development we are also beginning to understand that much more than pedagogy, instruction or teaching method is at stake. Teacher development, teachers' careers, teachers relations with their colleagues, the conditions of status, reward and leadership under which they work – all these affect the quality of what they do in the classroom.
>
> (Hargreaves and Fullan 1992: ix)

For those of you who are reading this and who are in the process of becoming a teacher there is one more fundamental issue which has to be addressed and that is the distinction between being a good teacher and someone who helps school students become good learners: those whom Claxton calls mentors (Claxton 1990). Claxton has set up a simple model to illustrate his point. He talks about the traditional 'good teacher' as someone who tells things clearly, points out the key features, and maximises the training procedures through which pupils 'perform smoothly and successfully in situations – like most exams – that ask them to apply familiar operations to familiar content' (Claxton 1990: 154). One consequence can be the development of an unimaginative and inflexible learner.

> Good pupils often perform well and look good but at the expense of precisely those qualities that distinguish good learners: resourcefulness, persistence and creativity. And it is just this kind of quality that mentors care about. Their main concern is to equip their pupils with the ability to be intelligent in the face of change.
>
> (Claxton 1990: 154)

Becoming a teacher is not just a matter of training in basic skills and classroom procedures, essential as these all are as a starting place. It is also a matter of choice and of various personal and professional decisions and judgements. That is why teaching is such a tantalising, challenging and rewarding occupation.

References

Bastiani, J. (ed.) (1989) *Parents and Teachers. Working with Parents 3. A Whole School Approach*. Windsor: NFER-Nelson.

Beynon, J. (1985) *Initial Encounters in the Secondary School: Sussing, Typing and Coping*. London: Falmer Press.

Claxton, G. (1990) *Teaching to Learn. A Direction for Education*. London: Cassell.

Delamont, S. (1990) *Interaction in the Classroom*. London: Routledge

Gewirtz, S., Ball, S.J. and Bowe, R. (1995) *Markets, Choice and Equity in Education*. Buckingham: Open University Press.

Hargreaves, A. and Fullan M.G. (eds) (1992) *Understanding Teacher Development*. London: Cassell.

Hargreaves, D.H. (1982) *The Challenge for the Comprehensive School: Culture, Curriculum and Community*. London: Routledge and Kegan Paul.

Head, J., Hill, F. and Maguire, M. (1996) Stress and the post graduate secondary trainee teacher: A British case study, *Journal of Education for Teaching*, 22(1): 71–84.

Munn, P. (ed.) (1993) *Parents and Schools: Customers, Managers or Partners*. London: Routledge.

Neill, S. (1991) *Classroom Nonverbal Communication*. London: Routledge.

Wootton, M.J. (1993) *Not Using Your Voice: Non-Verbal Communication Skills in Teaching*. Upminster: Nightingale Teaching Consultancy.

Further reading

Borich, G.D. (1995) *Becoming a Teacher: An Inquiring Dialogue for the Beginning Teacher*. London: Falmer Press.

Kohl, H.R. (1986) *On Becoming a Teacher*. London: Methuen.

2

Teaching in a new ERA

John Head, Meg Maguire and Justin Dillon

Introduction

Since you went to school, the education system has changed more radically than many people can remember. This chapter looks at the nature of the changes primarily brought about by the 1988 Education Reform Act (ERA). Prior to 1988, the most significant Acts of Parliament relating to education were:

- The 1870 (Forster) Act – which established universal elementary education.
- The 1902 Act – which established secondary education for the 'able', by enabling the provision of scholarships to grammar schools.
- The 1944 (Butler) Act – which established universal secondary education, initially a tripartite system (grammar, technical and secondary modern schools).

ERA is more complex than the earlier Acts, making it difficult to summarise. It represents a major shift in thinking about education by government and, to some extent, the wider community. Maclure (1988: v) believes that ERA is 'far-reaching' because 'it altered the basic power structure of the educational system'. Until 1988 teachers were, in general, left to get on with their jobs, working within the framework created by parliament. The local educational authority (LEA), democratically accountable to its local community, was obligated to manage and organise the provision. The 1988 Act changed this arrangement; it constrains teachers by the introduction of the National Curriculum and a national assessment system and by giving increased powers to school governors. Furthermore, the National Curriculum is influencing not just the overall shape of the curriculum but its detailed content and pedagogy (Ball 1993).

It is not possible here to unpack all the complexities, changes and amendments that have occurred since 1988. However, it is important to note that as a consequence of concerns about National Curriculum overload as well as debates within subject disciplines about the degree of prescription of the content, since 1988 there has been a period of almost constant change and subsequent discontent in many schools. Following national consultations with parents, governors, teachers, other specialist groups and local education authority advisers, Sir Ron Dearing, the chair of the School Curriculum and Assessment Authority (SCAA) produced a slimmed down version of the National Curriculum in 1993. This was circulated to schools and interested groups for comment and the resulting final version framed the National Curriculum until the year 2000.

However, the ERA is more than simply the National Curriculum. The complexity of the 1988 Act is shown by the fact that it runs to 284 pages. It has sections dealing with changing the educational system in London, dealing with the problem of bogus degrees, establishing City Technology Colleges, and reform of further and higher education. For more details about these parts of the ERA, see Maclure (1988). This chapter focuses on the provisions that affect mainstream state schools.

The National Curriculum

Compulsory schooling extends over a period of eleven years. Post-1988, a new system of numbering the years of schooling was brought in. The first year of schooling is known as Year 1 and so on. Pupils starting at secondary school find themselves not as 'first years' but as 'Year 7s'. It will take many years before this system becomes fully established in the vocabulary of teachers, parents and pupils so you will still hear people referring to the sixth form, third years, and so on.

The eleven years of compulsory schooling are separated into four key stages corresponding to the historical 'stages' of pre-1988 days:

- Key Stage 1 – Reception and years 1 and 2 (previously known as 'Infants');
- Key Stage 2 – Years 3–6 (previously known as 'Juniors');
- Key Stage 3 – Years 7–9 (previously known as first to third years);
- Key Stage 4 – 10–11 (previously known as the fourth and fifth years).

A new hierarchy of subjects has been introduced. All maintained (state) schools must provide schooling in three core subjects, English, mathematics and science, plus seven foundation subjects: art, geography, history, music, physical education, technology (that is, design and technology and information technology) and a modern foreign language (the last only in Key Stages 3 and 4). In addition, all schools must provide religious education, which normally should be of a mainly Christian character. Prior to the ERA, schools had to provide religious education, but its nature was not specified. Schools in Wales must also offer Welsh as either a core or foundation subject. Schools are allowed to apply for some measure of exemption from the National Curriculum for some of their pupils (for example, those with special education needs – see Chapter 21).

Schools originally assumed that the core and foundation subjects would occupy 70–90 per cent of the school timetable. However, schools began to find it extremely difficult to cover all the prescribed content in the time available. Primary school teachers became concerned that not enough time was available for reading or mathematics and in some secondary schools the pastoral (tutoring and counselling) programmes were constrained. Subjects such as classics, drama, media studies and social studies began to struggle for survival and many cross curricular programmes were discarded. Important elements of secondary school provision such as careers education were marginalised in the National Curriculum (there are cross-curricular themes which are not statutory: environmental education, health education, citizenship, careers education and industrial and economic understanding).

The ERA gave unprecedented powers to the Secretary of State for Education who has the legal responsibility for producing attainment targets, programmes of study, and assessment procedures for the core and foundation subjects (see Chapter 16). An attainment target is a general aim applied to a part of the curriculum of a subject. The programmes of study laid down a defined minimum of content which had to be covered, so what was to be taught was (for the first time in England and Wales) being determined by central government.

These programmes of study did not specify how things were to be taught. Teachers were considered responsible for devising an effective pedagogy for themselves. However, the issue of pedagogy is high on the political agenda and matters such as differentiation and mixed ability teaching, streaming and setting, the place and role of whole class teaching are being debated in schools as well as in the educational press and national media (see Millett 1996 and Chapter 15).

The Secretary of State initially appointed a National Curriculum Council (NCC) and Curriculum Council for Wales (CCW) to monitor and advise on the curriculum and a School Examinations and Assessment Council (SEAC) to provide policy on assessment. SEAC and the NCC were later amalgamated to form the School Curriculum and Assessment Authority (SCAA).

Assessment and testing

Chapter 16 deals with assessment and testing in more detail but, at this stage it is important to know that performance indicators (level descriptors) for each of the subject attainment targets are laid down for each key stage, indicating what the child of 7, 11, 14 and 16 should know, understand and be able to do. Originally, there were ten levels for each subject across the four key stages now there are eight across the first three key stages only (with another level for exceptional performance). The first three stages are tested by national tests and by teacher assessment and Key Stage 4 by the GCSE which are run by private examination boards.

In Chapter 6, Paul Black explains the background to the development of the national assessment policy. The Government wanted each key stage to be nationally tested and wanted the results published in league tables to show the 'best' as well as the 'failing' schools. This has been a major area of controversy. Specifically, at Key Stage 3, the teacher unions, spear-headed by the National Association of Teachers of English (NATE) operated a boycott of the national tests, then known as SATs (Standard Assessment Tasks). Teachers' concerns have essentially fallen into two areas: first, some of the test items were regarded as being poorly designed and too time-consuming; secondly, the publication of league tables, it was argued, was manifestly unfair. Schools with selected intakes of able academic students from privileged backgrounds were going to do better in raw scores than some inner city comprehensive schools although the quality of teaching might be identical in the two schools.

In 1996, children in Key Stage 2 sat national tests the results of which, the Secretary of State had said, would not be published in league tables as the tests were 'bedding in'. Policy changed and primary schools were told that their results would be published so that parents could compare school with school. Governing bodies in over 1000 schools instructed their headteachers not to report the scores to the Department for Education and Employment (DFEE), thus making league table publication virtually impossible. The controversy over testing, standards and assessment will continue (see Chapters 6 and 16).

The Dearing Report

As we noted earlier, the initial National Curriculum was regarded as being overloaded and to simplify matters some changes were made in 1991. These did not go far enough and the Government eventually acknowledged that the concerns expressed by parents, school governors and teachers were justified and that something more radical needed to be done; 'lessons have been learned' (Millett 1996: 11). Sir Ron Dearing, who had been in charge of the Post Office for many years, was appointed to review the curriculum and assessment systems. It is generally accepted that Dearing did a good job, and, more importantly, was seen to listen to a range of points of view. He made the following suggestions:

- That the existing National Curriculum in Key Stages 1–3 be streamlined to release a day a week for schools to use at their discretion.
- A reduction in curriculum content for this age group to be concentrated outside the core subjects.
- That 14–16-year-olds needed greater flexibility to allow schools to offer a wider range of academic and vocational options.
- That teacher workload be cut through National Curriculum simplification, reduced testing and recording demands.
- That the ten-level scale be simplified and run only to the end of Key Stage 3.
- That National Curriculum subjects for Key Stages 1, 2, and 3 should be reviewed simultaneously for September 1995.
- That no further changes to the National Curriculum should be made for five years after 1995.

Local management of schools (LMS)

As a result of the ERA, all secondary schools and primary schools with more than 200 pupils were made responsible for their own financial management. The system is known by the abbreviations LMS (local management of schools) or LFM (local financial management). School governing bodies are now responsible for ensuring the implementation of the National Curriculum and must also exercise a high degree of budgetary control. Schools now manage their own income, largely determined according to the size of the enrolment, and have considerable freedom for expenditure on staff salaries, books and equipment. A school, therefore, has the choice to spend less on one area – for instance, staffing, in order to divert the funds to other expenditure – for example, buying computers. Local education authorities remain responsible for major capital expenditure, their own administrative costs and for providing advisers and inspectors (the number of both have fallen considerably). The LEAs can, though, delegate expenditure for items such as building maintenance, insurance, and school meals to individual schools.

The result of these changes has been that school governors and senior staff have greatly increased responsibilities, particularly for financial matters. Schools are 'competitive' in the sense that if birth rates fall some schools must lose pupils, and hence lose income. Each school has to seek to persuade local parents of the particular virtues of their provision. This is critical for secondary schools who need to attract children from primary schools in order to sustain (or increase) their roll (Gewirtz et al. 1995). One major problem has derived from the fact that schools now have to pay teachers' salaries. The budgets allocated to school have been calculated on average teacher salaries; thus the actual costs for teachers' pay may well exceed the allocation if the staff are older or more highly qualified than the average and thus more costly. This shortfall has to be made up from other parts of the budget or schools have to seek alternative ways of raising money. Schools in many senses have to become entrepreneurial, a consequence which raises many concerns. Not all schools are equally placed to raise sums from their local communities; not all schools believe that this is a valid part of their role in society.

Grant maintained schools

With the passing of ERA all maintained secondary schools (and larger primary schools) became eligible to 'opt out' of LEA control. The school is then funded directly (hence 'grant maintained') from the government at the same level as it would have been under the LEA. Various conditions are attached to the grant which are basically similar to those for LEA maintained schools under the LMS proposals. In order to 'opt out' a ballot of parents has to be held. If 50 per cent or more of registered parents vote on the first ballot, the issue is decided (if less, a second ballot must be held within 14 days). The result is determined by a simple majority.

The Conservative Party have an expressed commitment to grant maintained (GM) schools. As not enough schools opted out, the Government amended ERA so that schools were compelled to raise the issue of GM status every year at the Annual Governors' Meeting. Additionally, extra funds were made available to the early GM schools which many schools were unable or unwilling to resist. However, the GM story is rather more complicated that this implies. For instance, in one metropolitan Conservative LEA, all the secondary schools opted out together to avoid what they saw as the excesses of their 'Tory flagship' council. In another Conservative controlled shire county, one famous comprehensive school opted out of LEA control; the LEA was committed to making all its secondary schools selective and so the school opted out in order to retain its comprehensive status with the support of parents, school students, staff and governors. Although the move towards GM status has slowed down, and, prior to the 1997 election, almost stopped, the debate about the future of GM schools rumbles on.

One of the problems with schools becoming grant maintained is the reduction in the LEAs capacity to plan and manage places for pupils in its schools. Although one school may experience financial benefits from opting out, the consequences of this action can rebound on the remaining LEA controlled schools. In some cases, the schools which elected to opt out at an early stage had been earmarked for closure as they were undersubscribed. When they were allowed to opt out, other schools had to reduce their provision as surplus places were far too costly for the LEA to maintain. This caused ill feeling in some parts of the country. In the past, LEAs had centrally provided services such as teachers' centres, advisory teachers, psychological services, payroll facilities, central libraries, and so on. In some areas where several secondary schools opted out, it became harder to provide these services. It is debatable as to whether it is more or less cost effective to have schools attempting to provide some of these services on their own. However LMS and GM status have allowed schools to be selective in purchasing advisory services and in-service education.

Consequences of ERA

Who has won and who has lost as a result of ERA? Government rhetoric during the 1990s celebrated the rolling back of the power of the bureaucratic state in educational provision through a focus on individual choice in a setting of diversity. At the centre of the new education market stands the parent as chooser and consumer (Gewirtz et al. 1995). Parents can choose from a variety of secondary schools and they can use the league tables to select the 'best' school for their child. Overall it is argued that the twin market mechanisms of choice and competition will improve standards in primary and secondary schools.

However, research is indicating that popular schools are able to do their own choosing and that parents only have the right to nominate a choice – not to automatically get it. Clearly, this has implications for 'success' in the national league tables; selecting well-motivated and hard-working children from supportive families makes 'economic and market sense' for some schools, although it might not sit well with some schools' concern to serve their local communities.

Ironically, given the philosophy of the Conservative Party, central government has actually increased its power by imposing a National Curriculum and assessment system, and by dealing more directly with schools rather than going via the LEA. The LEAs have lost much of their power and their role as 'honest broker' has been seriously undermined. The governors of a school have been moved from the periphery, raising funds for marginal activities, to the centre, taking control for the budget and curriculum. This assumes that all schools are equally able to recruit well-qualified citizens, able to deal competently with the mass of paperwork which now falls to their (unpaid) lot. Heads and deputies have increased responsibilities, acting on behalf of the governors in dealing with the budget, maintenance, publicity in the community, and so on. Classroom teachers have lost the freedom to generate their own curriculum and have to conform to the prescribed national requirements for much, but not all, of their time. In return, pupils have an entitlement to a curriculum that is broadly similar throughout the system and schools have a greater degree of control over their own spending.

ERA marked a revolutionary change in education policy and provision. At its heart lie two main concerns; to improve and reform education through the insertion of quasi-market forces and thus to raise standards which, it has been argued, have fallen (see Chapter 6). It will take time to fully evaluate the effects of ERA by which point, schools and teachers, learning and teaching may have been radically restructured.

References

Ball, S.J. (1993) Education, Majorism and "the curriculum of the dead", *Curriculum Studies*, 1(2): 195–214.

Ball, S.J., Bowe, R. with Gold, A. (1992) *Reforming Education and Changing Schools*. London: Routledge.

Gewirtz S., Ball S.J. and Bowe, R. (1995) *Markets, Choice and Equity in Education*. Buckingham: Open University Press.

Lawton, D. and Chitty, C. (eds) (1988) *The National Curriculum*. London: Institute of Education, University of London.

Maclure, S. (1988) *Education Reformed*. London: Hodder and Stoughton.

Millett, A. (1996) Pedagogy – the last corner of the secret garden. King's Annual Education Lecture, King's College London, 15 July.

Various Authors (1992) *Education: Putting the Record Straight*. Stafford: Network Educational Press.

Further reading

Chitty, C. (ed.) (1993) *The National Curriculum: Is it Working?* Harlow: Longman.

Flude, M. and Hammer, M. (1990) (eds) *The Education Reform Act 1988: Its Origins and Implications*. London: Falmer Press.

Lawton, D. (1994) *The Tory Mind on Education, 1979–1994*. London: Falmer Press.

Rao, N. (1990) *Educational Change and Local Government: The Impact of the Education Reform Act*. London: Joseph Rowntree Foundation.

3

Values and schooling

Alan Cribb and Sharon Gewirtz

Introduction

In this chapter we explore some of the ways in which fundamental questions about values and schooling are currently 'asked' and 'answered'. We will argue that in many respects these questions are marginalised, or even buried; and that there is a widespread and understandable scepticism about them. But we will also argue that this scepticism is an important feature of what might be called 'the prevailing values climate' – a climate which has a neutral and common-sense face but which is by no means neutral. Most of the chapter will be given over to sketching out some of the features of this value climate. The first part of this sketch covers features of the general philosophical and ethical context, particularly the role of value scepticism and value neutrality. The second part of the sketch focuses in on aspects of the current social and political context of English schooling, and the value shifts inherent in recent reforms.[1] Such broad coverage makes it impossible to cover issues in much depth or to trace through all the themes, or possible links between the features discussed. However, we hope that there are also advantages in working on a broad canvas. In particular we hope to draw attention to a powerful compound of factors which serve to undermine the critical function of value debate.

What are schools for?

Virtually all questions about schooling are value questions. But some of these are fundamental in the sense that the answers we give to them determine our answers to the others. 'What are schools for?' is an example of one of the most fundamental value questions that needs to be asked. The issues raised by this question are the most far-reaching and arguably the most practical matters facing a prospective teacher. The way in which schools are organised, priority setting and the allocation of resources, the attitudes towards (and attention given to) different sorts of tasks, the general modes of behaviour, and the nature and quality of relationships will all be shaped by beliefs about the purpose of schooling. Mike Bottery makes this point nicely in his book, *The Ethics of Educational Management* (1992). He identifies a number of different philosophical perspectives on the ultimate purposes of education and argues that these produce very different relationships and approaches to management within schools. For example, the 'cultural transmission' perspective:

> values knowledge which is perceived as part of a country's cultural heritage. It sees the child as essentially a passive imbiber . . . Teachers, therefore, are seen as guardians, transmitters of appropriate values, and as headteachers will be transmitters, and supervisors of those below them who are also transmitting, the situation will be an essentially hierarchical one.
>
> (Bottery 1992: 12)

The 'child-centred' perspective, on the other hand:

> sees the curriculum as based on each individual child's experiences and interests, each of them being active, involved, unique constructors of their own reality . . . The teacher, in this situation, becomes a facilitator, a constructor of beneficial situations for the child, but in no way a transmitter . . . Hierarchy makes little sense, and one moves increasingly towards a model of democracy.
>
> (Bottery 1992: 13–14)

These are just examples. Others include the 'social reconstruction' perspective, which 'sees schools as essentially concerned with pressing social issues which need to be resolved', and the 'gross national product' perspective, which 'values knowledge which is conducive to the furtherance of national economic well-being' (Bottery 1992: 12). Such approaches are not necessarily all mutually exclusive and can be interpreted and combined in various ways. This is exemplified in the Australian sociologist, R.W. Connell's seminal 1985 ethnographic study, *Teachers' Work*. Connell's teachers hold a range of views on the fundamental purposes of education and this is reflected in their different approaches to teaching.

Our purpose here has not been to answer the question 'what are schools for?' but merely to underline its fundamental nature for anyone pursuing a career in teaching. Although there is no doubt some wisdom, as well as a legal and moral obligation, in taking a lead from the policies and ethos generated by one's employing institution and one's colleagues, anyone who wants to make a contribution to the policy-making process operates, implicitly or explicitly, with a view of schooling. And even if a teacher were to retreat to a position of mere employee, virtually every practical decision they made, every conversation they had in the classroom or the corridor, would betray a personal conception of what schools are for.

Thus the challenge could be issued to everyone embarking on a career as a teacher – 'How will you affect the balance of the debate? What are your conceptions of the aims of education, and of schooling? What do you see as the role of schools in society?' Perhaps it would be foolish to start a career with a set of confident and dogmatic answers, yet not to have any answers might be deemed professionally negligent.

But it is not as simple as this. There are a whole array of factors that militate against individuals forming such a personal vision of the role of education. In fact when it comes to answering questions about values and schooling there are a loosely related range of 'licensed avoidance tactics'. In answer to the question 'What are schools for?' you could say, in short, (i) 'There are no right answers'; and/or (ii) 'There are different answers – and you have to be neutral between them' and/or (iii) 'You need to use a neutral mechanism to determine what people want from schools.' These avoidance tactics will be explored further in the sections that follow; but they all have the effect of marginalising both value debate and teachers' own personal value positions.

Scepticism

It is easy to stress the practical importance of questions about values and schooling, but it is much more difficult to answer them. What is an individual teacher to do? What is the appropriate stance towards ethical and political issues? This is where scepticism enters the picture.

At base, scepticism is the view that knowledge of something is impossible – in this case ethical or political matters; that there is no procedure for arriving at, or demonstrating, the truth or falsity, rightness or wrongness, of value claims. This is not the place to discuss the nature of scepticism in any depth, but perhaps it is worth mentioning that it is very difficult to argue convincingly against scepticism in any area of knowledge. However, for a number of reasons scepticism about value judgements is peculiarly pervasive in everyday culture. Indeed, the phrase 'It's a value judgement' is often treated as synonymous with expressions like 'It's just a personal opinion' or 'Who can say?'.

The growth of value scepticism has been a long and complex process (MacIntyre 1985). But to a large extent it is the product of the modern fixation with certain models of knowledge, in particular models of rationality, observability and testability associated with the natural sciences which seek to separate out the 'hard' public realm from the 'soft' realm of personal beliefs and feelings; the 'objective' from the 'subjective'; facts from values. In this century a number of philosophical theories have been advanced to the effect that ethical judgements are nothing more than expressions of emotions, attitudes, or preferences. At one extreme these would entail that no ethical position is better grounded, or more warranted, than any other. Something very like this has also become a major current in common-sense thinking. But if this was treated as the whole story the implications would be drastic. There would be no basis on which to criticise any ethical or political position. A teacher would be on an equally strong footing whether they pulled their value judgements out of a hat or whether they deliberated carefully about them. Asking about the aims of schooling would be asking a question for which there were no right answers.

But although value scepticism is prevalent in theoretical and popular discourse, it is only part of the picture. Other aspects of everyday culture tell a different story. First, there are of course people who are comfortable maintaining that they do have good grounds, and justified beliefs, as regards their moral and political judgements. The most clear-cut, and most visible, being religious fundamentalists of one kind or another. Secondly, even people who dismiss the idea that they operate with defensible moral convictions tend to change their minds in practice if certain lines are crossed (for example, if their flat-mate turns out to be a cannibal). Thirdly, very many people take overt moral and political stances, and show conviction and commitment in the pursuit of these stances, and may simply leave the question of the epistemological status of these stances on one side (although, once again, in practice they will typically offer reasons and arguments in the defence of these stances). The powerful convictions surrounding conflicts around racism or animal welfare testify to the limits of scepticism in practice.

These two facts about current values talk – the widespread currency of scepticism and the vigorousness of moral challenge and argument – appear to be contradictory. However, they are probably better seen as two complementary facets of a new orthodoxy.

Neutrality

Whether or not ethical systems are rationally defensible, ethics does not require a rational foundation. All that is required is a shared tradition and framework of beliefs, feelings and habits. Within such a tradition there can be scope for rational debate and disagreement about principles and ideals, and how they should be interpreted and applied. The difficulty is to know what to do if the reality, or even the idea, of a shared tradition breaks down and is replaced by a situation of moral or value pluralism. In many respects value scepticism is a response to value pluralism. Ours is a society which is suspicious of the controlling use of ethical traditions and systems, one which contains people with different world views, which encompasses different cultures and traditions, and in which there is increasingly less consensus about the right starting point for debate.

In the context of pluralism, the combination of scepticism and conviction mentioned above appears more coherent. Although this combination is perhaps better understood as a consequence of the 'privatisation of morality' and as a weak version of moral relativism, which allows scope for value divergence between individuals and groups within society but which draws the line at stronger versions of relativism. (Stronger versions would accord equal status to outlooks which sought to destroy this equilibrium.) This combination is characteristic of what might be called a 'liberal ethic', which is arguably the dominant outlook in the contemporary values climate and the orthodoxy of value pluralism! A liberal ethic allows for alternative beliefs about 'what is good' to operate at the private level, or within relatively self-contained groups, while preserving a 'thin' framework of public morality. The latter is necessary to protect the private sphere and to ensure that people 'rub along' together satisfactorily

(Mulhall and Swift 1993). The primary value in a liberal ethic is autonomy, and respect for autonomy. According to liberal political philosophy the role of the state is to be, as far as possible, neutral between 'competing conceptions of the good'. Individual conceptions of the good are to be autonomously determined and pursued. We can have our personal value convictions providing we do not use the public realm to 'impose' them on anyone else.

From this standpoint, developing and promoting the autonomy of young people becomes the central aim of education. The role of schools as public institutions is to introduce young people to the different perspectives which make up the pluralist culture and to support them in finding their own path through it and arriving at their own convictions. This approach is largely incompatible with the advocacy of any particular value position, and some might feel it should entail playing down the overt ethical and political dimensions of education.

The problem for this sort of liberalism is that, not only do public institutions tend not to be neutral in practice, but it is far from clear that neutrality is a possibility even in principle. This is particularly evident in the case of schools. In practice, a liberal ethos is overlaid with some favoured value system. The role of Christianity or particular attitudes towards sexuality will serve as examples. But how could a school be organised in such a way as not to favour certain world views? This may be a useful ideal for some purposes (up to a point it would serve to support a tolerant, respectful and inclusive ethos) but is surely not a realisable one. One reason it is unrealisable is that a liberal ethos can conflict with some of the standpoints it might seek to embrace – for example, how could a school be neutral between sexual equality on the one hand and anti-homosexual beliefs on the other?

Scepticism and neutrality provide avoidance tactics for teachers who are asked to make value judgements about the purpose, content and organisation of schooling. Indeed, there are good reasons for teachers to be cautious. It would seem arrogant to set oneself up as an authoritative arbiter of political and ethical matters. Surely it is necessary to recognise that there are very different beliefs about these matters, and there is a need to recognise this diversity, and to treat different views with respect? Perhaps those people who determine the organisation and ethos of schools should try to steer a 'middle course', and to avoid extremes? Up to a point this attitude is plausible but it is also highly prone to exploitation. Forms of scepticism and neutrality serve as very fertile conditions for the spread of dominant norms and ideologies. Teachers who retreat behind them – as a way of avoiding engagement with challenging value questions – may be in an unwitting conspiracy with some strongly 'non-neutral' stances.

Effectiveness and efficiency

In the practical contexts of politics and policy making there is not very much talk about 'neutrality'; the idea is rarely advocated explicitly, but it is an important implicit dimension of real world politics. Some very sophisticated mechanisms exist to present value laden positions as if they were value neutral. In fact, one aspect of the politics of policy making is to 'neutralise', and thereby help to legitimise, certain value judgements – to render ideology into common sense. A good example of this manoeuvre in recent UK politics has been the championing of the goals of effectiveness and efficiency in the reformed public sector.

It would be perverse not to be in favour of effective schools, or to favour wasteful schools. Here is a language which everyone can share, which – at least on the face of things – is outside of ethical and political ideology. However, in reality the use of these ideas within education policy has been part and parcel of the deliberate imposition of a specific ideological framework on schooling and the reinforcement and creation of specific value environments for schools. We will look at some features of this process in more detail below, but first we will briefly review the two main 'neutralising mechanisms' of efficiency:

Utilitarianism

Faced with the task of evaluating social institutions, and given the diversity and contestability of possible criteria, there is a tendency to identify, or stipulate, some lowest common denominator to serve as the arbiter of success or effectiveness, and as the means of comparing performance over time or between institutions. These measures of 'output' or performance indicators will need to be publicly observable and easily measurable. An efficient institution will be one which achieves the highest score of success at lowest cost. Of course this has the effect of replacing all of the complexity and value debate (about, for example, what schools are for) with whatever measure happens to be identified or stipulated. There will always be pressure to introduce more sophisticated and multi-dimensional criteria of success but equally inevitably there will always be countervailing pressures to simplify complex measures in order to provide definitive and decisive scores and comparisons.

Markets

Resorting to 'markets' of one kind or another represents the other main mechanism for smoothing out value diversity and conflict. The market can be represented as a neutral mechanism for efficiently aggregating and responding to the variety of 'consumer' preferences; for providing what it is people actually want. The market, it is claimed, merely reflects preferences rather than imposing some external standard on institutions, which would also mean deliberately imposing a contestable value position on people who do not share it. But it does not follow from the fact that a market mechanism may be an effective way of circumventing open-ended value debate that its effects are more defensible or acceptable, or that its consequences because 'unplanned' amount any less to an imposition. War is another mechanism which serves to circumvent debate but it is common to resist the accompanying idea that 'might is right'.

Although they are only two threads of a complicated picture, utilitarian and market thinking are undoubtedly important currents in recent public and education policy. In some varieties they are in strong tension with one another, because utilitarianism tends towards simple specified yard-sticks, whereas market ideology emphasises process and diversity. But they can be combined in various ways and they are linked by a preoccupation with efficiency and the attempt to cut through the contestability of values. It is this combination which makes them – along with the language of 'standards' and 'effectiveness' – suitable vehicles to import a specific value climate under the guise of neutrality.

Recent reform in England

We now want to turn to more concrete matters and in particular to sketch the specific form in which utilitarian and market principles have been combined in the restructuring of the English education system during the last decade. We will then look at some of the particular ways in which this restructuring has begun to generate a shift in the values climate of the English school system. In doing so, our aim is to use the concrete example of school reform in England to illustrate the general point that utilitarianism and markets represent key policy mechanisms for imposing, under the guise of neutrality, a particular set of values on schooling. We should say at once that the account which follows is only one interpretation of this specific values shift, our main intention is to draw attention to the process which is taking place. This is an important task, because in order for practising teachers to be reflexive about their own values they need to be aware of the ways in which these values, and the opportunities to act on them, are shaped and constrained by the values embedded within the structures of the school and the education system as a whole.

Those currently working within schools do not only suffer from living within a general philosophical climate which marginalises value debate. They are also being bombarded with a particular genre of 'new manager-ialist' literature designed to help them 'improve' and be more 'efficient' and 'effective' (Angus 1994). Most of this literature tends to neglect the social and value context of schooling, except in so far as it relates to the 'image' of the school in the education 'marketplace'. Some of it goes fur-ther and seeks positively to discourage school managers and teachers from concerning themselves with such things which are deemed to be beyond their control and an unnecessary distraction from the core tasks of being efficient and effective.

The 1988 Education Reform Act (ERA) established four key mechanisms that together were designed to create a market in schooling. These were choice, diversity, per capita funding and devolved management. In the rhetoric justifying the legislation, choice and freedom were presented both as good things in themselves and as mechanisms for raising standards. Standards would improve, it was suggested, because within the market 'good'/'strong' schools would thrive, while 'poor'/'weak' ones would 'go to the wall' or have to improve. In this survival-of-the-fittest approach to educational provision, good schools and colleges are defined as those which are popular with consumers (parents and/or students[2]), and poor schools as those which are unpopular.

However the market enshrined in the legislation cannot be characterised as a free market, nor as a neutral mechanism of resource allocation, but is more accurately described as a form of what Hayek (1980) has termed 'ordered competition'. This is because in addition to the market mechanisms of choice, per capita funding and devolved management, mentioned above, the state also provides a set of specific performance indicators based on a centrally prescribed National Curriculum and a system of national testing at four key stages. These components incorporate utilitarian aspects into the reforms.

The system of information established by the 1988 Act is supposed to be constituted by published league tables of national test results based on the National Curriculum, as well as league tables of attendance and school leaver destinations. This information is meant to enable consumers to compare the performance of schools and assist them in making their choices. The legislation is therefore designed to encourage schools to respond to consumer wishes, but at the same time it would seem that the government is trying to send very clear messages about what consumers should be looking for in a school.

We would argue, therefore, that these ostensibly neutral formal arrangements inevitably 'carry' a set of beliefs about what schools are for and about how those involved in managing them should behave. For example, although on the surface the legislation values freedom of choice, that value seems to be compromised by an alternative set of values embedded within the legislation. First, the ERA devalues the concept of neighbourhood schooling through the effective abolition of catchment areas. Neighbourhood schooling is based on the idea that children should go to their local school with other local children. Within the legislation it is assumed that consumers (or responsible ones at any rate) will only choose the local school if it performs well in the league tables. If sufficient parents in a neighbourhood choose not to send their children to a local school, then there is, in effect, no longer a neighbourhood school for other parents in that area to choose. This means that freedom of choice, as defined within the legislation, does not necessarily include the choice of a neighbourhood school. Second and relatedly, the emphasis within the 1988 legislation appears to us to be mainly focused upon the instrumental goals of education. More specifically, the legislation appears to be geared towards the improvement of 'standards' which are narrowly defined in terms of *output*: test results, attendance levels and school leaver destinations. The implication is that 'good' schools are those which perform well in league tables. The information required to be published is limited, and some important characteristics are ignored. For example, there is no requirement for schools to publish information on: the expressive, co-operative and community aspects of schooling, on levels of enjoyment, happiness, stimulation and challenge for teachers and students, on degrees of innovation and creativity in school approaches to teaching and learning, on the quality of special needs provision, on the pastoral, social and extra curricular dimensions of schooling, nor on collaborative relationships within and between schools. Good attendance might be a reflection of these things, but then again it may well be a reflection of other factors, such as the kind of students who attend the institution.

Values drift

It can be argued that the overall effect of the new arrangements for the control and management of schools is a process of values drift. This argument (set out in much greater length as part of research reported in Ball 1994, Gewirtz *et al.* 1995, and Gewirtz 1996) suggests that in practice the market constitutes an incentive structure that rewards schools for particular kinds of behaviour and values and penalises them for others. The argued drift consists of a diminishing concern with need, equity, community and co-operation and an increasing concern with image, discipline, output measures, academic differentiation and competition. (This drift is meant to be a simplification, and to reflect a tendency the effects of which are partial and patchy – not a universal before-and-after switch!).

It is argued that values drift occurs in large measure because school managers perceive that their schools will be judged on the basis of their exam league table performance. This leads them to implement policies which they feel will make their schools more attractive to children with a high measured ability. Such students are likely to enhance the schools' league table performances at lowest cost. At the same time, many schools seem to be concerned not to attract too many students with learning, emotional or behavioural difficulties. Such students demand a high level of investment while producing little 'return' in terms of exam league table performance (Housden 1993).

According to this interpretation, it appears that prospective students are effectively being divided into two categories by schools – those students which they desire to attract and those which they do not. The former category consists of children of a high measured ability, those who are perceived to be committed to education and those with supportive parents. A particularly desirable category of children are girls, who are perceived as behaviourally more amenable than boys and academically more highly achieving. Some groups of South Asian students are also treated as valuable 'commodities' in the marketplace. The second category of consumers, the 'undesirables', consists of the less 'able', children who have emotional problems or who are behaviourally disruptive, working-class children whose parents are viewed as not valuing education, who 'just' send their children to the school because it is local, and children with learning difficulties and other special needs (although there are some exceptions) who are expensive to educate and who threaten 'balanced' intakes. Schools with strong special needs departments need to be concerned about the 'image' conveyed by strength in this area as well as by the financial consequences of having large numbers of children with learning difficulties. As yet there is no direct evidence which suggests that schools are identifying particular ethnic groups within the 'undesirables' category, but national statistics on exclusions do suggest that African-Caribbean boys are at least covertly being assigned to this group (Bourne *et al.* 1994).

Within some schools resources appear to be effectively shifting from students with special needs to students defined as being more able. While special needs departments are contracting, a number of schools are establishing and drawing attention to programmes for 'gifted children' and increasingly schools are investing energy and resources on students deemed to be at the threshold of achieving more than five A–Cs or at least one A–G at GCSE. (These are the key indicators used to compile the exam league tables.)

Developments noted by other researchers lend support to the argument that values drift is a reality in English schools. For example, Woods (1993) in his study of 11 secondary schools in three LEAs point to 'indications ... of senior staff in the case study schools giving emphasis to middle-class parental perspectives, by making changes which it is assumed will be attractive to them.' Among the changes the authors note are more attention to discipline, uniform, homework and examination policies. Two of their case-study schools systematically identify the primary schools whose pupils achieve the best GCSE results in order to target their promotional activity. Fitz *et al.* (1993) noted what they refer to as a 'reinvigorated traditionalism' in a number of the grant maintained schools they studied:

> several had strengthened their dress codes and reinforced school uniform codes; others were giving increased emphasis to customary standards of pupil behaviour, including ways of approaching and addressing teachers; while at least one had banned the use of 'biros' in favour of fountain pens.
>
> (Fitz *et al.* 1993: 73)

Once again it is plausible that the 'reinvigorated traditionalism' which Fitz *et al.* describe represents efforts to make schools more attractive to middle-class students with good GCSE potential who will help to raise the league table position of the schools.

At the heart of the 'values drift' thesis is a concern that the fundamental value axis of English schooling is changing; that there is a gradual erosion of the principle 'that the education of all students is intrinsically of equal value' (Daunt 1975) which underpinned much educational thinking (if not always practice) in the pre-1988 'comprehensive era'. In opposition to this principle, it is argued, forms of marketisation and utilitarianism are working to promote the values of competitive individualism within the English school system.

Conclusion

Whether or not credence is given to the idea that the value climate of English schooling is fundamentally changing, and is moving away from an equal commitment to all, and whether or not the explanation set out in the values drift thesis is a sufficient one, there are clearly significant changes taking place. Changes in the social and political context of schooling and in the control and management of schools have implications for conceptions of schooling: for what is possible, for what is deemed desirable, for whose voices are influential and so on. The way in which the question 'What are schools for?' is answered in practice inevitably changes over time, and the recent reforms are only one – albeit significant – example of this process. Within individual schools the balance which is struck between different educational and schooling perspectives evolves through conflict and adjustment. In some settings aspects of child-centredness and 'social reconstruction' may well be losing out to a new emphasis on cultural transmission and economic instrumentalism. It is within the framework of these kinds of value conflicts that an individual teacher has to orient himself or herself both theoretically and practically.

We would argue that, faced with these fundamental questions about values and schooling, the role of professionals – individually and collectively – is not only to take up stances but also to enter into explicit value debate with one another and with the wider community. This debate about the purposes of schooling, and the respective merits of equality, freedom, and other basic principles, is both intellectually and emotionally challenging. There is an understandable temptation to take refuge in forms of scepticism and neutrality. But, as we hope to have illustrated, teachers contribute to changes in their values climate either self-consciously or by default.

Notes

1 Parallel reforms to those made in England were introduced in Wales, Scotland and Northern Ireland. However, there are differences in the legislation and in the structure of the educational systems in these countries. In order to be precise, therefore, we refer throughout this chapter specifically to England.
2 In the debate about choice in education at school level, it is the parents who are more often than not described as the consumers, not their children.

References

Angus, L. (1994) Sociological analysis and educational management: the social context of the self-managing school, *British Journal of Sociology of Education*, 15(1): 79–92.

Ball, S.J. (1994) *Education Reform: a Critical and Post-structural Approach*. Buckingham: Open University Press.

Bottery, M. (1992) *The Ethics of Educational Management*. London: Cassell.

Bourne, J., Bridges, L. and Searle, C. (1994) *Outcast England: How Schools Exclude Black Children*. London: Institute of Race Relations.

Connell, R.W. (1985) *Teachers' Work*. Sydney: George Allen and Unwin.

Daunt, P. (1975). *Comprehensive Values*. London, Heinemann.

Fitz, J., Halpin, D. and Power, S. (1993) *Education in the Market Place*. London: Kogan Page.

Gewirtz, S. (1996) Market discipline versus comprehensive education: a case study of a London comprehensive school struggling to survive in the education market place, in J. Ahier, B. Cosin and M. Hales (eds) *Diversity and Change: Education, Policy and Selection*. London: Routledge.

Gewirtz, S., Ball, S.J. and Bowe, R. (1995) *Markets, Choice and Equity in Education*. Buckingham: Open University Press.

Hayek, F. (1980) *Individualism and Economic Order*. Chicago: University of Chicago Press.

Housden, P. (1993) *Bucking the Market: LEAs and Special Needs*. Stafford: Nasen.

MacIntyre, M. (1985) *After Virtue: A Study in Moral Theory*. London: Duckworth.

Mulhall, S. and Swift, A. (1993) *Liberals and Communitarians*. Oxford: Blackwell.

Woods, P. (1993) Responding to the consumer: parental choice and school effectiveness, *School Effectiveness and School Improvement*, 4(3): 205–29.

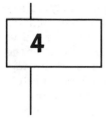

4 Teacher education[1]

Meg Maguire and Justin Dillon

Introduction

How should teachers be trained? Who should be responsible for training them? Is training the correct word or should we say educating? This chapter addresses these questions and charts the spate of policy shifts and legislative changes which have been enacted, particularly during the 1980s and 1990s, in order to reform initial teacher education (ITE). At the centre of these changes has been a concern to integrate the work of higher education institutions (HEIs) with the school-based elements of teacher education courses. However, before we undertake this task we will highlight a number of key issues that have always bedevilled teacher education and which continue to vex policy makers, practitioners and teachers alike.

These issues are constructed around questions such as: are good teachers born or 'made'; how long does it take to train a good teacher; isn't a practical job like teaching better learned alongside an able practitioner; aren't schools and teaching experience the best way to learn; doesn't a teacher just need to know their subject and enjoy working with young people; won't 'the rest' just take care of itself; is teaching an academic enterprise, a craft skill or a mixture of both? All these questions impinge on the overall issue of how courses are structured and what they should contain. These sorts of questions have reverberated down through the history of teacher education and different issues have been foregrounded in policy and practice at specific moments in time. It is not possible here to do justice to the history of teacher education/training (Alexander *et al.* 1984; Dent 1977; McBride 1996) but we will point up a number of fascinating and recurring dilemmas.

In the nineteenth century, teacher training, as it was called, was a highly regulated, low status concern. Teachers were trained on the job in elementary schools where they worked as apprentice teachers. This was intended to produce humble, moral and uncritical teachers, but the policy changed when it was realised that this method of training produced less than adequate teachers. Teachers who chose to work in fee-paying schools did not have to be (and still do not have to be) trained or educated to teach in any way. They could, and still can, move into teaching after the completion of a first degree. Indeed it was not until 1974 that it became compulsory for state secondary school teachers to be trained (or educated, as it was now referred to in official documents). Until then, secondary teachers in state schools had simply moved into teaching after their first degree. Since 1974, all teachers wishing to be employed in state maintained secondary schools have had to obtain the Postgraduate Certificate in Education (PGCE) or an equivalent teaching qualification.

Perhaps most importantly, teacher education has always been regarded as a lower-status activity. Until the mid-1970s, non-graduate teachers were trained to teach in primary schools and in the secondary modern schools which predominantly served the 'less academic' working-class child. For these sorts of reasons, teacher training has been caught between the world of the university and the school 'belonging to neither' yet susceptible to criticism from both (Taylor 1969: 12). So the state has always been able to intervene in the training of teachers in a way which would not be possible for other higher status professional training routes, such as medicine or law.

The major characteristics of teacher education in the UK are inscribed in its humble origins, in its subordinated power relations with the state and in its history of a provision to match the needs of a differentiated school system (differentiated on the basis of social class as well as age). At specific moments in time there has been some space within course design and development, where teacher educators could exert some influence and we would want to highlight, in particular, the moves to develop educated and reflective teachers. But powerful regulating discourses of 'respectability', the teaching of 'basic skills' and moderation have been ever-present.

Reforming teacher education

Broadly speaking, until 1979, teacher training provision was driven by issues of cost as well as the need to match supply to demand; always a tricky consideration. In the main, teacher training courses were built round a consensus on what constituted good practice; considerations of child development, learning theory, teaching styles, issues drawn from sociology and philosophical questions, as well as subject content and teaching methods. The intention was to develop sound professional practitioners who were able to critically reflect on their classroom practice. Changes were usually introduced after a process of public debate. This process provided some important and sometimes influential checks and balances.

However, 1979 marked a significant shift: the traditional policy processes of open debate, consultation and the hammering out of some degree of consensus gave way to a new regime under which policy making became more clearly political in nature and was ideologically driven. This change was facilitated by a wide range of well publicised, sustained attacks on teacher education. It was argued that teacher education was frequently more concerned with indoctrination than education (Scruton 1985); more with issues of equality and 'social engineering' than effective education. What was needed was a 'common-sense' approach to teacher training. The Conservative Government, newly elected in 1979, had promised wholesale shifts in the provision and 'delivery' of state services. In education, these promises were realised in the Education Reform Act of 1988 (see Chapter 2). 'Standards' were to be raised and schools made more accountable to their 'consumers' (see the section on 'standards' in Chapter 6). From this it followed that if schools were to be improved then the teachers and their pre-service training would have to be improved at the same time.

First moves

In 1983, *The Content of Initial Training* (DES 1983a) was published, closely followed by a White Paper on *Teaching Quality* (DES 1983b). One recommendation put forward was that a national accreditation committee be set up to approve courses in relation to a set of national criteria. It was also argued that teacher trainers needed to go back and teach in schools in order to make their courses more relevant to the everyday needs of classrooms. More account needed to be taken of school-based training. Finally, it was suggested that the Department for Education and Science (DES) be responsible for the inspection of teacher training institutions. At the time this particular suggestion was seen as an erosion of professional autonomy in higher education; central government had not intervened in teacher education in this manner ever before. Today, it seems uncontroversial.

The next development was the publication of Circular 3/84. All teacher training courses were to be evaluated and approved by the Council for the Accreditation of Teacher Education (CATE). It has been argued that the significance of CATE lay in its attempt to 'define the content and structure of initial teacher education' for the first time (Furlong 1992: 164). But CATE also signalled a move away from pedagogical issues, reflectivity and critical autonomy in teacher education courses and towards reconstituting the school teacher as a deliverer of a centrally agreed subject content; a step, perhaps, towards the de-professionalisation of school teachers.

One policy development which echoed this shift was the attempt to produce Articled and Licensed teachers. In a Green Paper (DES 1988a) it was argued that there were many people who would make excellent teachers simply by being trained on the job. Articled teachers would be graduates who could be trained mainly in school but with some input from a local institution of higher education. The licensed teachers were to be recruited from suitable candidates, over twenty-six years of age (later reduced to twenty-four to increase take-up rates) who had experienced two years of higher education. They too could be trained on the job and the governing body of their school could recommend them for the award of Qualified Teacher Status (QTS) after one or two years. Some of the teachers who have used this second route successfully have been 'ethnic minority' teachers whose overseas teaching qualifications were not previously recognised – the scheme did have some potential for breaking bureaucratic racism.

It would be naive (as well as inaccurate) to argue here that there existed a 'golden age' of superb teacher education which has been displaced. What has to be acknowledged is the almost constant pressure for the reform of teacher education. At various points in the last fifteen years it has been argued that newly qualified teachers needed 'modernising' – they needed 'hands-on' experience with technology, they needed an industrial dimension in their courses, if they were successfully to meet the challenges of the next century. It was argued that student teachers needed to spend more time on a traditional subject in their time in college, related, since 1988, to the National Curriculum. One perspective suggested that an induction into a subject is all that would be needed; love of children and some practical classroom experience would accomplish the rest. A further dimension to this position was that teaching is essentially a practical skill best picked up on the job. Furthermore, all of this needed to be achieved in the most cost-effective manner possible. One possible way forward, it was argued, could be through the insertion of quasi-market forces, diversity and financial competition between providers, to ensure 'efficiency' and 'value for money'.

All of these contradictory themes and critiques emerged in the arguments for the deregulation of statutory teacher education. The introduction of the licensed and articled routes were contrived to present a cheap and easy method of covering teacher vacancies as 'common sense', through utilising a complaint made of teacher education that practical matters were not always fully addressed. Somewhat paradoxically, the 'traditional' routes into teaching were being reconstructed on the basis of the need for greater professionalism and a better educated teaching force while the new routes, led by expediency and short term needs, were based on an assumption that teaching is a simple practical job which almost anyone could do. As was noted at the time, 'Part of the tension in teacher training at the moment is that both these concepts are endorsed by the government' (Wragg 1990: 24).

The licensed teacher route was adopted, in the main, to fill shortages in the supply of school teachers. It was widely attacked in the education press and is now a minor route used for retraining and as a way in for overseas educated teachers. The articled teacher route was less susceptible to attack as the intended participants had to be graduates, but this route proved to be expensive and not very successful when compared with the traditional PGCE route. However, the importance of these routes lay in their ideological effect in that they resembled the nineteenth-century apprenticeship schemes. This signalled an intention to break the 'producer capture' of the HEIs over teacher education as well as an intention to deregulate entry to teaching. They also privileged practical-technical classroom routines over critical and reflective professionalism.

Major changes

In 1989, the publication of Circular 24/89 (DES 1989a) led to the restructuring of CATE in a way that extended the government's interventions into teacher education. One outcome was that the student teachers' main teaching subject was now to have direct application to the National Curriculum. Certain subjects, for example, sociology, classics and philosophy were no longer available to be studied by intending primary teachers. Students enrolling on a PGCE course had to have a first degree which closely corresponded to a National Curriculum subject. But while CATE was changing the entrance requirements for the traditional courses, none of this applied to the licensed teacher routes.

At the same time, key individuals within what is loosely called the 'new right' were expressing more fundamental concerns. For them, teacher education was a waste of time. They wanted to 'restore' a traditional 'academic' view of the teacher as a scholar, immersed in their subject – the teacher from the grammar school sector.

> Teachers with Cert. Ed. after their names have studied nonsense for three years. Those with BEd for three or four years. Those with PGCE have had a rest for one year studying nonsense after doing a proper subject and those with MEd or Adv. Dip Ed have returned for super nonsense.
>
> (Anderson 1982: 11)

Her Majesty's Inspectorate (HMI) began to publish reports which were somewhat critical of teacher education: *Quality in Schools* (DES 1987) and *Initial Teacher Training in Universities* (DES 1988b). Another report suggested that 'while the training system had considerable strengths there were also important weaknesses, particularly in the quality of the students' experience in school' (DES 1991: 1). It was evident then that more 'reforms' of ITE were in the pipeline and, as usual, an HMI investigation signalled the direction of the ensuing trend. It is worth noting that the HMI report only gave a cautious welcome to school-based work and underlined the need for the 'essential knowledge and experience from higher education'. They argued that 'the main challenge in initial training is bringing these two kinds of essential expertise together in the most effective way' (DES 1991: 31) and thought that 'for a variety of reasons, secondary training is better placed at present than primary for such a development' (DES 1991: 36). They sounded a number of clear warnings related to inappropriate or 'poor' schools and the need for careful selection of the school teachers to be involved in teacher education and warned about the resources needed to achieve all this. But despite all this, the emphasis on the need for more school-based and school-focused teacher training was clear. The main conclusion of the report was that simply providing more time in school was not enough. The concept of school-based training was not to be merely a quantitative one but should include also the quality of teacher involvement in planning, providing and assessing training and the quality of co-operation between higher education and schools (DES 1991: 36).

Shortly afterwards Circular 9/92 (DFE 1992) was published which dealt with the training of secondary school teachers. Schools were now to take the 'lead role' in initial teacher education; institutions of higher education were to recruit, administer and validate the programmes although they had only 12 weeks for their input to the course (24 out of the 36 weeks of full-time secondary PGCEs had to be spent in school). The document outlined a set of competencies which all intending teachers had to meet. These were categorised into: subject knowledge and its application; class-room management; assessment and recording progress; and further profes-sional development. Funds were to be transferred from the higher education institutions to the schools to reflect the change in the locus of training, although precise amounts were never specified. All courses had to match these specifications by 1994. A vision of 'the teacher' as an enactor of practical competencies and subject knowledge was being articulated rather than that of a reflective practitioner.

Furlong (1992: 181) argues that the contemporary reforms in teacher education were based on technical rationalist principles, that is, he believes that attempts have been made to reduce teacher education to a functional-ist and utilitarian version of 'emphasising only what will be professionally useful to teachers', a form of instrumental knowledge which is typically portrayed as neutral and value free, where education is a means to given ends and all that is needed is a checklist of competencies which should be achieved. It can also be argued that the current emphasis on technical-rational goals has sidelined other issues, such as the need for critical reflec-tion, the need to focus on learning rather than teaching, as well as issues of social justice and equity.

Moving on

When the Major government was re-elected in April 1992 for a further five years, John Patten became Secretary of State for Education. One of his first projects was to extend the work of Circular 9/92. He offered one million pounds to clusters of secondary schools that would provide the total preparation for the award of QTS. The courses would be totally school-based and accredited by a local institution of higher education (which need not have any experience in school-teacher education). Patten also promised to add to the reforms of primary teacher training.

A draft circular was published in June 1993 (DFE 1993a) which argued that many people could easily become teachers of young children. Non-graduate mothers, armed with the experience of bringing up their own children could manage (after a one-year course) to take full responsibility for nursery and infant (Key Stage 1) children. The document made other proposals in relation to undergraduate and postgraduate routes and it was sent to schools and teacher education institutions 'for consultation'. The scheme met with derision and rejection almost immediately. The scheme was labelled as a 'Mums Army' approach and many primary school headteachers said that they would not operate it. Embarrassingly, Patten even failed to obtain support from his appointed CATE committee for the idea. However, the other plans for fragmenting the primary teacher educa-tion routes, providing differentiated courses focused more directly on particular ages and the development of 'specialist' courses were pushed through; with the concern and debate around the 'Mums Army' perhaps providing the smoke screen behind which primary teacher education was reconstructed. As with secondary training, primary schools were encouraged to 'take the lead' and take the funds. As with the reforms for secondary teachers, competencies for prospective primary school teachers were produced.

In September 1993 the Department for Education (DFE 1993b) published a Green Paper, *The Government's Proposals for the Reform of Initial Teacher Training*. It proposed that more teacher training should be moved into the school, that the funding for teacher education be managed through a new quango, the Teacher Training Agency (TTA), and asserted that 'the government will continue to promote additional routes into teaching'. The development of the TTA, with almost total control over teacher education provision, made up of personal appointees of the Secretary of State, was perhaps the most ingenious move yet. Additionally, the Green Paper proposed new arrangements under which the Secretary of State would take advice from those best placed to give it, including the new TTA, as and when he saw the need to revise course criteria, rather than maintaining a standing body to advise him on such matters (DFE 1993b: 2).

The paper, which was described as 'a singularly dishonest document' (Newsom 1993: 20) argued that around one-third of lessons taken by new teachers were unsatisfactory according to evidence from inspections. Teacher education reforms would have to be radical if standards were ever to rise. However, as Newsom pointed out, evidence from the Office for Standards in Education (Ofsted) stated that 'in 1992, over 90 per cent of headteachers considered their new teachers to have been adequately prepared for their first teaching post and over 70 per cent of lessons were considered by HMI as satisfactory or better'. Newsom argued that there was no evidence to suggest that 'fresh upheavals would contribute to the improvements needed'. Newsom commented that the major 'distortion' lay not in the way in which the research evidence was presented but in the attempt to 'conceal, under a cloud of clichés, the true intentions underlying the upheavals now proposed.'

One intention behind the Green Paper was to unravel the relationship between higher educational institutions and teacher education and to invest greater control in the central state. In setting up the TTA, the government removed several layers of balances and checks, which had been used to maintain some form of independent stance on ITE. In addition, the strong financially supported moves towards school-centred initial teacher training (SCITT) signalled the moves to insert market forces into teacher education. The Green Paper also argued that funding for research into teaching was also to be distributed by the TTA. As Brighouse put it at the time:

> Suspicions that government moves to ever-more school-based courses of initial teacher training are a prelude to dispensing altogether with the input of higher education are not easily dispelled. After all, the invitation to a few selected schools – mainly grant maintained and city technology colleges and regarded as fairly reliable friends of government – to mount PGCE courses at high unit costs and with university involvement limited to validation, seems to suggest sinister intent. Moreover, any research and evaluation which is funded by curriculum and assessment quangos is often on terms which are inimical to disinterested enquiry and sometimes can preclude publication. Practising

teachers' in-service needs are decreasingly funded by local education authorities at school level. To be paranoid does not preclude the possibility that someone is out to get you!

(Brighouse 1993)

In November 1993 the Conservative Government published yet another Education Bill that, among other things, sought to restructure teacher education yet further. The Bill contained most of the proposals drawn from the Green Paper. It established the TTA and promoted the school-based teacher education courses.

Reform comes full circle

Currently, teacher education is based on a partnership model of integration between HEIs and schools. 'Such a model holds out important opportunities for the development of highly effective forms of initial teacher education' (Furlong *et al.* 1996: 33). But there are some issues which need to be raised. In our view, teachers need to be educated; that is, they need to be exposed to a wide range of the research and debates which inform and sustain sound practice. Teachers need a breadth as well as a depth of vision and they also need a 'healthy scepticism'. As McBride (1996: 276) has put it, 'a professional teacher operates in largely non-routine situations, especially when children's learning is taken into account, and therefore teachers have to have some freedom to make judgements. We cannot educate teachers by giving them lists of simple rules.' However, research conducted by Dart and Drake (1993) suggests that, in some partnerships, the students were unable to question the practices which they observed and that school-based training could lead to a very conservative practice which merely reinforced the in-school status-quo. Additionally, there are also very real questions of resourcing which need consideration if the opportunities of partnership are to be realised.

In 1996 the Government proposed a National Curriculum for Initial Teacher Training and the TTA was to produce an initiative on teaching methods to provide, among other things:

legitimate national standards for teaching and to ensure that teacher trainers, whether in higher education or school-based, are clear – thanks not least to the new national curriculum for initial teacher training – about what teachers have to know, understand and be able to do, and what they as teacher trainers need to know, understand and be able to do in order to prepare the teacher-professionals of tomorrow.

(Millett 1996: 13)

We want to end by asking some open questions about the reforms in teacher education/training. First, what are we to make of the paradox which allows the Government to blame poor schools for poor performances yet at the same time seeks to train teachers in these very institutions? Secondly, the almost constant allegations of poor quality and low standards in British schools seems unlikely to attract 'able' recruits; after all, who wants to be part of an under-performing service? After 17 years of almost constant 'reforms' in initial teaching (with more proposed) does it seem reasonable that teachers and teacher trainers should be regularly singled out as responsible for 'poor standards' in education?

Finally, it seems to us that one thing, at least, is certain; teacher education will continue to evolve, incorporating different stances on the sorts of questions we outlined at the start of this chapter. Our hope is for evolutionary, incremental, research-driven 'reforms' which incorporate the views of school teachers, trainee teachers as well as college tutors. Our fears are that without a critical, reflective and co-operative approach towards teacher education, our schools and our children will be less well served.

Note

1 This chapter draws on an earlier work by Maguire and Ball (1995).

References

Alexander, R.J., Craft, M. and Lynch, J. (eds) (1984) *Change in Teacher Education: Context and Provision since Robbins*. London: Rinehart and Winston.

Anderson, D. (1982) *Detecting Bad Schools: A Guide for Normal Parents*. London: Social Affairs Unit.

Brighouse, T. (1993) Strong forces for change, *Times Higher Education Supplement*, 10 September.

Dart, L. and Drake, P. (1993) School-based teacher training: a conservative practice?, *Journal of Education for Teaching*, 19(2): 175–89.

Dent, H.C. (1977) *The Training of Teachers in England and Wales, 1800–1975*. London: Hodder and Stoughton.

Department for Education (DFE) (1992) *The Initial Training of Secondary School Teachers*, Circular 9/92. London: HMSO.

Department for Education (DFE) (1993a) *The Initial Training of Primary School Teachers: New Criteria for Course Approval*, Draft Circular. London: HMSO.

Department for Education (DFE) (1993b) *The Government's Proposals for the Reform of Initial Teacher Training*, Draft proposals, 7 September. London: HMSO.

Department of Education and Science (DES) (1983a) *Teaching in Schools: The Content of Initial Teacher Training*. HMI Discussion Paper. London: HMSO.

Department of Education and Science (DES) (1983b) *White Paper; Teaching Quality*, Cmnd 8836. London: HMSO.

Department of Education and Science (DES) (1984) *Initial Teacher Training: Approval of Courses*, Circular 3/84. London: HMSO.

Department of Education and Science (DES) (1987) *Quality in Schools: The Initial Training of Teachers*, Her Majesty's Inspectors Survey. London: HMSO.

Department of Education and Science (DES) (1988a) *Qualified Teacher Status – Consultation Document*, Green Paper. London: HMSO.

Department of Education and Science (DES) (1988b) *Initial Teacher Training in Universities in England, Northern Ireland and Wales, Education Observed 7*. London: HMSO.

Department of Education and Science (DES) (1989a) *Initial Teacher Training: Approval of Courses*, Circular 24/89. London: HMSO.

Department of Education and Science (DES) (1989b) *Future Arrangements for the Accreditation of Courses of Initial Teacher Training – A Consultation Document*, Circular 3/89. London: HMSO.

Department of Education and Science (DES) (1991) *School-based Initial Teacher Training in England and Wales – HMI report*. London: HMSO.

Furlong, J. (1992) Reconstructing professionalism: ideological struggle in initial teacher education, in M. Arnot and L. Barton (eds) *Voicing Concerns: Sociological Perspectives on Contemporary Education Reforms*. Oxford: Triangle Books.

Furlong, J., Whitty, G., Miles, S., Barton, L. and Barrett, L. (1996) From integration to partnership: changing structures in initial teacher education, in R. McBride (ed.) *Teacher Education Policy: Some Issues Arising from Research and Practice*. London: Falmer Press.

McBride, R. (ed.) (1996) *Teacher Education Policy: Some Issues Arising from Research and Practice*. London: Falmer Press.

Maguire, M. and Ball, S.J. (1995) Teacher education and education policy in England, in N.K. Shimahara and I.Z. Holowinsky (eds) *Teacher Education in Industrialised Nations: Issues in Changing Social Contexts*. London: Garland Publications Inc.

Millett, A. (1996) Pedagogy – the last corner of the secret garden. King's Annual Education Lecture, King's College London, 15 July.

National Curriculum Council (1991) *The National Curriculum and the Initial Training of Student, Articled and Licensed Teachers*. York: National Curriculum Council.

Newsom, P. (1993) 'Pestered with a Popinjay', *Times Educational Supplement*, 17 September.

Scruton, R. (1985) *Education and Indoctrination*. London: Education Research Centre.

Taylor, W. (1969) *Society and the Education of Teachers*. London: Faber and Faber.

Wragg, E.C. (1990) The two routes into teaching, in M. Booth, V.J. Furlong and M. Wilkin (eds) *Partnership in Initial Teacher Training*. London: Cassell.

5

Teachers and the law

Dylan Wiliam

Sources of law

There are two main sources of law in England and Wales: common law and statute law. Common law is not written down in Acts of Parliament but rather has been built up over the centuries. Statute law, on the other hand, is the law that comes from the work of Parliament in passing Acts like the 1988 Education Reform Act. A teacher's responsibility (and the same applies to student teachers) for children derives largely from common law, not statute law. The crucial part of this responsibility is the notion of a *duty of care*.

Everyone has a duty of care to everyone else. If I ran down a busy street and knocked someone over, causing injury, I might well be held liable in a court for the injury I had caused. This general duty of care extends only to what I do, rather than what I do not do. If someone else knocks someone over in the street, I have no legal obligation to help the injured person.

However, the role of the teacher (or the student teacher) in school is different, because they have taken on what is called a 'special relationship' in respect of the children in the school. If a child is hurt in the school playground, teachers have a duty to help the child, because of the special relationship. Being in a special relationship with someone else places a duty of care that includes what you do not do (acts of omission) as well as what you do (acts of commission).

Whether a special relationship exists or not depends on what a person professes to be, rather than what they are. So for example, if someone says 'Let me through, I'm a doctor' in a crowd of people surrounding a road casualty, that person does have a special relationship with the casualty, whether the person is, in fact, a doctor or not. Similarly, a student teacher teaching a class is in a special relationship with the individuals in that class even though an experienced teacher from another school who was just in the classroom as a visitor would not.

The interpretation of particular laws, whether derived from common law, or brought about by statute, is built up over time by referring to what has been determined in similar cases in the past. This is *case law*. The 'ground rules' of case law are that if a higher court decides a case in a particular way then a lower court must follow that ruling and any court at the same level should take notice of it, but a higher court does not have to. So, for example, the High Court would have to follow a ruling decided by the Court of Appeal, but the House of Lords does not. A selection of the most important cases relating to the teacher's role is included at the end of this chapter.

There is another kind of law called 'delegated legislation'. This is a means by which an Act of Parliament does not specify the details of the legislation, but instead grants powers to some other person or agency to specify the details of the law. For example, the part of the 1988 Education Reform Act that relates to the National Curriculum covers only three pages. The section that brings the National Curriculum into being is very brief. It states, 'The Secretary of State may by order specify in relation to each of the foundation subjects such attainment targets, such programmes of study and such assessment arrangements as he considers appropriate for that subject.' That is all that is in the Act, but it grants power to somebody else to make law. In this case, it is the Secretary of State for Education, who, by signing his or her name to an Order, makes it statutory.

The reason for such 'delegated' legislation is very sensible. For example, every year teachers' pay is renegotiated. The framework for this process is established in statute law but without some mechanism for delegated legislation, the actual details would have to be dealt with by Parliament every year, taking up a great deal of parliamentary time.

What is very disturbing is the number of such legal powers that have been given to secretaries of state in recent years. The 1988 Education Reform Act, for example, gave over *two hundred* new powers to the Secretary of State to make statutory regulations. As a consequence, it is very difficult to keep up with the current state of the law. Furthermore, the speed and lack of opportunity to debate and examine legislation before it becomes law that we have seen means that the regulations which are made are often flawed. For example, the Education (School Performance Indicators) regulations which were published in August 1993 contained three errors, which had to be rectified by publishing the Education (School Performance Indicators) No. 2 regulations!

The good news for new teachers is that hardly any of the recent legislation (as many acts in eight years as in the previous 40) impacts directly on the classroom teacher. The impact of almost all recent educational legislation has been at a management or a policy level. The task of the ordinary teacher is to carry out any 'reasonable' instruction from the headteacher. Even where certain tasks are not necessary in law, if it is a reasonable instruction, then it is part of a teacher's contractual duty to carry it out. If you are given an instruction that you consider unreasonable you might refuse to carry it out. But then you would run the risk of being formally disciplined, either by the headteacher or the governors of the school. Even if you successfully appealed against a disciplinary action, you could well end up with a headteacher who hated you forever! Because of this, a teacher's job really comes down to two things: carrying out the headteacher's instructions, and discharging your duty of care to the pupils that you supervise.

Duty of care

The earliest definition of what a duty of care might mean in the context of schools and teaching was established in *Williams* v. *Eady*: 'The duty of a schoolmaster is to take such care of his boys as a careful father would take of his son.' This creates the clear impression that there were neither girls nor female schoolteachers around in these days, but then it is a very old judgement (1893). That was the earliest definition of what exactly that duty of care amounted to in the educational setting – a careful father. Now, there is plenty of evidence to suggest that over the intervening years – certainly the past fifty years – the duty of care has been interpreted more precisely. That is the big strength of common law established through case law: as public perceptions change, interpretations of the law can shift, without changing the 'letter' of the law.

In September 1993, for example, a schoolteacher was suspended for sticking masking tape over a pupil's mouth. Now, that in itself is not surprising because local authorities have the power to suspend people for a range of disciplinary offences, very few of which relate to the law. What was unusual in this case is that the police were involved, because in the past, they have been rather unwilling to act unless the level of harm to the child was relatively serious. Such action would certainly not have been regarded as a matter for the police (or probably even the education authority) in 1893.

In 1938 the notion of a careful parent was reaffirmed in a judgement that held that 'the courts [would] not put on the headmaster [*sic*] any higher standard of care than that of a reasonably careful parent'. However, two decades later the requirement had shifted somewhat. Because of the way that case law is built up (as described above), the central notion of a reasonable, prudent or careful father cannot be overturned, but more recent judgements have attempted to re-interpret the original judgement. By 1962, the common law duty of a schoolmaster is held to be that 'of a prudent parent bound to take notice of boys [*sic*] and their tendency to do mischievous acts, not in the context of home but in the circumstances of school life, and extends not only to how pupils conduct themselves but also to the state and condition of the school premises'. There is an implication that there are more risks at school than at home and therefore a teacher needs to be aware, and take account, of this. In 1968, it was held that 'it is a headmaster's duty, bearing in mind the propensities of boys and girls [at last!] between the ages of 11 and 18 to take all reasonable and proper steps to prevent any of the pupils under his care from suffering injury from inanimate objects, from actions of their fellow pupils or from a combination of both'. So while the *standard* of care required is the same for teachers and for parents, teachers are expected to take account of the special circumstances pertaining in school in discharging this duty.

The same standard of duty of care applies to student teachers, but the law does recognise that by virtue of their lack of training and experience, they are less able than their colleagues to anticipate events and to take appropriate action. If while a student is teaching a class, something goes wrong and their inexperience leads to a pupil being injured, it could well be the case that the student would not be found negligent whereas an experienced teacher acting in exactly the same way could be. While teachers are relatively inexperienced the law does not expect as much as it does when they are fully trained, provided, of course, that they do exercise a minimum level of responsibility.

Negligence

In practice, most court cases relating to duty of care come under the general heading of negligence. To prove negligence one has to establish that there was a duty of care, that it was breached, that there was damage, that the breach caused the damage, and that the damage was reasonably foreseeable. The last of these has been very important in the past. In 1984, a pupil brought an action against a teacher who had tackled the boy round the neck in a 'staff vs. students' rugby game causing the boy relatively severe injuries. The teacher *was* found to have been negligent because the court held that it *was* reasonably foreseeable that a 14-stone teacher tackling an 8-stone pupil around the neck would cause injury. As a result, the boy was awarded substantial damages. These were paid by the local education authority (LEA), because although it was the teacher and the school who were actually being taken to court, all local education authorities are exposed to what is known as *vicarious liability* as regards the negligence of their employees. Even if a teacher has acted against local authority guidance, the authority can still be liable, and since they tend to have more money than most teachers, most actions are brought against the LEA in addition to the school or an individual teacher.

However, as can be seen from the dates of the important cases relating to negligence, actions against schools and teachers are rare. Very few actions actually reach the courts. In this sense, teaching is not a 'high-risk' activity unlike medicine where malpractice suits are much more common. It is important to remember that most teachers never find themselves accused of anything in their whole teaching career. However, it is also important to know what one's professional duties are.

Of the responses that a teacher can make to claims of negligence, the two most important are a) that there was no breach of duty, or b) that what happened would have happened anyway. For example, if one pupil suffers injury as the result of an assault from another pupil during morning break would the school be held to be negligent? If the attack was unpredictable or completely unexpected, then it is likely that an action for negligence would not succeed – the courts have always held that something that would not have been prevented had there been supervision is not negligence. However, if the attacker was known to the school to be a bully and given to random and unprovoked attacks, then an action for negligence could well succeed.

Another response to an action for negligence is illustrated by the following case. A primary school teacher was going to take two young girls out, and had them dressed ready to go when another child came along with a cut hand. The teacher attended to the child with the cut hand during which time one of the two other little children ran out of the school gates, causing a car accident in which the driver was killed. The family of the driver sued the teacher and the LEA for negligence. In this case, the teacher was found *not* to be negligent, because the court held that the teacher had behaved reasonably in dealing with the injury to the other child first. The fact that a teacher is distracted by a more serious or urgent incident is a defence. Even though the law places a higher burden on the teacher than on the proverbial 'man on the Clapham omnibus', it still only requires that the teacher behaves reasonably in the circumstances. But even in this judgement, the court was careful to point out that the ruling depended on the fact that it was an *infant* child with a cut hand. A 15 year-old with the same small cut would probably not be grounds for leaving younger children alone, and an action might still succeed against whoever left the school gates open so that the child could run out into the road. The important message here is that the law only requires you to act reasonably – provided you do so, you will not be held liable.

The criterion of reasonableness also governs whether student teachers can teach classes without a qualified teacher present. It would probably not be held to be reasonable to leave a student on her or his own with a class during the first week of teaching practice. A court might also hold that it was unreasonable to leave a teacher on her or his own with a class known to be particularly difficult, even towards the end of teaching practice. However, it is generally accepted that there are times when student teachers have to be left alone in the classroom to establish that they can actually manage. The courts have generally followed the principle that the test of what is reasonable in ordinary, everyday affairs may well be answered by experience arising from 'practice adopted generally and followed successfully for many years'.

Sanctions

The most important remaining aspects of educational law – or at least the ones that everybody seems to want to know about – are sanctions: discipline, confiscation, punishments and such matters. Can a teacher confiscate cigarettes from a pupil? The important thing about confiscation is that one must not permanently deprive someone of something – that is theft. So, confiscating cigarettes from a pupil may be quite reasonable, but smoking them oneself later is not.

But the duty of care also plays a part here. If, for example, one discovered that a student had a flick-knife, which was subsequently used to injure another pupil, it is quite possible that one would be found negligent if one had *not* tried to confiscate it, or at least reported the matter to someone else (because of the responsibility for omission as well as commission in a special relationship, and one's duty of care to all the pupils at a school).

Most schools have a procedure laid down for what to do with confiscated items. Personal hi-fis might be kept in the headteacher's office until the end of the day and then returned, cigarettes might be returned only to parents, and flick-knives would probably be handed over to the police. The important thing here is to find out what your school's policy is and follow that.

The same applies to detention. Most schools have policies laid down about the length of detentions that can be given and the notice required. Many schools allow detention for 15 or 30 minutes without notice, with 24 hours notice being required for longer detentions, but again, the important thing is to find out what your school's policy is.

Detention through the use of physical force would probably constitute a trespass to the person. The defence to this has generally been that it was reasonable and appropriate as a punishment, but it is unlikely that using physical force to keep a pupil in detention would be regarded as reasonable.

The use of physical force *can* be justified in order to prevent pupils from injuring themselves and from injuring one another provided the force used is the minimum necessary. The justification lies in the special relationship which the teacher has to protect and preserve the interests of the pupils. I have seen a pupil in such a rage that he was repeatedly banging his own head against a brick wall. In such a situation, it is likely that you would be in breach of your duty of care if you did *not* try to stop him from injuring himself further. If two pupils are fighting, then you should either separate them or, if you do not consider yourself physically able to do this, take steps to alert other members of staff. You can also use physical force to prevent damage to property (the law is nothing if not capitalist!). If a child is insisting on damaging school property or any other property you may use physical force to prevent this, but it has to be reasonable. The definition of 'reasonable' in this context is that it is the minimum force necessary to achieve what is required.

The courts have also held that schools' supervision of pupils extends to the pupils' journey to and from school. This principle was reinforced in a ruling concerning the case of two boys who were caught smoking on the way to school and were caned. One of the parents took action against the school but the court decided that from the moment they has stepped out of the door then the pupils were under the school's jurisdiction, and could certainly be punished for deeds committed on the way to and from school. Furthermore, one does not have to take into account what a *particular* parent might do or want to have done. Generally, a teacher's actions will be defensible if they have done what a reasonable parent would do even though that particular child's parent would not have acted in that way.

Corporal punishment

Until relatively recently, the law regarding corporal punishment treated teachers looking after students in the same way as a parent. The teacher was *in loco parentis* or 'in the place of the parent'. The law condones a parent hitting a child as 'proper chastisement', provided it is not excessive.

The first definition of what was reasonable in terms of corporal punishment in schools was given in 1860: 'Punishment must be reasonable and moderate and not for the gratification of passion or rage or excessive in its nature or degree or protracted beyond the child's endurance.'

Until 1986, decisions regarding corporal punishment in state schools were delegated to local education authorities. Some LEAs had banned all corporal punishment; those that had not were required to set up procedures for administering corporal punishment. For example, in most schools only a small number of teachers were allowed to administer corporal punishment and it had to be entered into a punishment book. But it is important to remember that, even in schools that allowed the use of corporal punishment, the kind of 'clipping across the ear' that used to happen informally was probably illegal, and certainly a breach of the teacher's contract. As far as most teachers were concerned, the changes made in 1986 did not change the position of individual teachers with respect to corporal punishment, but only whether one could send a pupil to somebody else to be beaten.

The change in the law came because two Scottish parents wanted the right to exempt their children from corporal punishment in school. Having lost their case at every level of the domestic legal system the action went before the European Court of Human Rights where the judgement was overturned. The British Government's original response was to allow a situation in which individual parents had the right to withdraw their children from corporal punishment. There was a great deal of concern that this would create a situation in which two students guilty of exactly the same offence in school might receive very different punishments because of what their parents had said. For this reason, sections banning the use of corporal punishments in state schools were tagged onto the end of the 1986 Education (No. 2) Act – an Act largely concerned with the governance of schools – which happened to be going through Parliament at the time.

Thus a teacher may not hit students, nor physically restrain them, except to prevent injury to themselves, or to others, or damage to property, and even then, the force used must be reasonable – that is, the minimum necessary.

The same law, of course, protects the teacher. If a student assaults you, then you have recourse to law. The difficulty is that the police are unlikely to prosecute unless there is actual bodily harm. However, the teacher can still bring private prosecutions or civil actions, and if a member of a trade union, may receive legal support in doing so.

Defamation

Most people are familiar with the distinction between slander and libel. Defamatory speech is slander but if it is in any kind of permanent form (writing, audio tape, etc.) it is libel. Interestingly enough, if someone writes something defamatory on a blackboard, even though it is easily removed, that technically is probably libel rather than slander. The distinction between slander and libel is important, because in order to succeed with an action for slander, in most cases one generally has to prove some financial loss as a result of the untrue remark, whereas in libel it is only necessary to prove that one's standing in other people's eyes would be lowered, such as an assertion that a particular teacher is incompetent. The reason I emphasise this point is not to encourage student teachers to sue anyone who says they are not doing very well on teaching practice, but to point out that one must be careful about what one says about other teachers. I have heard student teachers say things about other teachers in a staff room that would certainly be actionable, and I think it is also important to bear in mind that pupils have exactly the same rights. Although actions for defamation are very rare, the safest course is to avoid saying anything 'that would be calculated or likely to reduce somebody's standing in the eyes of their peers'.

Copyright

The area in which teachers are most likely to break the law or run into trouble is copyright. A new agency set up as a result of the 1988 Copyright Designs and Patents Act insists that its poster is displayed by all photocopiers in schools that have signed up for a special agreement permitting limited copying of copyright documents. The poster specifies exactly what one can and cannot copy. One can for example, make class sets of certain materials for use in teaching provided both the school or the LEA and the author of the work are signatories to the agreement. Certain kinds of publications are designed to be photocopied, in which case the copyright agreement would allow unlimited photocopying within the purchasing institution.

The traditional length of copyright in the United Kingdom has been 50 years from the death of the author. So, for example, the work of Alfred Lord Tennyson came out of copyright 50 years after his death. However, as part of the harmonisation of legislation within the European Union, the length of copyright has now been extended to 70 years after the author's death. The transitional arrangements mean that work by authors who died between 1926 and 1946, which has been out of copyright in Britain (but not, for example, in Germany) have come back into copyright, which now lasts for 70 years after the end of the calendar year in which the author died.

However, published editions have a copyright of 25 years irrespective of the date of the author's death so if one photocopied a page of a book of Tennyson's poems one would not be infringing the author's copyright, but one could be infringing the *publisher's* copyright in the 'typographical arrangement'. Copying out the poems by hand would not infringe the copyright in the typographical form, nor would manually keying the poems into a wordprocessor, printing it off, and making multiple copies of the printout. However, because electronic scanners do make an internal image of the page – albeit only temporarily – scanning a page of poems and then using text-recognition software to produce a wordprocessor file of the poems probably *would* infringe the publisher's copyright in the typographical arrangement.

However, the area in which schools break copyright laws most frequently would appear to be that of computer software, simply because most commercial business software is not copy protected. Computer games that are bought predominantly by adolescent males have very extensive precautions to prevent them being copied because the manufacturers know that this is the sort of thing that adolescent males do all the time. However, the business market has, in recent years, put a great deal of pressure on the software manufacturers not to impose 'copy-protection' on business software because it makes the software more difficult to use, and as a result most 'business' software is not copy protected. A single copy of such software can be used on more than one machine quite easily. Schools often reason like this: 'Why should I spend £5,000 buying multiple copies of a desk-top publishing package when it's only going to be used by one class for two weeks in the whole year?' Nevertheless, what they are doing is illegal and some LEAs have been 'raided' and found to be using software illegally.

As far as the new teacher is concerned, the only safe course of action is to ask the member of staff at the school responsible for IT (information technology) before using any software, and you should certainly not install any software on a school computer without asking someone first.

Health and safety at work

Another important piece of legislation is the Health and Safety at Work Act of 1974. This Act makes provision concerning the health, safety and welfare of employees and the health and safety of visitors to any work premises. Strangely, for the purposes of law, pupils count as visitors, rather than workers in educational institutions, although it is not clear why that is. This law is important in that it gives the duty of care some 'criminal teeth'. If, for example, there was a nail sticking out of a table, which the teacher knew about, and one day a pupil walked past it cutting their leg, the teacher would be in breach of their duty of care and there would be a possibility of successful civil action against the teacher and the school or LEA. However, the Health and Safety at Work Act would also allow the Health and Safety Executive to bring a *criminal* prosecution against the school and the individual teacher for having dangerous premises. What actually happens in practice falls short of the ideal envisaged in law.

A teacher might find that their classroom was dangerous for some reason or another (window catches that would not secure, nails sticking out of objects, and so on). The response of the school management in such a situation would typically be to move the teacher and her or his class into a different classroom while the problem was rectified. However, teachers often do not want to do this because all their teaching resources are in that classroom. As a result, teachers are sometimes reluctant to report anything dangerous in their classrooms. Nevertheless, one does have to provide for the health and safety of pupils in one's classes and if one knows about anything that is likely to cause a risk then one must do something about it. Inconvenience is no excuse, and it is certainly no defence in law.

Professional responsibilities

An important element of any course of initial teacher education is a process of 'enculturation', of discovering what 'being a schoolteacher' entails. They do not look like it, but even the smallest schools are extremely complex organisations. The ability to displace all the energy that students bring in every day requires some very sophisticated mechanisms and many of these run on the assumption that people do what they are meant to do. Consider the following example.

A teacher is on the way to school by train one very cold winter morning. Due to frozen points, the train had been completely stationary in the middle of nowhere for about half an hour and has just come to a station. With no more stoppages, there is a reasonable chance that if she stays on this train she will get to school about five minutes late. However, if she gets off this train at this stop to telephone the school there is no telling when the next train would arrive. What should she do? To an experienced teacher this would be a 'no brainer' – a decision that is so easy to make that it requires no thinking at all. You get off the train and call the school. It gives the school a chance to cope. It is much easier for the school to know that somebody is not turning up so a supply teacher, or somebody else who is free, can be there to cover. If a class is unsupervised, things can go seriously wrong.

Summary

Inevitably, this chapter has focused on the 'pathology' of school teaching. As a teacher you will have important responsibilities, but it is important to keep things in perspective. As long as you use physical force only to prevent injury to students or damage to property, and then only the minimum necessary; as long as you think the consequences of your actions through; as long as you act reasonably, then you will be alright. No one will sue you or take you to court, and it is extremely unlikely that you will be assaulted in any way. And you will, like most teachers, enjoy the job.

Relevant case law

The extracts from legal judgements given below are taken from *Legal Cases for Teachers* by Geoffrey R. Barrell (1970).

Punishment

- Punishment must be reasonable and moderate and not for the gratification of passion or rage or excessive in its nature or degree, or protracted beyond the child's endurance (*R* v. *Hopley* [1860] 2 F&F 202).
- A teacher acts *in loco parentis* and detention of a parent of his/her own child is unlawful if it is for such a period or in such circumstances as to take it out of the realm of reasonable parental discipline (*R* v. *Rahman* [1985]).

Negligence

- The duty of a schoolmaster is to take such care of his boys as a careful father would take of his son (*Williams* v. *Eady* [1893] 10 TLR 41).
- The courts will not put on a headmaster any higher standard of care than that of a reasonably careful parent (*Hudson* v. *Rotherham Grammar School and Johnson* [1938] *Yorkshire Post*, 24 March 1938 and 25 March 1938).
- The common law duty of a schoolmaster is that of a prudent parent bound to take notice of boys and their tendency to do mischievous acts, not in the context of the home but in the circumstances of school life, and extends not only to how the pupils conduct themselves, but also to the state and condition of the school premises (*Lyes* v. *Middlesex County Council* [1962] 61 LGR 443).
- It is a headmaster's duty, bearing in mind the propensities of boys and girls between the ages of 11 and 18, to take all reasonable and proper steps to prevent any of the pupils under his care from suffering injury from inanimate objects, from actions of their fellow pupils, or from a combination of both (*Beaumont* v. *Surrey County Council* [1968] 66 LGR 580).
- A defendant who through training or experience, may have grounds to visualise more clearly the results of his acts in a particular sphere than would be expected of the proverbial man in the street owes a higher duty of care (*Baxter* v. *Barker and others* [1903] *The Times*, 24 April 1903 and 13 November 1903).
- School authorities must strike some balance between the meticulous supervision of children at every moment when they are under their care, and the very desirable objects of encouraging the sturdy independence of children as they grow up; such encouragement must start at quite an early age (*Jeffery* v. *London County Council* [1954] 52 LGR 521).
- The mere fact of the fall of a blackboard is not evidence of negligence (*Crisp* v. *Thomas* [1890] 63 LT756).
- It is negligence for a teacher to order a child to undertake a dangerous operation (*Foster* v. *London County Council* [1928] *The Times* 2.3.28).
- It is, I think, impossible to avoid the conclusion that it was a most unfortunate, unforeseeable and quite unpredictable thing which occasioned the accident on this day. [. . .] It appears that this was the first time such a thing had happened. In those circumstances, I find it is impossible to say on the facts than any negligence was shown on the part of the defendant (*Wright* v. *Cheshire County Council* [1952] 2 All ER 789).
- The test of what is reasonable in ordinary everyday affairs may well be answered by experience arising from practices adopted generally and followed successfully for many years (*Wright* v. *Cheshire County Council* [1952] All ER 789).
- Where a course of action follows general and approved practice an action of negligence will not lie (*Conrad* v. *Inner London Education Authority* [1967] *The Times*, 26 May 1967).
- An action for negligence cannot succeed if it is founded on an event which is simply an accident (*Webb* v. *Essex County Council* [1954] *Times Educational Supplement*, 12 November 1954).

- A school master is not liable for a sudden act which could not have been prevented by supervision (*Gow* v. *Glasgow Education Authority* [1922] SC 260).
- Where there is no evidence of lack of supervision or that, assuming there was supervision, it would not have prevented an accident, there is no liability (*Langham* v. *Wellingborough School Governors and Fryer* [1932] 101 LJKB 513).
- It is not incumbent upon a local education authority to have a teacher continuously present in a playground during a break (*Ricketts* v. *Erith Borough Council and Browne* [1943] 2 All ER 629).
- The duty of a schoolmaster does not extend to the constant supervision of all the boys in his care all the time; only reasonable supervision is required (*Clarke* v. *Monmouth County Council* [1954] 52 LGR 246).
- Even if there is failure of supervision, the question arises whether the best supervision could have prevented the accident (*Price* v. *Caernarvonshire County Council* [1960] *The Times*, 11 February 1960).
- When a class of nine or ten are using pointed scissors, it is not necessary to wait until after a lesson, or to make sure that the rest of the class put their scissors down before giving individual attention to one child (*Butt* v. *Cambridgeshire and Isle of Ely Council* [1969] *The Times* 27 November 1969).

Reference

Barrell, G.R. (1970) *Legal Cases for Teachers*. London: Methuen.

Part 2 | Social and political issues

6

Ideology, evidence and the raising of standards[1]

Paul Black

Introduction

The system in which new teachers find themselves working has been influenced, more than at any time in recent years, by policy makers and their informants. This chapter develops ideas about national education policy, starting, in the first section, with some reflections on developments in England and Wales since the National Curriculum and assessment were first put in place by the Education Reform Act of 1988 (the ERA). This leads, in the second section, to a more general account of the way in which policy has developed in relation to ideological pressures and in the third section to some comparisons with the policy approaches of other countries. Finally, in the fourth and final section, I want to suggest some ways in which our policy thinking ought to develop. This chapter should be read in conjunction with Chapter 2, which focuses on the ERA and Chapter 16, which explains some of the more technical aspects of assessment.

TGAT – An impossible dream?

In 1987, the Cabinet Minister then responsible for education, Kenneth Baker, invited me to chair the Task Group on Assessment and Testing (TGAT) to advise on assessment policy for the new National Curriculum. I accepted because my experience made me optimistic that valid, and therefore helpful, external national tests could be set up. I was also optimistic because government statements seemed to recognise the importance of teachers' own assessments in any national scheme (DES 1987: para. 29; DES 1988a: Appendix B).

The TGAT proposals (DES 1988a, b) were at first accepted as government policy, and then abandoned one by one in the next few years (Black

1993a; 1996). It was clear at an early stage that Baker's acceptance of the TGAT report might not have wholehearted support from his Prime Minister:

> The fact that it was then welcomed by the Labour Party, the National Union of Teachers and the *Times Educational Supplement* was enough to confirm for me that its approach was suspect. It proposed an elaborate and complex system of assessment – teacher dominated and uncosted. It adopted the 'diagnostic' view of tests, placed the emphasis on teachers doing their own assessment and was written in an impenetrable educationalist jargon.
>
> (Thatcher 1993: 594–5)

A more explicit rejection was delivered later by Thatcher's new Education Minister, Kenneth Clarke:

> The British pedagogue's hostility to written examinations of any kind can be taken to ludicrous extremes . . . This remarkable national obsession lies behind the more vehement opposition to the recent introduction of 7 year old testing. They were made a little too complicated and we have said we will simplify them . . . The complications themselves were largely designed in the first place in an attempt to pacify opponents who feared above all else 'paper and pencil' tests . . .
>
> (Clarke 1991)

What in fact was happening at that time was a tussle within the Conservative Party in which the 'new right' prevailed. Sir Malcolm Thornton, the Conservative chairman of the House of Commons Select Committee on Education explained this clearly in commenting on events following the appointment of Clarke:

> From that point on, I believe that both the wider debate and the ears of Ministers have been disproportionately influenced by extremists – extremists whose pronouncements become even wilder and further from the reality of the world of education which I recognise, in which I work in and for which I care deeply. And who are they to foist upon the children of this country ideas which will only serve to take them backwards? What hard evidence do they have to support their assertions?
>
> (Thornton 1992, quoted in Chitty and Simon 1993: 45–60)

The TGAT argued strongly for priority to be given to supporting assessment by teachers as essential to the raising of standards and its view was accepted by Kenneth Baker. However, the agencies responsible for developing the national assessment policy devoted hardly any of their time or resources to it – they concentrated on external testing (Daugherty 1995; Black 1996). This should not have been a surprise in view of earlier reversals. Consider, for example, Baker in 1989:

> The balance – characteristic of most GCSE courses – between coursework and an externally set and marked terminal examination has worked well. I accept the Council's judgement that assessment by means of coursework is one of the examination's strengths . . .
>
> (Kenneth Baker, July 1989, quoted in Daugherty 1995: 131)

In 1991 the Prime Minister, John Major, reversed this conclusion:

> It is clear that there is now far too much coursework, project work and
> teacher assessment in GCSE. The remedy surely lies in getting GCSE
> back to being an externally assessed exam which is predominantly
> written. I am attracted to the idea that for most subjects a maximum
> of 20 per cent of the marks should be obtainable from coursework.
> (John Major, July 1991, quoted in Daugherty 1995: 137)

This speech led to government directives to reduce the coursework
component of GCSE; a change which was not preceded either by public
consultation or by any review of evidence.

I would like to contrast this history with three developments in other
countries. In the USA, well-funded projects have made substantial progress
in replacing multiple choice tests with valid and therefore longer assessment tasks. Their research shows that even in well-controlled situations,
pupils' performance on science investigations varies so much, between
one particular task and another, that the bare minimum for any reliable
assessment is to use the average score over at least three tasks (Shavelson
et al. 1993; Gao *et al.* 1994). Thus, the capacity to use one's knowledge to
tackle new problems, without which that knowledge is surely of little
value, cannot be assessed at all by short external tests. It has to be done
over time by teachers.

In France, the national tests in mathematics for all pupils at 8, 11 and
14 are taken at the beginning of the school year and the new teachers of
these pupils then have to consider how to adapt their teaching to meet
the variety of needs that the tests reveal (Black and Atkin 1996). Thus,
national testing is deployed, not to blame teachers at the end of a teaching year, but to help them to collaborate to raise the standards of their
teaching. The research literature on assessment by teachers (Black 1993b)
shows both that such development raises standards and that most teachers
need help to develop the skills of designing and using assessment to
improve learning.

Other work with schools (Fairbrother *et al.* 1995a) has shown that science teachers anxious to improve learning and assessment soon see the
need to develop pupils' self-assessment. Other countries are making this
a national priority, for example, the National Board of Education in Fin-
land have written (1994: 29) that:

> The task of evaluation is to encourage the student – in a positive way
> – to set his [*sic*] own aims, to plan his work and to make independent
> choices. For this to take place, the student gradually needs to learn to
> analyse his own studies and those of others through the use of self-
> evaluation and group evaluation ... The ability to do that in the future
> means the ability to survive in a situation where there is more and
> more uncertainty and where the individual is subjected to all kinds
> of choices and sudden changes.

I have given these three examples to show the contrast between intelligent and thoughtful initiatives in other countries and the development of
policy in this country.

I believe that this country's policy will not raise standards because it has led to a system where short, written, external tests will dominate the curriculum. Such tests cannot reflect some of the important aims of education, yet the pressure on schools to do well in them means that they will distort and damage learning (ASE 1992; Fairbrother *et al.* 1995b; Gipps *et al.* 1995); there is also alarming evidence that while above average pupils are improving on tests, the absolute standards of those well below the average have fallen (Bell 1995). Furthermore, as schools concentrate on drilling pupils to do well in sets of short test items, they can give less attention to developing in pupils the skills needed to apply their learning to complex and realistic tasks.

To make matters worse, it is also clear that the test results are bound to be of limited reliability. All the evidence that I have reviewed (Black 1963; 1990; Wiliam 1995) indicates that if we had sound data about their reliability for the short national tests, or for GCSE, or for A levels, these would all turn out to involve rather large margins of error. However, while these tests are the basis on which teachers are to be judged and pupils' life chances determined, such data are not available.

Nostalgia, fear and myth

The world of politics is driven by a mixture of rationality, myths and political expediency. In education, three powerful myths have driven political thinking and public opinion.

The first is that standards have fallen. This myth is not supported by the review of evidence prepared for the National Commission on Education (Foxman *et al.* 1993). Its main conclusion was that we do not have an effective system for monitoring changes. So while policy is driven by selective evidence and hearsay, there is no plan to provide reliable and impartial evidence.

Between 1970–71 and 1991–92 the percentage of pupils obtaining no graded examination results as school leavers fell from 44 per cent to 6.2 per cent (due in part to the raising of the school leaving age), while the percentage of those leaving school before the age of 17 who gained five or more higher grades at GCSE (or the earlier equivalents) rose from 7.1 per cent to 13.2 per cent (DFE 1994). This points to the enormous success of teachers in our comprehensive schools.

A second myth is that this 'fall in standards' has been due to the adoption of 'progressive' methods of teaching. Again this flies in the face of the evidence of Eric Bolton (one-time HM Chief Inspector), based on his experience of thousands of hours of observation by the HMI, the national inspectorate:

> The evidence of inspection is that poor standards of learning are more commonly associated with over-direction by teachers, rather than with teachers opting out and allowing pupils to set the pace and style of learning.

Far from having an education service full of trendy teachers led, willy-nilly, this way and that by experts and gurus (the 'Educational

Mafia'), we have a teaching profession that is essentially cautious and conservative: a profession that is highly suspicious of claims from within or without its ranks that there is a particularly fool-proof way of doing things. Teachers are too close to the actual, day-to-day complexity of classrooms, and to the variability of people and pupils, to be anything else but pragmatic and commonsensical in their thinking and actions.

(Bolton 1992: 16–19)

The third myth is that learning would be improved by a return to traditional methods. Here again the evidence contradicts the myth. Numerous research studies have shown the debilitating consequences of rule bound traditional learning (e.g. Benezet 1935a, b; 1936). The study of Nuthall and Alton-Lee (1995) on the methods pupils use to answer tests, shows that long-term retention depends on the capacity to understand and so reconstruct procedures, and the work of Boaler (1993; 1994; 1996) shows that more open methods produce better attitudes and performance in mathematics than traditional methods. The results of such studies are entirely consistent with contemporary research on the ways that children learn. Consider the following from a review of such work:

even comprehension of simple texts requires a process of inferring and thinking about what the text means. Children who are drilled in number facts, algorithms, decoding skills or vocabulary lists without developing a basic conceptual model or seeing the meaning of what they are doing have a very difficult time retaining information (because all the bits are disconnected) and are unable to apply what they have memorised (because it makes no sense).

(Shepard 1992: 303)

This dominance of mythology is linked to neglect of research. The report of the National Commission on Education (NCE 1995) deplored the rapid decline in government spending on research in education and the absence of any significant research into the effects of its own reforms. The following quotations help to explain this neglect (the first is about a former Conservative Minister, Sir Keith Joseph):

Here Joseph shared a view common to all conservative educationists: that education had seen an unholy alliance of socialists, bureaucrats, planners and Directors of Education acting against the true interests and wishes of the nation's children and parents by their imposition on the schools of an ideology (equality of condition) based on utopian dreams of universal co-operation and brotherhood.

(Knight 1990: 155)

Tories really do seem to believe in the existence of left-wing, 'education establishment' conspiracies.

(Lawton 1994: 145)

Thus one can understand why research evidence is untrustworthy – those responsible for this evidence are part of the conspiracy.

One possible origin for this conspiracy theory is suggested by Lawton:

The dominant feature of the Tory Mind that has emerged from this study is, unsurprisingly, an exaggerated concern for tradition and past models of education and society. But what did surprise me when reading so many speeches and autobiographies was the Tory *fear* of the future and of the non-traditional. I was even more surprised by the kind of fear which took the form of an almost paranoid belief in conspiracies among the 'educational establishment'.

(Lawton 1994: 144)

Another relevant policy initiative has been the application of the ideology of the marketplace to education – more eagerly taken up because it promised to weaken local education authorities and the comprehensive system. The application of a market model to education has been criticised by many, notably in the reports of the National Commission on Education (NCE 1993; 1995), in the analysis offered by Stephen Ball (Ball 1994: ch. 7), and in a review of the effect of over a decade of parental choice of schools in Scotland:

Parental choice has led to an inefficient use of resources, widening disparities between schools, increased social segregation and threats to equality of educational opportunity.

(Adler 1993: 183)

A market implies consumer choice between expensive products of high quality and cheaper products of poorer quality, while demand is linked to willingness and ability to pay, not to need. The right-wing Hillgate Group has commented that 'Consumer sovereignty does not necessarily guarantee that values will be preserved' (McKenzie 1993). Keith Joseph's 'blind, unplanned, uncoordinated wisdom of the market' implies that some 'businesses' can spiral down and go bankrupt. What is to be done about the permanent damage to children caught in this spiral? It is also clear that markets favour those who have the knowledge and the power to choose wisely – the children of the less well informed will suffer.

My conclusion here is that our educational policy seems to be based on a combination of nostalgia and fear of change with an inappropriate market model for education. This foundation is supported by myths which are protected by a neglect of evidence, so that we shall not learn from experience, let alone from the experience of others.

Real attempts to tackle real problems

I present here some examples from other countries of policies in education which contrast sharply with our own and do not share our weaknesses.

On the central issue of the framework for the curriculum, the Finnish policy document (National Board of Education 1994) discusses changes in social needs and values, and goes on to emphasise that our new understanding of learning shows the need to stress 'the active role of the student as the organiser of his [*sic*] own structure of knowledge' and the need for 'organising teaching into inter-curricular issues and subjects'.

The Norwegian Ministry document on the Core Curriculum (Royal Ministry of Church, Education and Research 1994) is in chapters with titles as follows:

- the spiritual human being
- the creative human being
- the working human being
- the liberally educated human being
- the social human being
- the environmentally aware human being
- the integrated human being.

Here we have governments who wish to present to their country a deeply argued rationale for the aims of their curriculum. By contrast, our National Curriculum has concentrated on ten required subjects as if they were self-evident goods with no intellectually serious basis to underpin this approach (White 1990).

Other comparisons are equally striking. Many countries share a concern about the changing world of the child and the adolescent. Changes in family stability and in the stability of employment, and the increasing power of the media, has meant that young people face an environment which is rich in information and vicarious experience, poor in first-hand experience, weaker than it ever was in emotional security and support, and overshadowed by the threat of unemployment. Where the world of the child has been impoverished, the task of the school is both more complex and more vital. Yet it has to be carried out in a society where the authority of teachers, as with other professionals, is no longer taken for granted.

A nostalgia-driven return to 'basics' ignores such problems, and cannot provide the qualities in young people which society needs. A statement from a group of European industrialists (ERT 1995) stresses the importance of literacy, numeracy and of science and technology, but adds to these critical thinking, decision-making, the need to be able to learn new skills, ability to work in groups, willingness to take risks and exercise initiative, curiosity, and a sense of service to the community. British employers see the same needs (see also Ball 1990: 103).

Can we find new directions?

While the nostalgic ideology of the New Right cannot meet the needs of our society, the task of shaping a new ideology for education is a daunting one, not least because our society lacks consensus about ultimate beliefs and values. I wish here only to discuss six issues which need clarification in any attempt to achieve a new formulation of policy.

The first is concerned with the process of change. An OECD review of 23 case studies, spread over 13 countries, which examined the progress of different educational innovations, revealed striking differences between the models of change that were adopted (Black and Atkin 1996). At one extreme there were top-down models in which central authority tells everyone what to do. Where this was done, either very little happened at classroom level, or teachers, being disoriented, delivered an impoverished interpretation of the intentions.

The opposite approach, which was to leave as much as possible in the hands of schools and of teachers, also had difficulties, for the process was slow and such delegation implied that only a very general framework could be prescribed. However, there are powerful arguments, of principle and from empirical evidence, that this is the most effective and acceptable strategy (Fullan 1991; Posch 1994). Where matters are interlinked in complex ways and where one has to be sensitive to the local context in which this complex is situated, then only those who have freedom of manoeuvre can then turn a good idea into a really effective innovation. This approach has been adopted in business and industry (Peters and Waterman 1982), where the response has been to move from long hierarchical chains to so-called 'flat' management structures.

> Recent business experience has shown that in times of chaotic change, the centralisation of administration of any complex system can become a veritable obstacle to adapting to new circumstances. While the existence of central national institutions is necessary to guarantee social equity in education and to supply guidelines and expertise, it is essential that educational institutions at every level should have autonomy to implement the changes they see as necessary.
>
> (ERT 1995: 18)

Thus if new aims for education are to be achieved, we have to give teachers freedom to work out the best ways for their school. This need is stronger if schools are to form those links with local communities and with local employers which they need if they are to help pupils to make successful transition from schools to working life.

A second main finding was that change at classroom level cannot happen quickly. It takes several years for the majority of teachers to grasp new curriculum ideas and to put them into practice through changes in their classroom work. This timescale is long compared with the interval between elections. More alarmingly, it may be too long in relation to the pace at which our society is changing and, therefore, at which its needs in education are changing.

Teachers are the focus of my second issue. Where teachers have low status, they become targets for blame, and are treated with remarkable insensitivity:

> We are struck by the extent to which German and French education systems place responsibility on the shoulders of professional teachers. It contrasts sharply with the mood of distrust of professionals which has grown in this country in recent years, not without government encouragement. This mood has been carried too far and must be reversed.
>
> (NCE 1993: 340)

Such treatment is not only unjust, it is also counter-productive, for in any but the most narrow mechanical view of teaching, it must be recognised that teachers are the sole and essential means to educational improvement. If they do not share the aims, and do not want to do what needs to be done, it cannot happen effectively.

Furthermore, to define teachers as mere providers of the market goods that the parent customers require is to misconstrue their fundamental role. A former chair of the Headmasters' Conference, Father Dominic Milroy, wrote:

They [parents] know that, for the child, the encounter with *the teacher* is the first major step into outside society, the beginning of a long journey towards adulthood, in which the role of the teacher is going to be decisive . . . all education is an exercise in collaborative parenting, in which the profession of teaching is seen as a complement to the vocation of parenthood . . . Teachers are, therefore, not in the first instance agents either of the National Curriculum Council (or whatever follows it) or of the state. They are bridges between individual children and the culture to which they belong . . . This culture consists partly of a heritage, which links them to the past, and partly of a range of skills and opportunities, which links them to the future. The role of the teachers is, in this respect, irreplaceable.

(Milroy 1992: 57–9)

This rejects the notion of teachers as paid agents, and replaces it with a concept of partnership in which teachers, by virtue of their role, must take authority for developing young adults. Indeed, parents give this authority to the school and the teachers because they want their children to learn the myriad of ideas and behaviours that they cannot themselves give them, and society reinforces this when it sets up a curriculum within which parents are not free to pick and choose if their children go to schools funded by their taxes. Thus, the teacher is the pivotal agent of change, sharing authority with parents for the development of children, and representing society as the agent to put into effect any nationally agreed plans for education.

A third issue is the need to clarify what society wants teachers to achieve, which is to say that we need a fresh consensus about the educational aims that society wants schools to pursue. This is lacking because of rapid social change, because our society is divided about its fundamental beliefs and values and because society has weakened in many ways the support given to the developing child outside school.

A National Curriculum that stresses details of subjects, flimsily related to a few very broad aims, leaves schools in a very difficult position. It might make sense to give schools no direction at all. It might be better to set out for them the broad framework of aims that society wants them to achieve and leave them to find the detailed ways to achieve such aims. It surely makes no sense at all to specify the detailed ways but to leave them to decide the overall aims.

My fourth issue has already been discussed in the first section above. We need a new policy for assessment, one which will support the assessment aspect of teachers' work, which will have helpful rather than damaging effects on good teaching by assessing those aspects of learning which young people need to be effective in a changing society, and which will give information, to individuals and to the public, that is both fair and trustworthy.

The fifth issue is that we need to have a proper respect for evidence, which means that we have to be willing to review existing evidence, to monitor the progress of our educational changes and to research in depth some of the most important problems that they raise. This implies that the level of investment in research in education should be very sharply increased above the derisory level to which it has sunk in recent years.

If we are to be able to work effectively at these five issues, I believe we shall need to take up a sixth, which is that we need to build up a much better public understanding of the complexities of teaching and learning.

The public ought to be far better informed about educational issues than at present. Myths about our schools are too powerful and policy thinking about our education is too weak. There ought to be a sustained effort to help the public, and especially politicians and their policy advisers, to achieve a more realistic, and therefore more complex, understanding of the realities of schools, of classrooms, of testing and of educational change.

Note

1 This chapter is based on 'Ideology, evidence and the raising of standards', the Second King's Annual Education Lecture given on 11 July 1995 (Black 1995).

References

Adler, M. (1993) An alternative approach to parental choice, in NCE *Briefings*. London: Heinemann.

ASE (1992) Key Stage 3 Monitoring Group: report on the monitoring of Key Stage 3, *Education in Science*, November: 18–19.

Ball, S.J. (1990) *Politics and Policy Making in Education*. London: Routledge.

Ball, S.J. (1994) *Education Reform: A Critical and Post-structural Approach*. Buckingham: Open University Press.

Bell, C. (1995) In a different league?, *British Journal of Curriculum and Assessment*, 5(3): 32–3.

Benezet, L.P. (1935a) The teaching of arithmetic I: the story of an experiment, *Journal of the National Education Association*, November: 241–4.

Benezet, L.P. (1935b) The teaching of arithmetic II: the story of an experiment, *Journal of the National Education Association*, December: 301–3.

Benezet, L.P. (1936) The teaching of arithmetic III: the story of an experiment, *Journal of the National Education Association*, December: 241–4.

Black, P.J. (1963) Examinations and the teaching of science, *Bulletin of the Institute of Physics and the Physical Society*, August: 202–3.

Black, P.J. (1990) APU Science: the past and the future, *School Science Review*, 72(258): 13–28.

Black, P.J. (1993a) The shifting scenery of the National Curriculum, in C. Chitty and B. Simon (eds) *Education Answers Back – Critical Responses to Government Policy*. London: Lawrence and Wishart. Also, in P. O'Hear and J. White (eds) *Assessing the National Curriculum*. London: Paul Chapman.

Black, P.J. (1993b) Formative and summative assessment by teachers, *Studies in Science Education*, 21: 49–97.

Black, P.J. (1995) Ideology, evidence and the raising of standards. Second King's Annual Education Lecture. King's College London.

Black, P.J. (1996) Whatever happened to TGAT? in C. Cullingford (ed.) *Assessment vs. Evaluation*. London: Cassell.

Black, P.J. and Atkin, J.M. (eds) (1996) *Changing the Subject*. London: Routledge.

Boaler, J. (1993) Encouraging the transfer of 'school' mathematics to the 'real world' through the integration of process, context and culture, *Educational Studies in Mathematics*, 25: 341–73.

Boaler, J. (1994) When do girls prefer football to fashion? An analysis of female underachievement in relation to 'realistic' mathematical contexts, *British Educational Research Journal*, 20(5): 551–64.

Boaler, J. (1996) Learning to lose in the mathematics classroom: a critique of traditional school practices in the UK, *Qualitative Studies in Mathematics*, 9(1): 17–33.

Bolton, E. (1992) The quality of teaching, in various authors, *Education: Putting the Record Straight*. Stafford: Network Education Press.

Chitty, C. and Simon, B. (eds) (1993) *Education Answers Back – Critical Responses to Government Policy*. London: Lawrence and Wishart.

Clarke, K. (1991) Education in a classless society, 'The Westminster Lecture', given to the Tory Reform Group, June 1991.

Daugherty, R. (1995) *National Curriculum Assessment. A Review of Policy 1987–1994*. London: Falmer Press.

Department of Education and Science (DES) (1987) *The National Curriculum 5–16 – A Consultation Document*. London: Department of Education and Science and the Welsh Office.

Department of Education and Science (DES) (1988a) *Task Group on Assessment and Testing: A Report*. London: Department of Education and Science and the Welsh Office.

Department of Education and Science (DES) (1988b) *Task Group on Assessment and Testing: Three Supplementary Reports*. London: Department of Education and Science and the Welsh Office.

Department for Education (DFE) (1994) *Educational Statistics for the United Kingdom*. Statistical Bulletin 1/94. London: Department for Education.

ERT (1995) *Education for Europeans: Towards the Learning Society*. Brussels: The European Round Table of Industrialists.

Fairbrother, R.W., Black, P.J. and Gill, P. (eds) (1995a) *Teachers Assessing Pupils: Lessons from Science Classrooms*. Hatfield: Association for Science Education.

Fairbrother, R.W., Dillon, J. and Gill, P. (1995b) Assessment at Key Stage 3: teachers' attitudes and practices, *British Journal of Curriculum and Assessment*, 5(3): 25–31 and 46.

Foxman, D., Gorman, T. and Brooks, G. (1993) Standards in literacy and numeracy, in NCE *Briefings*. London: Heinemann.

Fullan, M.G. with Stiegelbauer, S. (1991) *The New Meaning of Educational Change*. London: Cassell.

Gao, X., Shavelson, R.J. and Baxter, G.P. (1994) Generalizability of large-scale performance assessments in science. Promises and problems, *Applied Measurement in Education*, 7(4): 323–42.

Gipps, C., Brown, M., McCallum, B. and McAlister, S. (1995) *Intuition or Evidence? Teachers and National Assessment of 7-year-olds*. Buckingham: Open University Press.

Knight, C. (1990) *The Making of Tory Education Policy in Post-war Britain, 1950–1986*. London: Falmer Press.

Lawton, D. (1994) *The Tory Mind on Education,1979–94*. London: Falmer Press.

McKenzie, J. (1993) *Education as a Political Issue*. Aldershot: Avebury.

Milroy, D. (1992) Teaching and learning: what a child expects from a good teacher, in various authors, *Education: Putting the Record Straight*. Stafford: Network Education Press.

National Board of Education (1994) *Framework for the Comprehensive School, 1994*. Helsinki: Painatuskeskus (in English).

National Commission on Education (NCE) (1993) *Learning to Succeed: Report of the National Commission on Education*. London: Heinemann.

National Commission on Education (NCE) (1995) *Learning to Succeed: The Way Forward*. London: National Commission on Education.

Nuthall, G. and Alton-Lee, A. (1995) Assessing classroom learning: how students use their knowledge and experience to answer classroom achievement test questions in science and social studies, *American Educational Research Journal*, 32(1): 185–223.

Peters, T. and Waterman, R. (1982) *In Search of Excellence*. New York: Harper and Row.

Posch, P. (1994) Strategies for the implementation of technology education, in D. Layton (ed.) *Innovations in Science and Technology Education, Vol. V*. Paris: UNESCO. 201–12.

Royal Ministry of Church, Education and Research (1994) *Core Curriculum for Primary, Secondary and Adult Education in Norway*. Oslo: Akademika a/s (in English).

Shavelson, R.J., Baxter, G.P. and Gao, X. (1993) Sampling variability of performance assessments, *Journal of Educational Measurement*, 30(3): 215–32.

Shepard, L.A. (1992). Commentary: What policy makers who mandate tests should know about the new psychology of intellectual ability and learning, in B.R. Gifford and M.C. O'Connor (eds) *Changing Assessments: Alternative Views of Aptitude, Achievement and Instruction*. Boston: Kluwer.

Thatcher, M. (1993) *The Downing Street Years*. London: Harper Collins.

White, J. (1990) *Education and the Good Life: Beyond the National Curriculum*. London: Kogan Page.

Wiliam, D. (1995) It'll all end in tiers, *British Journal of Curriculum and Assessment*, 5(3): 21–4.

7

Diversity and social justice

Kelly Coate Bignell and Meg Maguire

Introduction

> Learning to listen to different voices, hearing different speech challenges the notion that we must all assimilate – share a single, similar talk – in educational institutions.
>
> (hooks 1993: 106–7)

This chapter aims to introduce the concepts of diversity and social justice in education through an historical overview. What do these concepts suggest to you? Perhaps such terms as equal opportunities, affirmative action, multicultural education, anti-racism and anti-sexism come to mind. These are all concepts which are frequently under attack from various sectors of society and their aims are often misunderstood through reactionary debates in the popular media. In fact, throughout the 1980s and early 1990s there has been a growing trend by the Conservative Government to drastically undermine issues of social justice (Griffiths and Troyna 1995) and adopt a stance of what has been termed 'equiphobia' by those working in the field of social justice (Myers 1990). Yet as a teacher, the value you place on these concepts will help shape the education and experiences of all your pupils. This chapter is designed to provide a background to the development of social justice issues in order to raise questions in your mind which to varying degrees may influence your professional development as a teacher. The authors believe that a concern with social justice has been a valuable contribution to society and to education, and have kept the following quote in mind:

> It is only by recognising the value of cultures and experiences other than their own and by working together to develop and refine anti-racism and anti-sexist practice that teachers can genuinely begin to think about education and equality as compatible notions.
>
> (Brah and Minhas 1985: 25)

First initiatives

One of the starting points for society's concern with issues of social justice was the 1944 Education Act, when the state set up secondary schools for all. Prior to 1944, education had a long history of availability only to upper-class men, and what education women did receive often prepared them for a traditional, domestic life. Secondary schools were an attempt to enact the new belief that everyone should have a right to education, and thus education was seen as a mechanism for egalitarian reform. At the time there were considered to be three 'types' of children: academically inclined children, practical children and 'the rest'. There were therefore three types of schools which made up the tripartite system: the grammar school, the technical school and the secondary modern school. Children were selected through tests (the 11+) and were allocated secondary school places accordingly. The only difference recognised among school students was related to 'ability' and consequently it was seen as socially just to make separate provision according to 'ability'. This meritocratic system attempted to catch the 'clever' children and give them an academic education regardless of their capacity to pay.

There were several problems with this early attempt to provide education for everyone. The most serious flaw was that the system was not truly meritocratic. For instance, only the high status, academic, grammar schools were perceived to offer the potential for good chances in life and so those placed elsewhere often felt they were in effect being relegated to a limited future. Another problem was that, nationally, more girls than boys attained the highest marks in the 11+ examination. As this was thought to be 'unfair' to boys, the raw scores of children were standardised through a conversion grid in which girls had to be far more successful than boys in order to qualify for a grammar school place. This was justified on the grounds that although boys were not performing as well as girls on the 11+ exam, they had greater future potential than girls. Finally, this 'meritocratic' initiative led to a movement of the middle classes from the independent sector into the state system. Overwhelmingly, the intake of the grammar school consisted of middle-class children. Academic aptitude and ability seemed to correlate neatly with socio-economic background (Rogers 1986).

While some of these problems have been mitigated by abolishing the 11+ in many parts of the country, schools and society gradually became aware of other forms of discrimination. Since 1944, there have been many changes in society which have led to a growing concern with social justice in education. It is impossible to do full justice here to the wide ranges of influences for egalitarian reform, however, one major influence was a growing political activism in the late 1960s and early 1970s. The Civil Rights Movement in the USA where African Americans asserted their rights as full citizens and the second wave women's movement from the late 1960s both provided an impetus for change. In the UK two critical pieces of legislation were enacted with far-reaching consequences: the Sex Discrimination Act (Great Britain 1975) and the Race Relations Act (Great Britain 1976).

Accordingly, research in education began to focus on gender and 'race'[1] in an attempt to understand whether schools were in fact contributing to inequalities in society. This research was ground-breaking as it began to focus in-depth for the first time on female school students and Black[2] students, and the results painted a rather depressing picture. Feminist researchers focusing on girls in schools found that girls were being provided with a different education from boys; they were encouraged to pursue traditional, 'female' subjects such as home economics (Grafton *et al.* 1987) and were missing out on maths and science (Spender and Sarah 1980). They were receiving distorted images of themselves in school texts and were under-represented in science and maths textbooks (Kelly 1987). Research on Black students found that many were being marginalised through stereotyping into sports and music rather than more traditional academic subjects, and that they were underachieving academically (Carrington 1983). Through the evidence of the research it gradually became clear that education had a part to play in tackling sexism and racism.

The education system began to respond to these critiques and various tactics were proposed. During the 1970s and 1980s many local education authorities (LEAs) developed policies which promoted multi-cultural education and 'girl friendly' schooling initiatives. These initiatives were an attempt to develop curriculum and resource materials which reflected Black and female achievements more positively. It was also argued, for example, that there was a need for more Black teachers and more women mathematics and science teachers. These and many other suggestions were designed to enhance the self-esteem of certain groups of students. Efforts to promote positive images were based on a liberal notion of equal opportunities which presumes that equality will be achieved if all students are given the same opportunities and access to education. It is dependent upon the underlying assumption that students should be encouraged to broaden their own horizons, which implies that it is the students' perceptions and attitudes which need to be altered. This perspective, to a certain extent, alleviated the responsibilities of educational institutions.

The differences between multicultural education and anti-racist education, and equal opportunities and anti-sexist education came to be recognised as crucial distinctions. Multicultural education was premised on the assumption that schools needed to add more about other cultures to the curriculum rather than fundamentally alter their own structures. On the other hand, anti-racist policies would be an admission that racism existed in the school. Equal opportunities policies were based on the notion that equality would be achieved if everyone had equal access whereas anti-sexist initiatives would again imply that sexism exists and needs to be challenged. So it was much easier for schools to have, as examples, lunch-time girls' meetings, steel bands, or female visitors advocating careers in engineering than deal more directly with the sexism and racism which existed in many schools. In other words, the students were indirectly blamed for their own alleged lack of attainment. However, a minority of LEAs and schools, notably those in the metropolitan areas, did start to confront sexism and racism head-on.

Reforming schools – reforming the curriculum

In 1988 the Education Reform Act was passed. Although there are many critiques of this massive piece of legislation one positive move forward was that the ERA was conceptualised as an 'entitlement' Act. All children, regardless of 'race' or gender were entitled to receive a broad education in three core subjects and seven foundation subjects as well as Religious Education. For the first time in the history of mass schooling in the UK, all students had to follow a common curriculum until 16. In this legislation, difference was not directly acknowledged but social justice was to be achieved through equity of provision for all. The National Curriculum Council expected that:

> Dimensions such as a commitment to providing equal opportunities for all pupils, and a recognition that preparation for life in a multicultural society is relevant to all pupils, should permeate every aspect of the curriculum. In order to make access to the curriculum a reality for all pupils, schools need to foster a climate in which equality of opportunity is supported by a policy to which the whole school subscribes and in which positive attitudes to gender equality, cultural diversity and special needs of all kinds are actively promoted.
>
> (NCC 1990: 2)

The fact that ideas concerning social justice had filtered through to actual legislation marks an advancement, even though the Act has been criticised for promoting a nationalistic culture through the curriculum (Donald and Rattansi 1992). Another problem is that the vague suggestions contained in this legislation still left it up to the schools to make their own policies and commitments. Considering that the Sex Discrimination Act (Great Britain 1975) and Race Relations Act (Great Britain 1976) were about fifteen years old at this time, there were still many prejudiced attitudes in schools which equal opportunities policies would be ineffective against. In the meantime, the social justice movement had developed even more sophisticated and critical analyses of discrimination.

A focus on diversity

In the 1980s, particularly as a consequence of the multicultural and anti-racist movement, activists started to challenge the essentialist assumptions within the field. The question of essentialism arose through the tendency of certain groups to claim that their members shared commonalities while neglecting diversity among the members of their group. While some members of ethnic groups felt that identifying as Black would raise awareness of discrimination, others were unhappy to be categorised as 'black': for instance, some critics have suggested that South Asian identity is marginalised when black is used as a political category[3] (see Brah 1992). Many non-white communities argued strongly that their own specific histories and cultures were unique and should not be subsumed within a wider social movement.

In the feminist movement, Black women and lesbians raised similar points. The previously unifying concept of 'women', it was argued, frequently stood only for white, middle-class, heterosexual females (Knowles and Mercer 1992). It was also argued that patriarchy was experienced in different ways by different groups, and therefore the theory of the patriarchal family as the prime source of oppression needed revision if it was only based on a model of Western, white, nuclear families. For instance, Carby presented an alternative perspective: the Black family, she asserted, was a source of resistance, support and defence against endemic racism (Carby 1982). In a similar vein, lesbian feminists were influential in not only stressing the oppressive nature of heterosexual relations but also the reluctance of heterosexual feminists to recognise the ways in which lesbians face different forms of discrimination. Through all of these arguments the complexities of social justice issues came to be recognised and the tendency of large, disadvantaged groups to form political alliances without recognising diversity among their members was challenged.

Gradually it has been understood that diversity and differences work in complex, multi-faceted dimensions. This recognition was not simply an enlightened, rational and egalitarian process; rather it was accelerated by the formation of politically active campaigning groups who were fighting for their civil rights, access rights and sometimes simply recognition. Campaigns which have raised awareness of the complexities of social injustice are the HIV/AIDS campaigns; disability rights activists who draw attention to the patronising charity stunts which position them as 'victims' in the need of help; and gays who are campaigning (as yet unsuccessfully) for the age of consent to be equal. All of these campaigns have ensured that issues of equality are not always limited to 'race', class and gender.

Social justice literature now encourages the need to consider diversity in pluralist and complex societies across a range of elements such as 'race', class, gender, ability, motivation, previous experience, language, age, physical and intellectual capacity, sexuality, power, status, qualification, religion, and schooling. More importantly, the ways in which these themes weave together and interact at different points is now acknowledged. For example, Audre Lorde has powerfully expressed how she experienced multiple identities:

> I was born Black and a woman. I am trying to become the strongest person I can become to live the life I have been given and to help effect change toward a liveable future for this earth and for my children. As a Black, lesbian, feminist, socialist, poet, mother of two including one boy, and a member of an interracial couple, I usually find myself part of some group in which the majority defines me as deviant, difficult, inferior or just plain 'wrong'. From my membership of all these groups I have learned that oppression and the intolerance of difference come in all shapes and sizes and colors and sexualities, and that among those of us who share the goals of liberation and a workable future for our children, there can be no hierarchies of oppression.
>
> (Lorde 1983: 9)

Specifically in educational settings, the complex sets of diversities which this more sophisticated conceptualisation has suggested has meant that schools have had to carefully rethink their work and provision in relation to their students' needs. The recognition of the powerful interplay between factors such as 'race', class and gender and the growing awareness of diversity has raised wider questions for schools. Until now our focus has been on the broad context: in the next section we address one specific issue – underachievement.

Changing perceptions of underachievement

One of the most evocative debates for school teachers relates to the issue of underachievement in schools. This has been compounded by the publication of league table results and the growing public awareness of exam results. What has become apparent in these debates is that simple generalisations can be made far too easily. Early research focused on generalised divisions between 'race' and gender. For instance, the Rampton Report (DES 1981) published statistics which indicated that 'West Indian' school students were less successful than 'Asians' and 'Others'. In relation to the achievement of girls, the common understanding from the early research has been that girls tended to pass numerically more examinations than boys but the subjects which they gained were 'soft' rather than 'hard'. They did well in home economics, child development, office practice, languages and biology. Boys were more successful in physics, craft design and technology.

However, one of the problems with generalised accounts of achievement is the lack of recognition of diversity among students. For instance, in the Rampton Report (1981) no account was taken of gender or of ethnicity beyond 'Asian', 'West Indian' or 'Other'. This is a significant gap as, for instance, the position of Mirpuri Pakistani communities will differ from the Chinese community in Britain, and the situation for refugees will differ from that of long-established groups. Socio-economic class was also not factored into these statistics, even though this has been shown to be a significant influence and would have made the results of the groups more comparable (Rattansi 1992). Therefore the perceived educational disadvantages of having black skin were actually more a result of bias in information gathering (Gill *et al.* 1992). Similarly, research indicating that girls did better in single sex schools rarely brought socio-economic class into the analysis. Certain single sex schools attract girls from privileged backgrounds and therefore the complex interplay between gender, class and 'race' could be further explored in these instances.

When analysing issues of underachievement it is important not only to take into account the diversity among students, but also some of the factors which could influence educational outcomes. Instead of questioning the students' own ability, it is necessary also to look to the learning environment. Certainly one of the earlier concerns of anti-racists and feminists which is still on the agenda today is the enormous potential for stereotyping in schools (Delamont 1994). Stereotyping results when one group defines in an exaggerated and negative manner the values, beliefs, rules of conduct, behaviour, language and types of social interaction of another group. This easily leads to misinterpretation of behaviour.

There are certain stereotypes which have affected Black students in particular ways and can seriously affect their life chances. Cecile Wright (1987, 1992) has found that African-Caribbean students were placed in examinations well below their ability, and that teachers were more influenced by behaviour than by cognitive ability. There has also been research into the ways in which teachers misconstrue the activities of some of their Black students which leads to student exclusion, stereotyping and racism on the part of the teacher (Wright 1994). Mac an Ghaill's (1988) study illustrates how African-Caribbean students who behaved no worse than 'South Asian' or white boys were overwhelmingly singled out for their bad behaviour – sometimes for a simple matter such as the way they walked around the school.

There are different assumptions about Black female students which can be just as damaging. Many of the stereotypes of the 'Asian woman' as passive yet oppressed may work to limit opportunities of participation or reciprocity in classrooms. Recent studies, however, have indicated that African-British girls are doing better than white working-class girls (Mirza 1992). These successful girls recognise that schools are racist, nevertheless they work hard and hold high aspirations for themselves. Black female students particularly view education as an opportunity for better life chances (Fuller 1983). Like their male counterparts they flourish in further educational settings. However, it is at the crucial hurdle of career advice where many barriers are met and where the aspirations of young African-British women may be undermined by those giving advice (Safia-Mirza 1992).

The situation for non-white working-class males and females is complex. In the African-British community this contradiction is most evident. Overwhelmingly, males are being excluded from schools in disproportionate numbers as contrasted with any other group, while African-British girls are attaining good results (Bourne 1994). Recent communities which have settled in the UK, such as the Bangladeshi community, and who originally came from a mainly rural background, are still substantially underachieving in school.

The achievement of girls in schools is equally complex. It has recently been demonstrated that where teachers enter students for public examinations which have levels (foundation, intermediate, higher) the tendency is to set internal examinations and use these as a rough indication of aptitude. Teachers then tend to enter boys at a higher level than girls even where girls have achieved more in the school examination. The teachers often assume that the boys have been lazy and have not really done their best but will produce the results when it matters. Girls, on the other hand, are assumed to have tried their best and so they are entered at a level which relates to their internal grade (Stobart et al. 1992). Thus, teachers' expectations, stereotypical beliefs and misperceptions are revealed in the research to influence the opportunities offered to students. For example, Gipps and Murphy argue:

> The influence of teacher expectation in an assessment context is crucial. With the introduction in the UK in 1994 of differentiated exam entry based on teacher judgements in *all* subjects in GCSE *and* in national assessment at Key Stages Two and Three, the issue of differential teacher expectations must be of central concern in any debate about equity and assessment.
>
> (Gipps and Murphy 1994: 272)

Exam results are becoming an emotive and political issue, and it is important to retain a historical perspective within the debates. Traditionally, exam results have been interpreted according to the social and political culture of the time. For example, women's low achievement in the hard sciences was frequently interpreted as directly related to natural ability, as this explanation tied in with earlier notions of women as incapable of rational, logical thought. More recent research has pointed out that there are a significant number of factors involved, such as teachers' expectations, careers' advice, the masculine image of science, parental influences, and so on. Therefore it is important to monitor continually the ways in which current debates concerning achievement might reflect the particular social and political environment. It is also vital to understand that assessment in schools is not a pure indicator of 'ability'. Research has shown that performance in assessment is related to such factors as who wrote the exam questions, how the curriculum is shaped, what the socio-economic status of the school is, what the teachers' expectations of performance have been, and so many other factors that even whether the invigilator is Black or white can make a difference to the results.

Where are we now?

In this brief overview of some of the issues involved in the debates about diversity and social justice we have tried to illuminate what is a complex, shifting and contradictory issue for schools in the 1990s. What should schools be concerned with now? Are social justice issues to do with a 'natural waste of national resource' if we fail to capitalise upon the talents of all our young citizens or are these issues about the value of equality and fairness in society? The current situation is probably most noted for a publicised shift in rhetoric which questions the slight gains made in different areas of equal opportunities provisions.

In some schools it is possible to see aspects of policy provision which have been handed down from the 1970s and 1980s. In inner city schools (where inner city frequently stands for multi-racial, working class) there are some clear outcomes in multicultural or anti-racist education, anti-sexist work and, more obviously, work related to language issues. But increasingly there has also been a questioning of some of this. It has been argued that some of the earlier policy responses were authoritarian in style and in tone which alienated many teachers. Simplistic accounts which essentially 'blamed' white middle-class men for social injustices or which induced feelings of guilt and then rejection of the debates were not likely to result in any improvements in practice. It is quite common to hear that 'political correctness' has gone too far. What is less frequently stated is that the debilitating effects of racism and sexism are against the law and that changes which have attempted to eradicate these forces are marks of a civilised and democratic society.

Currently there are some attempts to ask more complex questions about equality, diversity and social justice in schools. Many mixed schools are finding it harder to recruit girls whose parents believe they will get a better deal in a girls-only setting. One co-educational comprehensive school has responded by reorganizing its subject teaching so that most subjects are taught in single-sex settings, although the students are in mixed form groups. Interestingly, the headteacher has stated that this move is not so much driven by his own belief in equality but in response to market forces. Although this scheme may be seen to work in favour of equality, it is interesting to consider the recent introduction of market forces rhetoric in education. Is education about competition, with winners and losers, or is it about ensuring that all members of society are provided with an educational background that will allow them to achieve to their full potential?

Another recent trend is a concern with the education of boys and young men. This takes a number of forms: one is a concern that girl friendly schooling initiatives did nothing to change the behaviour and attitudes of males which was the real problem; a second strand has been concerned with the way that boys have been exposed to a macho culture which has cut them off from their 'real' selves; and yet another strand has been concerned with boys underachieving in language subjects. It is interesting to speculate on whether any of this is driven by a feminist backlash. In a recent response to the raised attainments of girls fuelled by some anti-sexist provision in schools Barber (1994) asks, 'Have girls had it too good for too long, while society has complacently accepted that 'boys will be boys'?' Provocative statements such as these ignore the fact that a concern with social justice in education is a relatively recent phenomenon. Twenty years since the Sex Discrimination Act can hardly seem 'too long' considering the hundreds of years of virtual exclusion of women from education.

What happens in schools is directly related to the manner in which these dilemmas are construed and how or if they are translated from policy into practice. Some schools feel on firmer ground in dealing with issues of gender or disability. Some 'all white' schools do not accept they have a responsibility to deal with racism. Many schools are either unwilling or feel unable to deal with the fact that they have lesbian and gay school students as well as staff. In a time where Christianity is being espoused as the dominant national tradition, other faiths believe their responsibilities to their children are marginalised in state schools. In the moves towards the selection of students at 11, there are once again moves towards a 'meritocratic' system based on 'ability'.

Currently all state schools have to be regularly inspected and one of the key themes in the inspection is related to equality of opportunity. The requirements of the Education (Schools) Act 1992 place inspectors with the duty of reporting on a regular basis on 'the strengths and weaknesses in schools so that they may improve the quality of education offered and raise the standards achieved by their pupils'. The inspection schedule requires that all schools make arrangements for equality of opportunity which are evaluated. Schools have to provide specific evidence; monitored and recorded 'standards of achievement of individuals and groups'; a published policy document including reference to 'admissions policies, intakes and exclusions'; 'curriculum content and access'; 'classroom organisation and management, teaching and differentiation'; use made of language support teachers as well as evidence relating to 'pupil relationships' (Ofsted 1993).

Dilemmas related to difference and justice are not just issues in the research literature. They are practical issues for every school which have to be responded to at inspection time. They are issues for individual teachers too because schools do make a difference. How will you group your school students in your classroom? Will you spend more time with some students than others? Will you welcome the slower learner or will they be a 'nuisance' in your classroom better dealt with by a 'specialist'? How will your school react to students who are 'absent' during Eid celebrations? Who do you expect will do well and who do you expect will do less well in your classroom? How will you respond to racist and sexist name calling or stereotyping, not just in your class but maybe in the staffroom too? What you think about all these issues is critical because your views underpin and give shape to your own professional practice and the values you advocate as a future member of staff in a secondary school.

Notes

1 The term 'race' will be used with quotes to indicate that it is a socially constructed rather than biologically determined category.
2 Black will be used with a capital letter to denote that it is a political rather than descriptive term.
3 The origins of the use of the term Black stem from the Black Power movement in the USA and initially referred more specifically to Sub-Saharan African descendants. It was adopted in the UK by coalitions of various non-white groups as a way of asserting group identity in the powerful, positive way that Black political activists had attempted in the USA (Brah 1992).

References

Barber, M. (1994) Report into school students' attitudes. University of Keele, reported in *The Guardian*, 23 August: 2.

Bourne, J. (1994) *Outcast England: How Schools Exclude Black Children*. London: Institute of Race Relations.

Brah, A. (1992) Difference, diversity and differentiation, in J. Donald and A. Rattansi (eds) *'Race', Culture and Difference*. London: Sage.

Brah, A. and Minhas, R. (1985) Structured racism or cultural difference: schooling for Asian girls, in G. Weiner (ed.) *Just a Bunch of Girls*. Milton Keynes: Open University Press.

Carby, H. (1982) White woman listen: Black feminism and the boundaries of sisterhood, in Centre for Contemporary Cultural Studies, *The Empire Strikes Back*. London: Hutchinson.

Carrington, B. (1983) Sport as a side-track: an analysis of West Indian involvement in extra-curricular sport, in L. Barton and S. Walker (eds) *Race, Class and Education*. London: Croom Helm.

Delamont, S. (1994) Sex stereotyping in the classroom, in B. Moon and A. Shelton Mayes (eds) *Teaching and Learning in the Secondary School*. London: Routledge.

Department of Education and Science (DES) (1981) *West Indian Children in Our Schools*. The Rampton Report. London: HMSO.

Donald, J. and Rattansi, A. (eds) (1992) *'Race', Culture and Difference*. London: Sage.

Fuller, M. (1983) Qualified criticism, critical qualifications, in L. Barton and S. Walker (eds) *Race, Class and Education*. London: Croom Helm.

Gill, D., Mayor, B. and Blair, M. (eds) (1992) *Racism and Education: Structures and Strategies.* London: Sage.

Gipps, C. and Murphy, P. (1994) *A Fair Test? Assessment, Achievement and Equity.* Buckingham: Open University Press.

Grafton, T., Miller, H., Smith, L., Begoda, M. and Whitfield, R. (1987) Gender and curriculum choice, in M. Arnot and G. Weiner (eds) *Gender and the Politics of Schooling.* London: Unwin Hyman.

Great Britain (1975) *Sex Discrimination Act.* London: HMSO.

Great Britain (1976) *Race Relations Act.* London: HMSO.

Griffiths, M. and Troyna, B. (eds) (1995) *Antiracism, Culture and Social Justice in Education.* Stoke-on-Trent: Trentham Books.

hooks, b. (1993) Keeping close to home: class and education, in M.M. Tokarczyk and E.A. Fay (eds) *Working Class Women in the Academy: Labourers in the Knowledge Factory.* Amherst: University of Massachusetts Press.

Kelly, A. (1987) The construction of masculine science, in M. Arnot and G. Weiner (eds) *Gender and the Politics of Schooling.* London: Unwin Hyman.

Knowles, C. and Mercer, S. (1992) Feminism and antiracism: an exploration of the political possibilities, in J. Donald and A. Rattansi (eds) *'Race', Culture and Difference.* London: Sage.

Lorde, A. (1983) There is no hierarchy of oppressions, *Homophobia and Education.* Interracial Books for Children Bulletin, 14(3–4): 9.

Mac an Ghaill, M. (1988) *Young, Gifted and Black: Student–teacher Relations in the Schooling of Black Youth.* Milton Keynes: Open University Press.

Mirza, H.S. (1992) *Young, Female and Black.* London: Routledge.

Myers, K. (1990) Review of Equal Opportunities in the New ERA. Education, 5 October: 295.

National Curriculum Council (1990) *Curriculum Guidance 3; The Whole Curriculum.* London: HMSO.

Office for Standards in Education (Ofsted) (1993) *Framework for the Inspection of Schools.* London: HMSO.

Rattansi, A. (1992) Changing the subject? racism, culture and education, in J. Donald and A. Rattansi (eds) *'Race', Culture and Difference.* London: Sage.

Rogers, R. (ed.) (1986) *Education and Social Class.* London: Falmer Press.

Spender, D. and Sarah, E. (eds) (1980) *Learning to Lose: Sexism and Education.* London: The Women's Press.

Stobart, G., Elwood, J. and Quinlan, M. (1992) Gender bias in examinations: how equal are the opportunities?, *British Educational Research Journal*, 18(3): 261–77.

Wright, C. (1987) Black students – white teachers, in B. Troyna (ed.) *Racial Equality in Education.* London: Tavistock.

Wright, C. (1992) Multiracial primary school classrooms, in D. Gill, B. Mayor and M. Blair (eds) *Racism and Education: Structures and Strategies.* London: Sage.

Wright, C. (1994) Black children's experiences of the educational system, in B. Moon and A. Shelton Mayes (eds) *Teaching and Learning in the Secondary School.* London: Routledge.

Further reading

Epstein, D. (ed.) (1994) *Challenging Lesbian and Gay Inequalities in Education.* Buckingham: Open University Press.

8

Multicultural matters

Barbara Watson and Meg Maguire

Introduction

The period following the Second World War was typified by a demand for improvements to the education system in the UK. This period was also marked by large-scale movements of people from the ex-colonies and New Commonwealth countries who shared these heightened expectations. The overt discourses which shaped the post-war setting provided for equality of treatment before the law for these migrant citizens who were actively recruited to the 'motherland' in its need to supplement the labour force. However, many of the educational reports which started to appear in the 1960s reflected a growing unease and awareness of the inadequacies of the formal educational system in relation to these communities (and the working classes). These reports suggested disparity of achievement related to social class and argued that inner city decay, poverty and inappropriate pedagogy were factors in this unequal outcome (see, for example the Robbins Report (CHE 1962) and the Newsom Report (DES 1963)). It was argued by a Home Office study (Smith 1967) that since a degree of 'racial prejudice' existed in the UK and that as the cultures of 'minority' communities were not reflected in the school curriculum, some disengagement from the education process was inevitable for children from minority heritages. At the same time research was being undertaken which indicated that the black child in particular was failed by the school system (Coard 1971). The post war promise, quite simply, just had not been delivered.

In this chapter we argue that this pattern of exclusion has persisted for many (working-class) black children and their families who are still poorly served by the school system. We also consider some of the related issues that face intending teachers. First, we examine some of the theoretical dilemmas that are currently being debated. Theories are not arcane, abstracted irrelevancies because our ideas, beliefs and attitudes shape and underpin our practice. Second, we consider some of the contemporary social policy issues in this area as well as some of the implications of the 1988 Education Reform Act. Finally, we discuss briefly some of the key issues that schools have to consider if they are to meet the challenges and opportunities of a multiracial society and serve the needs of all their students in a socially just manner. Before we start, we want to make two points. Issues related to 'race', culture and difference are historically constituted and socially constructed. They are also contradictory, complex, changing and sometimes ambivalent (Rattansi and Westwood 1994). Thus there are wide-ranging and changing 'race' and cultural issues involved in education. In what follows we outline some of the central issues which seem to us to have particular relevance for the beginning teacher.

Theoretical issues

As general levels of awareness have grown and changed over time in response to political shifts, research findings and, not least, the campaigning activities of various minority communities, there have been marked critical linguistic shifts. 'In an area with a vast literature and a good deal of emotional as well as intellectual investment, terminology may be highly charged' (Klein 1993: 3). Language is a social phenomenon and, as such, is subject to fashion and politics as well as other cultural shifts. However, one of the most intractable of dilemmas exists in the ways in which people are identified, labelled or sometimes not recognised at all. For instance, in the educational setting, the language which is, or is not, used may send unintended signals to school students, their families as well as to other teachers in school. For example, the use of the word 'immigrant' is confusing. Most of those who currently migrate to the UK are white; most black people in the UK are not immigrants; they are second, third and sometimes fourth generation black British. There are also concerns about how to refer accurately (and collectively) to peoples who descend from and belong to different cultural, 'racial' or religious groups in the UK, other than the 'dominant' one. The expression 'ethnic minority' can cause difficulties; everyone belongs to an ethnic group and thus we are all ethnic minorities somewhere in the world. It is inaccurate to talk about world majorities (such as the Chinese) as minorities. There is currently a move towards utilising 'national minority groups' but there are obvious difficulties with this expression too.

Another dilemma is caused by the use of the word 'black'. The reclaiming of 'black as beautiful' and the Black Power Movement emerged from the civil rights uprisings in the USA in the 1960s. 'Black' came to denote a 'politics of solidarity' between those who experienced and resisted anti-colonial struggles as well as 'the social condition of post-colonial subjects in the heart of the British metropolis' (Brah 1993: 128). Indeed, some local authorities were able to design policies and target particular communities expressly through using the term 'black' (Gilroy 1987). However, recently the use of the word 'black' has been critiqued in the UK context (Brah 1993; Modood et al. 1994). It has been recognised that 'black' can usefully refer to South Asians in a political manner but that, in the main, it refers to the historical experiences of those of African descent. Essentialist expressions such as 'black' or 'Asian' which carry with them assumptions of homogeneity, are not always adequate. At some times, in some social contexts, black people share similar experiences – for example, of racism – where collective action is essential. At other times, issues of difference are more important.

In the USA there has been a trend towards signalling some of the dualisms which pattern social experiences; people identify as African-American or Irish-American which denotes heritage as well as full citizenship. In the UK there has been a move away from Black-British into differentiated naming systems. There is an awareness that African-Caribbean does not describe all those who came via the Caribbean and that other subtleties and distinctions need to be addressed such as those of Indo-Caribbean descent (Solomos and Back 1994). For an increasing number of people, Afrika and Afrikan is seen as appropriate. For those of South Asian descent, other factors, perhaps of faith or language may have as much to say about their identity as the actual place of origin. Additionally, people who are of mixed-race/dual heritage will have access to a wide range of cultural and material experiences. Contextual factors will frequently determine the way in which identity is most usefully expressed.

The recognition that identities are formed out of a multiplicity of 'raced', classed and gendered experiences does not in any way displace the debilitating impact of racism. Therefore a connected issue is still related to the need to challenge and eliminate racial discrimination and for those of us who work in educational settings, it is here that we have critical responsibilities. All this is of course premised on acknowledging the existence of racial discrimination in schooling as well as a recognition of the ethical and moral responsibility of the teacher in responding to this oppression. In numerous research projects some white teachers have argued that they simply just don't see the colour of their students; that there would be 'no problem here' if racial issues were not stressed so much (Gaine 1987). Ramdeen (1988) cites a school student's essay: 'My teacher is always telling me that she does not see my colour. If she does not see my colour then she does not see me.' However, the manner in which racism is conceptualised (or not) will have outcomes in policy. For example, in a 'colour-blind' world no action will be taken. In some schools racism will be regarded as individual unpleasantness and systematic discrimination will not be addressed. If racism is seen as a 'black problem' then all-white schools will not tackle the beliefs and values of their school ethos and their staff and student attitudes. (In this example it is clear that the way in which a dilemma is theorised or understood has outcomes and consequences for classroom practice). However, there is overwhelming evidence that black children and school students are subjected to low expectations on the part of their teachers, that they are on the receiving end of demeaning stereotyping and that racial harassment is a common part of daily life in schools in the UK (CRE 1987; Mac an Ghaill 1988; Mirza 1992). How schools deal with these matters, the whole school policies and strategies they employ in reducing and eliminating stereotyping, low expectation and racism will relate to how these issues are understood.

Currently our understandings, in the literature at least, have moved away from old essentialisms. We are working with 'more complex and fluid notions of race and identity that clearly articulate with contemporary theories of identity construction in late modernity' (Gillborn 1996: 176). This is an important and provocative move which will be returned to in our discussion of social policy shifts.

Social policy issues and resistances

Although changes are taking place in the way in which race relations and identity politics are being shaped in the 1990s, what needs to be recognised is that these developments are not of a piece and do not necessarily influence social policy formation in a direct or linear manner. Although it is possible to identify key shifts in policy responses towards race and schooling in the UK 'the phases do not reflect neat transitions in thinking across the whole population . . . neither should it be assumed that policies originating from earlier positions have been superseded by later thought and so have been altered or discontinued' (Gill 1993: 277). Old discourses of 'immigrant children' being seen as the problem are still influential in some schools today. For these reasons, it is useful to outline briefly some of the key moments in race relations policy in the UK.

In the early 1960s 'immigrant' children were seen as a 'problem'. The way forward, it was alleged, was to assimilate these children as quickly as possible to the 'host' culture. It was necessary to immerse these children in English if it was not their first language and then disperse them across schools, for if there were too many immigrant children in a school, this could 'hold back' the white children (a belief which still holds some currency). In some areas black children were 'bussed' to schools as part of a UK dispersal policy. Gradually, it was recognised that a 'gentler' process of integration was more appropriate. If teachers had a greater awareness of the diversity in their classrooms they would be able to teach these children more effectively – and thus promote assimilation. The publication in 1971 of Bernard Coard's work which detailed the manner in which African Caribbean children in particular were being wrongly assigned to special units, being labelled as 'less able' and in this way being denied access to the mainstream curriculum, clearly indicated that black children were being sidelined in their schools regardless of the tactics of integration or assimilation. During the 1970s and 1980s it was argued that multicultural education, which celebrated diversity would better promote tolerance and enhance in-school attainment. However, many theorists believed that multicultural education was ineffective as it failed to address the racism which, it was argued, was inherent in the UK school system (Troyna 1993). What developed was a form of dualism and polarisation between some multiculturalists and some anti-racists which persisted throughout the 1980s, at least in the research literature.

In the 1980s some local authorities started to move towards anti-racist policy making. The intention was to deconstruct racist practices and pedagogy. Schools, mainly in metropolitan areas, drew up antiracist whole school policies which covered the hidden and overt curriculum and attempted to ensure that racism was tackled and eliminated at an individual as well as institutional level. However when a student, Ahmed Iqbal Ullah was murdered in his school playground by a white boy, it was argued that the schools strong anti-racist policies had been too doctrinaire, polarised and thus counter-productive (Macdonald *et al.* 1989). This high-profile tragedy has led to a reconsideration of in-school tactics. As one consequence, the binary opposition of multicultural education (which sometimes only celebrated diversity through a reification of the more exotic/ historical aspects of various cultures) set against anti-racist education (which sometimes did little more than position black people as victims and white people as oppressors) was seen as limiting and irrelevant. It is now argued that through the contemporary reconstructions within race, identity politics and pedagogy, new possibilities are made visible.

> You can no longer conduct black politics through a strategy of a simple set of reversals, putting in the place of the bad old essentialist white subject, the new essentially good black subject. Now that formulation may seem to threaten the collapse of an entire political world. Alternatively it may be greeted with an extraordinary relief at the passing away of what at one time seemed to be a necessary fiction. Namely either that all black people are good or indeed that all black people are the same.
>
> (Hall 1992: 254)

However, these developments in national and educational race relations policy were and are taking place against a background of profound social and economic change. It is not possible here to do justice to the complexities and contradictions involved in this massive restructuring (see Ball 1994), but essentially there has been a rightwards move. In this move it has been argued that market forces are the best way through which to deliver social provisions such as health and education. Competition and choice (exercised by parents, the new consumers of education) will force up 'standards' and a National Curriculum, tested at regular intervals, will ensure a uniformity of provision and will provide consumer information. At the same time, this new Curriculum has been developed (in some ways at least) as a counterpoint to some of the egalitarian impulses of the 1970s and 1980s. At the 1987 Conservative Party Conference, Margaret Thatcher identified multicultural education with left-wing extremism and low standards in schools.

> In our inner cities where youngsters must have a decent education if they are to have a better future, the opportunity is all too often snatched away from them by hard-left education authorities and extremist teachers. Children who need to be able to count and multiply are learning anti-racist mathematics, whatever that is.
>
> (Margaret Thatcher, reported in Hughill 1987)

In many ways the impact of the Education Reform Act (1988) and in particular the National Curriculum, seem to take us back to a form of assimilationist tactics. Blair and Arnot (1993) argue that the National Curriculum has seriously reduced black perspectives and any multicultural dimension in the UK classroom. For example, the languages spoken by many British school children are not recognised in the National Curriculum. Blair and Arnot express concern that there is less space and time for individual teachers to respond to their students and children by drawing on their heritage and culture in an informed manner. They are concerned too, that the National Tests may be culturally biased. Importantly, they point out that there is no commitment in the National Curriculum to educate children and students about race relations and anti-racism.

It is important to set these assimilationist tendencies in policy against and alongside various resistances within the black communities who have consistently attempted to obtain good educational provision for their children. Where this has not been available and where parents have been fundamentally dissatisfied with an essentialist European-centred curriculum they have sought to restore some sense of balance and reality in their children's educational lives by setting up and using black supplementary schools. This strong network of schools has provided and continues to provide a supplement to the state system which many black parents believe is not adequately meeting the needs of their children. Black parents have expressed concerns that less is expected from their children, that their children are not taught the basic skills in an adequate manner and that, importantly, their children remain ignorant of their own histories and cultures which are sidelined in a reassertion of more traditional forms of curriculum and schooling (Ball 1994).

One response towards European centred education that has been influential in the USA and which is starting to impact on the UK context is the move towards African-centredness. When a community or 'nation' wishes to re-assert itself, its intellectuals tend to look to its classical civilisation for guidance, for an anchor which can afford a reorientation from which to move forward. The reconstruction of the Afrikan world view under the auspices of African-centrism is such a process. The classical civilisation for Africans is Kemet (Egypt). The link between Kemet and the rest of Africa is thought to be of such importance that Cheik Anta Diop concluded that the history of 'Africa will remain suspended in air and cannot be written correctly until African historians dare connect it with the history of Egypt' (Diop 1974: xiv). Central to the ideological basis of African-centricity is the idea that African people should analyse the world within and through the context of their (non-European) realities.

The argument is that Europe established international dominance in the colonial period through tactics such as military invasion and occupation; enslavement; erosion of language and tradition and other forms of political repression. At the height of the colonial period in the eighteenth and nineteenth century, these methods of control were underpinned by religious indoctrination and virulent 'scientific' discourses which positioned Africans and their cultures as 'uncivilised', 'barbaric', 'pagan' as well as 'underdeveloped'. The power of past images to influence contemporary beliefs and attitudes cannot be underestimated. Thus, Africans in the contemporary context are overwhelmingly referenced in the discourses of crime, single motherhood, drug abuse, unemployment and poverty.

The need to study Africa and Africans from an African-centred perspective becomes clear and even 'desperate' in order to challenge notions of an eternally dependent Africa and to offer another perspective. It has been

suggested that some African students are particularly vulnerable to ali-
enation in the European dominated educational system in the UK (and
elsewhere) due to a lack of any positive alternative cultural reservoir from
which to obtain validation. African students who were born in Britain
may self-identify as British, but are not always recognised as such by some
in the wider community. African British students are still referred to by
some teachers and in the media as 'West Indian' or even as 'immigrants'.
Although there is not enough space here to do more than mention African-
centricity as one form of resistance, we want to draw attention to the fact
that African British children (males in particular) are still 'underachieving'
in the mainstream school setting (but not in further education) and are
disproportionately being excluded from schools. What is also important
to point out is that African-centredness does not seek to displace a European perspective but works to provide an unbiased view of Africa. However, the Education Reform Act (ERA) has had a powerful effect on what
counts as knowledge and what counts as education in the UK and it may
be only through the supplementary independent school movement that
an African-centred perspective will be developed.

At the same time, there are a range of other important structural (and
ideological) issues embedded in the ERA which are starting to have an
impact on race and educational provision in the UK. Schools now test
children at key points in their educational career at 7, 11, 14 and 16 years
of age. The results at 16, and now 11 are published nationally so that parents can gain information about local schools. In this way, it is argued,
parental choice (and competition) is maintained. However, as is only too
obvious (Gewirtz *et al.* 1995) it is the popular and oversubscribed schools
which actually do the selecting. It may be that disaffected or 'difficult'
school students will find it harder to get their first choice. It may also be
the case that inner city (black) schools become increasingly less attractive
to white middle-class parents, so much so that the phenomenon of 'white
flight' which is apparent in many American cities may become a feature
of 1990s UK inner city schooling.

The effects of choice, competition and race relations in the marketplace
of schooling was recognised in a landmark case in 1987. An earlier piece
of Conservative legislation, the Education Act of 1981, had given parents
the 'right' to assert their choice of school. A group of white parents in
Dewsbury refused to send their primary aged children to a local multiracial
school as they wanted their children to receive a 'Christian' education
based on 'British culture'. In 1988, the Kirklees Education Authority allowed
the families to send the children to the school of their choice. After a
High Court case on the issue it was argued that parental choice overruled
the Race Relations Act of 1976 even if schools in consequence became
'ghettoised'. This is not to deny the contribution which might be made
by all-black schools, themselves a controversial issue (Brown 1994; Alston
1994). Rather, working-class multiracial schools, in inner city areas, will
be less able to draw on affluent parental support in order to supplement
any financial deficiency. This could have a knock-on effect on staffing,
resourcing and stability.

Since the ERA, however, secondary schools in particular have had to
ensure that they are attractive to parents (as their income is determined

by numbers of students on roll) and they have to ensure that their examination performance looks good too. It is easy to see why certain types of students will be less attractive and less desirable; they will also be more expensive to teach. For a variety of complex but interwoven reasons (see Bourne *et al.* 1994) schools have increasingly been resorting to excluding these sorts of students. The statistics are stark. Overwhelmingly, the students who are excluded are African Caribbean males (Bourne *et al.* 1994). It is worth quoting Bourne *et al.* at length at this point:

> Black families have come under growing social and economic pressures as a direct result of government policies, trapped as they so often are in the most deprived and neglected inner urban areas and concentrated among the lower income sectors of society. For it is these sectors which have suffered most from rising unemployment, regressive taxation and massive cutbacks in social spending, not least in subsidies for public housing. Black parents and children alike also face the additional disruption to their lives resulting from rising racial harassment and attacks. All these factors combine to increase the discontinuity faced by many black children as between the social dislocation imposed on their family and community life and the demands of the supposedly more 'disciplined' and orderly school community. It is hardly surprising that some black children present themselves as 'aggressive' in school, as this is a stance that society outside has taught them is necessary for survival. And, when racism spills over into the school itself, in terms of incidents or violence in the playground or in teachers' attitudes towards black pupils, black pupils are only confirmed in their aggression as a means of survival.
>
> (Bourne *et al.* 1994: 11)

What we are suggesting is that there are significant structural and ideological shifts which are having an impact on race relations and school provision in the UK. Individual schools caught up in this policy maelstrom need sound whole-school policies as well as an ethical commitment to and an understanding of issues of social justice if they are to withstand some of these pressures.

School issues

Some trainee teachers may be impatient with what is on offer in this chapter. If they have read this far they may well be asking themselves what can they actually do in their classroom. How should they cope with grouping students? How should they monitor their students' attainments? How can they deal with any stereotyping or racism which may occur? What can they do as trainee teachers if they are involved in discussions in the staffroom, or with parents, which make them feel uncomfortable? These sorts of issues become all the more problematic for a relatively powerless trainee teacher who may be placed in a school which has no whole school policy or supportive network of anti-racist teachers. The very first step in schools with no whole school policies is to link up with other colleagues who share these concerns. There is a useful body of research literature which describes in-school tactics and strategies in this area (Gillborn 1995; King and Reiss 1993; Klein 1993; Massey 1991). The main point to emphasise, however, is the need for a whole school approach which 'has total staff ownership' (Gould 1993) where issues are discussed, renegotiated and where all, including school students (see Gillborn 1996) are involved. However, as schools now control their budgets (through local management of schools) they decide themselves whether to employ specialist staff in this area or to dedicate funds towards in-service training in this field. As Blair and Arnot (1993: 264) say, 'The extent to which schools will be prepared to use their limited budgets in this way is now being tested.'

Conclusions

For over thirty years now, educationalists, researchers and policy makers have been concerned with multicultural/antiracist work in schools. Although the major impact has been experienced in inner city schools, controlled in the main by Labour-led local authorities, nevertheless in 1985 the Swann Report (commissioned by the Conservative Government) underlined the need for all educational institutions to prepare all children for life in a multiracial society. And despite some negative and ethno-centric aspects within the National Curriculum there are still opportunities for teachers who want to work in a multicultural and antiracist manner. 'It therefore depends upon the choice of teachers, schools and commun-ities as to whether multicultural education is affirmed or pushed to the periphery' (King 1993: 18).

References

Alston, K. (1994) Community politics and the education of African American males: whose life is it anyway?, in C. Marshall (ed.) *The New Politics of Race and Gender*. London: Falmer Press.

Ball, S.J. (1994) *Education Reform: A Critical and Post-structural Approach*. Buckingham: Open University Press.

Blair, M. and Arnot, M. (1993) Black and anti-racist perspectives on the National Curriculum and government educational policy, in A.S. King and M.J. Reiss (eds) *The Multicultural Dimension of the National Curriculum*. London: Falmer Press.

Bourne, J., Bridges, L. and Searle, C. (1994) *Outcast England: How Schools Exclude Black Children*. London: Institute of Race Relations.

Brah, A. (1993) Difference, diversity and differentiation, in J. Donald and A. Rattansi (eds) *'Race', Culture and Difference*. London: Sage, with Open University Press.

Brown, K. (1994) Do African American males need race and gender segregated education? An educator's perspective and a legal perspective, in C. Marshall (ed.) *The New Politics of Race and Gender*. London: Falmer Press.

Coard, B. (1971) *How the West Indian Child is made Educationally Sub-normal in the British School System*. London: Beacon Books.

Commission for Racial Equality (CRE) (1987) *Learning in Terror*. London: CRE.

Committee on Higher Education (CHE) (1962) *Higher Education Report* (The Robbins Report). London: HMSO.

Department of Education and Science (DES) (1963) Half our Future: A Report of the Central Advisory Council for Education (England) (The Newsom Report). London: HMSO.

Diop, C.A. (1974) *The African Origin of Civilisation: Myth or Reality*. Chicago: Lawrence Hill Books.

Gaine, C. (1987) *No Problem Here: A Practical Approach to Education and Race in White Schools*. London: Hutchinson.

Gewirtz, S., Ball, S.J. and Bowe, R. (1995) *Markets, Choice and Equity in Education*. Buckingham: Open University Press.

Gill, B.A.G. (1993) Assessment: social processes, in A.S. King and M.J. Reiss (eds) *The Multicultural Dimension of the National Curriculum*. London: Falmer Press.

Gillborn, D. (1995) *Racism and Anti-racism in Real Schools*. Buckingham: Open University Press.

Gillborn, D. (1996) Student roles and perspectives in antiracist education: a crisis of white ethnicity?, *British Educational Research Journal*, 22(2): 165–81.

Gilroy, P. (1987) *There Ain't no Black in the Union Jack*. London: Hutchinson.

Gould, D. (1993) Whole school issues, in A.S. King and M.J. Reiss (eds) *The Multicultural Dimension of the National Curriculum*. London: Falmer Press.

Hall, S. (1992) New ethnicities, in J. Donald and A. Rattansi (eds) *Race, Culture and Difference*. Buckingham: Open University Press.

HMSO (1985) *Education for All*, Cmnd 9453 (The Swann Report). London: HMSO.

Hughill, B. (1987) Dramatic steps that will carry Britain forward, *Times Educational Supplement*, 16 October.

King, A.S. (1993) 'Introduction', in A.S. King and M.J. Reiss (eds) *The Multicultural Dimension of the National Curriculum*. London: Falmer Press.

King, A.S. and Reiss, M.J. (eds) (1993) *The Multicultural Dimension of the National Curriculum*. London: Falmer Press.

Klein, G. (1993) *Education Towards Race Equality*. London: Cassell.

Mac an Ghaill, M. (1988) *Young, Gifted and Black: Student-teacher Relations in the Schooling of Black Youth*. Milton Keynes: Open University Press.

Macdonald, I., Bhavani, R. Khan, L. and John, G. (1989) *Murder in the Playground* (The Burnage Report). Longsight Press.

Massey, I. (1991) *More than Skin Deep: Developing Anti-racist Multicultural Education in Schools*. London: Hodder and Stoughton.

Mirza, H.S. (1992) *Young, Female and Black*. London: Routledge.

Modood, T., Beishon, S. and Virdee, A. (1994) *Changing Ethnic Identities*. London: Policy Studies Institute.

Ramdeen, L. (1988) Primary consideration: young children's education and the GERBIL, *Multicultural Teaching*, 6(2): 26–30.

Rattansi, A. (1994) 'Western' racisms, ethnicities and identities in a 'postmodern' frame, in A. Rattansi and S. Westwood (eds) *Racism, Modernity, Identity on the Western Front*. London: Polity Press.

Rattansi, A. and Westwood, S. (eds) (1994) *Racism, Modernity, Identity on the Western Front*. London: Polity Press.

Smith, D. (1967) *Racial Discrimination in Britain*. London: Population and Economic Planning.

Solomos, J. and Back, L. (1994) Conceptualising racisms: social theory, politics and research, *Sociology* 28(1): 143–63.

Troyna, B. (1993) *Racism and Education*. Buckingham: Open University Press.

Further reading

Asante, M.K. (1988) *Afrocentricity*. New Jersey: Africa World Press Inc.

Asante, M.K. (1992) *Kemet, Afrocentricity and Knowledge*. New Jersey: Africa World Press Inc.

Marshall, C. (ed.) (1994) *The New Politics of Race and Gender*. London: Falmer Press.

Tomlinson, S. and Craft, M. (eds) (1995) *Ethnic Relations and Schooling: Policy and Practice in the 1990s*. London: Athlone Press.

Troyna, B. and Carrington, B. (1990) *Education, Racism and Reform*. London: Routledge.

Troyna, B. and Hatcher, R. (1992) *Racism in Children's Lives*. London: Routledge.

9 Understanding the urban experience: inner city schooling[1]

Meg Maguire and Justin Dillon

Introduction

The majority of new teachers work in urban environments – many in inner cities. Many teachers want to work in inner cities, some do not and others have no choice. What is so special about inner cities? Our intention here is to provide an account of and a background to the urban school that is essential in any attempt 'to improve the education of the urban poor' (Grace 1994: 45). We argue that teaching in inner city schools offers a particular set of challenges, that these have been constructed over time and that they have fundamental implications for society at large.

First then, we want to explore what is meant by urban education and in order to do this it is necessary to locate the urban in its historical context. The nineteenth century modern industrial form was distinguished by a 'great movement of population from the land to the towns, from village to factory' (Hall 1977: 8). During this century, a developing awareness of the brutalisation and inhumanity of urban life and the oppression of the industrialised factory system 'pointed clearly to the limits of the market as a mechanism for 'invisibly' securing the greatest good for the greatest number' (Hall 1977: 8). It was recognised that some form of social intervention was essential; issues of urban sanitation, the amelioration of poverty, disease and child labour were all regarded as critical causes for social improvement. Education was not initially regarded as a fundamental concern.

Gradually it was recognised that some form of basic schooling needed to be provided by the central state and this was based on two main justifications. First, the urban masses needed some form of minimal literacy to sustain the growth and expansion of capital. Educational provision in other European (competitor) nations was far in advance. An uneducated mass workforce was no longer economically viable. Secondly, and just as important, it was recognised that an unruly inner city 'mob' had the potential for revolution (as had been the case in France). Thus, as Hall puts it, while the cities had to be improved, they also had to be controlled. It is worth quoting Hall at length on this issue for many of the sentiments expressed seem peculiarly appropriate in the current climate.

> Some way had to be found to create, within the ranks of the urban-industrial masses, an inner attachment to society's goals, a positive commitment to the social order. Respectability, thrift, sobriety, self-discipline were required, to form – as it were from inside – an impulse, a 'formed sentiment', among the masses to adapt to the logic, rationale and mores of industrial capitalism. Thus, education took its place, along-side chapel, tract, self-improving societies, temperance movements, improving popular fiction, as a major cultural force reshaping the inner sentiments and aspirations of the masses. Like other missionary crusades, it was only a partial success.
>
> (Hall 1977: 9)

The urban schools, the old elementary schools, whose wonderful build-ings are still present in our cities, were set up specifically to school the urban working class. They were set up to 'gentle' the masses but not to 'gentrify' them. Their curriculum was 'basic' and their intention straight-forward enough. Schooling was used, as it still is, to reproduce society; education distributes life chance and education legitimates 'failure'. After all, if everyone has the opportunity to succeed in a meritocratic system, then 'failure' can be individually constituted. Throughout the first half of the twentieth century, a pattern of limited provision persisted (see Chap-ter 10). A small minority of working-class people climbed 'the ladder' of success. As one of this small group recalls:

> In practice the school unconsciously orientated its teaching to the exceptions among us . . . who were going to be lifted up into a higher social class. How many of these? That was the point . . . Always the pride that prevailed in this working class school was that it succeeded in turning out less recruits for the working class than any other of its kind in the district. That less was still the majority, mind you . . . but the school's official boast was not of them.
>
> (Common 1951, cited in Hargreaves 1982: 75–6).

However the majority of working-class youngsters were not so 'success-ful'. In many ways, their compulsory schooling – for education it was not – seemed almost irrelevant. When work was plentiful, educational achieve-ment was not important; when work was scarce, education was used to keep them off the streets (the compulsory dole schools of the late 1920s and early 1930s, forerunners, perhaps, of current youth 'training' projects). The coercion to attend school was not always met in a compliant way. Grace has recorded some incidents of school-room life in the nineteenth century which do not seem so distant from contemporary experiences:

I had occasion to punish a boy slightly this morning: he swore most horribly and rushed from the school . . . I was suddenly startled by a large stone passing my ear. I got out of the reach of stones thrown through the window and continued the lesson.

(Grace 1978: 32)

Compare that with:

Paper planes, knobs of chewing gum and once a gravel filled condom (apparently looted empty from a pastoral studies class) just miss my head as I attempt to write a French irregular verb on a ravaged blackboard pitted with holes.

(Owen 1990)

What we want to underline is that inner city schools have always served a distinct section of society; the working-class urban poor. Their schools 'in and around the inner city stand' as 'beacons and landmarks of working class education' (Hall 1977: 11). In contrast, the privileged schools, have, in the main, remained outside the city while in the city, some grammar schools have developed in either the middle-class suburbs or within middle-class areas of urban gentrification. As Hall (1977: 11) presciently put it:

there has never been, in England, anything remotely approaching a 'common' or 'comprehensive' school experience for all classes of children. Each kind of school has been absorbed into its socio-geographic segment, and taken on something of that imprint.

Some 'urban' issues have persisted over time. School children and school students, in the past as in the contemporary inner city school, are not passive recipients of the educational system. Neither are their teachers. However, all are caught up in a maelstrom of dilemmas; what sort of education should be on offer in our inner city schools? Is the current curriculum, at which so many have persistently 'failed,' an appropriate offer? If some children were to be offered a different curriculum, what would this do for their chances? Do teachers (mainly white middle-class) hold reduced aspirations and expectations of working-class and minority children? What can be done to motivate inner city young people in the current situation of high youth unemployment?

The contemporary city

It is now argued that if post-war Britain was characterised by profitable manufacturing industries which provided high levels of employment and good salaries, homes, health and schooling for its citizens, then Britain in the 1990s is undergoing the trauma of deindustrialisation (Bettis and Stoeker 1993; Weis 1990). Manufacturing jobs have declined. Employment is becoming fragmented by short-term contracting and by a move to part-time rather than full-time jobs. However, deindustrialisation does not occur in a 'uniform' manner or in isolation from other structures. Regions and cities experience its effects differentially.

Some cities have experienced significant overall decline while others have experienced localised outer-city growth set alongside inner-city decay (Bettis and Stoeker 1993: 6). Particular communities have experienced the differential effects of post-Fordist labour market restructurings. For example, a recent Labour Force Survey has estimated that 62 per cent of black young men in London were unemployed as contrasted with 20 per cent of white men in the same age cohort (TUC 1995).

Thus, the urban setting makes 'visible' some of the fundamental contradictions within the wider society (Grace 1978: 3). In London (the first industrialised city) the impact of deindustrialisation is significant. From the city business zone which contains empty office buildings through Docklands, where investments have been made in bricks and mortar with almost no job creation for local people, to areas of new settlement like Tower Hamlets or Stoke Newington; from housing 'ghettos' like Thamesmead, with no local amenities for recreation to gentrified housing locales such as parts of Islington and Hackney, the poorest live across the road from some of the richest in the country. Maden (1996) has argued that this polarisation was exacerbated by post-war urban planning through which skilled workers were resettled in new towns and 'greenfield' developments outside metropolitan areas; what Newsam (1996) has described as the 'planned dereliction of the inner city'.

Hutton (1995) has characterised the UK as the 'thirty, thirty, forty society' where the bottom 60 per cent are 'disadvantaged', 'marginalised' and 'insecure'. He describes a society where 'segmentation of the labour market . . . is sculpting the new and ugly shape of British society' (Hutton 1995: 108). He underlines the fact that more than half of the people in the UK are 'living either on poverty incomes or in conditions of permanent stress and insecurity' and so it has been much harder to sustain relationships let alone parent children adequately in contemporary society.

While these conditions are not unique to urban settings, it is in inner cities where the highest concentrations of the marginalised and dispossessed are to be found. Between 1981 and 1991 'the degree, intensity and extent of poverty increased markedly in inner London and other large metropolitan areas' (Maden 1996: 20) and 'in the list of England's thirty most deprived areas, all inner London boroughs are there' (Maden 1996: 21). Six London boroughs are listed in the worst ten areas of deprivation in the UK where deprivation is measured in relation to employment, housing, education credentials, race, crime, lone caring, and so on. London thus provides a cockpit in which to view in a concentrated manner, many of the inequities of contemporary policy making writ large (Grace 1978).

Welfare spending and the 'culture of contentment'

It might be argued that as deindustrialisation has impacted on western societies in consequence of global capitalism, individual nation-states are unable to resist this change. However, western democratic capital states do have some options at their disposal. One of these is in relation to social welfare spending for the public good. However in the UK, successive Governments have dealt with the economic shifts of deindustrialisation through appropriating a neo-liberal ideology which now underpins social and economic policy in Britain.

Essentially there has been a massive disruption in national ethics and values, an attempt to shift from 'a culture of commitment to relative public good to a defence of relative private interest' (Grace 1994: 53). Grace argues that this shift is characterised by the reification of private and individualised self-interest. Once again, a belief in the 'justice' inherent in a meritocratic society is being asserted. If an individual has achieved in school for example, the acquisition of this cultural capital is regarded as an individual asset which can be exchanged for material advancement. For example, the old, traditional, elite higher educational system (as opposed to the 'new' universities) which richly rewards its students with access to higher salaries (and 'satisfying' careers as opposed to tedious jobs) is paid for by the majority and provides for (in the main) a rich and powerful elite who justify their claim to privilege, and free higher education, on the basis of merit.

At the same time a powerful constituency, which Galbraith has called the 'contented electoral majority' or the 'culture of contentment' actively resists the 'burden' of redistributive taxation (Galbraith 1992). Individuals have the right to hold onto as much of their money as possible, it is argued, while ensuring that they maximise their capacity to access state provisions – health, welfare and education. This can be done through moving house to access a 'good' state school, or activating cultural capital to 'interview' successfully and obtain a place in a suburban selective school (see Rosen 1996). All these individual measures are less available to inner city working-class families. As Grace (1994: 46) says, the constituency of contentment contains within itself a 'relative unwillingness to look at longer term social, economic, or environmental planning, if these threaten present contentment'. With Grace, we believe that it is the urban poor who are on the losing side of this value shift and it is to their education that we now turn.

Schooling in the city

> The majority of schools situated in inner cities have some characteristics in common. Chief among these is the presence of large numbers of pupils from social backgrounds where education is not as highly valued as it is in other areas. In many cases, these are also schools where there are large numbers of pupils who suffer from various forms of disadvantage.
>
> (HMI 1991: 1–2)

In 1991, the HMI recognised the distinctiveness of inner city schools where 'a higher than average proportion of pupils were disadvantaged'. They acknowledged the 'extra challenge' of teaching in the city, particularly London, and highlighted a number of professional dimensions which they believed to be particularly relevant to teaching in urban schools. These were: multi-cultural education; language development, including English as a second language (ESL), class management, behavioural problems and absenteeism; low expectations and achievement. However, we would want to suggest that all this exemplifies a 'problem' or 'deficit' discourse on the inner city which neatly hides the structural underpinnings which support and frame urban disadvantage. So, it is the family that does not value education which is to blame for its own 'failure to succeed'.

In many ways urban schooling has always been mythologised through individualised 'deficit' rather than structural disadvantage. Our initial examples of dissent and disruption capture the sense of 'crisis' and panic which surrounds the inner city school. 'Inner city' does not mean the gracious boys' grammar school set well in the heart of the city – simply, it stands as a signifier for the schools which are attended by black and white working-class 'difficult and disruptive' children. Therefore the 'solution' has frequently been to improve these schools, through tactics like the effective schools movement, specific strategies such as 'assertive discipline', the use of 'positive role models' or to close them down. These tactics have not significantly impacted on inner city schools. As Grace (1994) has argued, what is needed is a stronger conceptualisation than one of mere 'deficit' as well as the political will to tackle structural disadvantage.

As we have already argued, the most drastic effects of de-industrialisation, recession and social restructurings such as cut backs in social welfare, housing and health have been disproportionately experienced by those who are most vulnerable; the unemployed, the single parent, the refugee, the recent migrant. Children who go to school 'in the most economically deprived areas of the inner cities will be faced with declining resources, a scarcity of experienced teachers, poorer plant facilities, reduced educational support, and in some cases their local school will close' (Ball 1990: 99). In the 'culture of contentment' who will defend these schools, now often constructed as 'failing' or 'underachieving' schools? Who will want to teach in them? Whose children will attend them?

The shift from public concern to private interest has been particularly evident in the attack on the Inner London Education Authority (Jones 1992). ILEA was a 'high spender' because it needed to be. ILEA also stood for a commitment to 'race', gender and class issues. As such, the ILEA could not be tolerated – its views were in direct contrast to neo-liberal low public spending ideologies – thus ILEA was abolished. London is now the only city without a cohesive cross-city educational authority in the UK.

London is a cosmopolitan city; well over 160 languages are spoken by London children. Some schools serve a community composed mostly of recent migrants and refugees who may well still be traumatised by their experiences. Other schools serve the needs of one local community; perhaps white working-class or British Bengali. The range of differences and the range of needs is enormous, yet patterns of inequality persist and become reinforced by contemporary social policies and material reality.

For example, parental choice at primary/secondary transition has not yet delivered school improvement. In the inner city, choice becomes a subtle form of 'discriminatory sorting' (Moore and Davenport 1990: 221). Whitty (1991: 19–20) has argued that the current reforms of ERA will have particular consequences for the predominantly working-class and black urban populations. While they never gained a fair share of resources under social democratic policies, the abandonment of planning in favour of the market seems unlikely to provide a solution. It is worth quoting Maden (1996) at length in relation to this issue.

Peter Newsam has shown how secondary schools in the inner London area have increasingly moved beyond a simple first and second class division to a much more hierarchical and qualitatively polarised system. In his analysis, over three quarters of children in the top 25 per cent of the ability range are now in half the available schools, including the selective independent schools (which represent a third of this favoured half). The other half represents schools which contain very few and sometimes no pupils who are in the top 25 per cent of the ability range. These are best classified as 'other' and 'secondary modern' schools and, as Sir Peter comments 'such schools are no more failed comprehensives than a Brussels sprout is a failed cabbage'. Over half of inner London's secondary age pupils are in such schools.

(Maden 1996: 22)

In a small study of classroom life in London urban primary schools (Pratt and Maguire 1996) teachers reported a wide range of difficulties. They argued that non-attendance at school was sometimes caused by factors such as family difficulties or illness due to poor housing conditions. They stated that inadequate sleeping facilities and overcrowding resulted in tired children who came late for school. Lack of money at home resulted in children coming to school hungry

A child comes to school having slept ten to a damp room with no breakfast, telling me the electricity has been cut off and petrol poured through the letter box. How would you feel? Could you concentrate on learning?

(Teacher cited in Pratt and Maguire 1996: 24)

The teachers did make positive suggestions which could help resolve some of the difficulties resulting from home circumstances, e.g. providing breakfast facilities. They suggested strategies to support parents and local communities – all of which had resource implications. Teachers believed overwhelmingly that the main work needed to be done through improved government policies on education, employment, housing and health: 'Deprived areas need more resources' as one teacher said. Some schools had been forced to make cuts following changes in the funding arrangements. In consequence, some schools now had less Section 11 teaching support (for children for whom English is not their first language) and had increased class sizes.

What to do?

Currently in the UK there is a movement towards school improvement; the effective schools movement. The effectiveness research highlights the key attributes of a 'good' school which can be reproduced elsewhere. In this way it is possible to 'blame' individual schools for their failure to succeed (where success is measured in relation to GCSEs obtained or scores in the national tests – see Chapters 6, 16 and 23). However, there are some contradictions involved in relation to urban schools.

> Inevitably however, any school improvement that takes place is likely to benefit those from advantaged families – those better able to make use of the new opportunities – more than those from families which are facing difficulties . . . Thus, though overall national standards may rise, the difference between the most and the least advantaged will probably also increase.
>
> (Mortimore 1995: 17)

In addition, less attractive 'poorer' areas in the inner cities may find it harder to attract and retain teachers. Schools in suburban settings or middle-class urban enclaves are able to draw on parental financial support in a way which is closed to urban schools. 'Those living in the inner cities may increasingly become the only groups in society receiving merely the basic state provision' (Whitty 1990: 113).

Urban schools and trainee teachers

In conclusion we want to make two main points in relation to the contemporary reforms of teacher education as these have specific impact on the inner city experience (see Chapter 4 for a discussion of recent reforms in teacher education). If trainee teachers are spending the majority of their time in schools, coping and surviving in difficult circumstances, without much more than a cursory appreciation of the urban context, it may well be that trainee teachers 'blame' their school students for the difficulties they face in their teaching (which could indirectly contribute towards low expectations and achievement). 'The urban poor, however they are constituted in ethnic, gender or class terms in various societies, and wherever they are located, are a challenge to established institutions' (Grace 1994: 45). This 'challenge' is not always easy for teachers to manage but perhaps more importantly, without any knowledge or theoretical exploration of the urban context, it is perhaps understandable that some schools may 'blame' the students for the disruptions they sometimes pose.

Perhaps the most intractable and contradictory dilemma that faces teachers in the inner city is the paradox of recognising the social and material realities in which the school is placed, while at the same time ensuring that aspirations and expectations are not reduced by these challenges. But the greatest challenge lies beyond individual and localised responses:

> Adequate human and material resources are fundamental to the renaissance of effectiveness and of hope in urban education. Only those who have not taught in the inner city assert otherwise. With such resources the capacity of urban schools to respond to the new informational economy and its consequences could be greatly enhanced. The children, youth and adults of the inner city and of other deprived urban locations could realise the skill and knowledge capacities which they undoubtedly have.
>
> (Grace 1994: 52)

Note

1 This chapter draws on an earlier paper (Maguire and Dillon 1997).

References

Ball., S.J. (1990) Markets and ERA, *The Urban Review: Issues and Ideas in Public Education*, 22(2): 85–99.

Bettis, P.J. and Stoeker, R. (1993) New urban sociology and critical education theory: framework for urban school reform in an era of deindustrialisation. Conference Paper, Annual Meeting of the American Educational Research Association, Atlanta, April.

Common, J. (1951) *Kiddar's Luck*. London: Turnpike Press, cited in Hargreaves, D. (1982) *The Challenge for the Comprehensive School: Culture, Curriculum and the Community*. London: Routledge and Kegan Paul.

Galbraith, J.K. (1992) *The Culture of Contentment*. London: Sinclair-Stevenson.

Grace, G. (1978) *Teachers, Ideology and Control*. London: Routledge and Kegan Paul.

Grace, G. (1994) Urban education and the culture of contentment: the politics, culture and economics of inner-city schooling, in N.P. Stronquist (ed.) *Education in Urban Areas: Cross-national Dimensions*. London: Praeger.

Hall, S. (1977) Education and the crisis of the urban school, in J. Raynor and E. Harris (eds) *Schooling the City*. Glasgow: Ward Lock in association with The Open University.

Hargreaves, D. (1982) *The Challenge for the Comprehensive School: Culture, Curriculum and Community*, London: Routledge and Kegan Paul.

HMI (1991) *Training Teachers for Inner City Schools*. London: HMSO.

Hutton, W. (1995) *The State We're In*. London: Jonathan Cape.

Jones, C. (1992) Dogma, equality and excellence: education in London, in D. Coulby, C. Jones and D. Harris (eds) *Urban Education: World Yearbook of Education 1992*. London: Kogan Page.

Maden, M. (1996) Divided Cities: 'Dwellers in Different Zones, Inhabitants of Different Planets'. The TES/Greenwich Education Lecture 1996. London: University of Greenwich and *The Times Educational Supplement*.

Maguire, M. and Dillon, J. (1997) The inner city experience, in M. Fuller and A. Rosie (eds) *Teacher Education and School Partnerships*. Lampeter: Edwin Mellen Press.

Moore, D, and Davenport, S. (1990) Choice: the new improved sorting machine, in W.L. Boyd and H.J. Halberg (eds) *Choice in Education: Potential and Problems*. Berkeley: McCutchan.

Mortimore, P. (1995) Better than excuses, *Times Educational Supplement*, 7 July.

Newsam, P. (1996) Take the terminology to task, *Times Educational Supplement*, 22 March.

Owen, M. (1990) School for scandal, *The Guardian*, 1 May.

Postner, M. (1989) *Critical Theory and Poststructuralism: In Search of a Context*. Ithaca: Cornell University Press.

Pratt S. and Maguire, M. (1996) Inner city children and their schooling, *Primary Teaching Studies*, 9(2): 22–28.

Rosen, M. (1996) The old school lie, *New Statesman*, 26 January.

Trades Union Congress (1995) *Young People in the Labour Market in 1995*. Report prepared for the 1995 Youth Conference. London: TUC.

Weis, L. (1990) *Working Class Without Work*. New York: Routledge.

Whitty, G. (1990) Creeping privatization and its implications for schooling in the inner city, *The Urban Review*, 22(2): 101–13.

Whitty, G. (1991) Teacher education: next in line for the treatment? Education reform and teacher education in the 1990s. Inaugural Lecture, Goldsmith's College, University of London.

Further reading

Gewirtz, S., Ball, S.J. and Bowe, R. (1995) *Markets, Choice and Equity in Education.* Buckingham: Open University Press.

Grace, G (1984) *Education and the City: Theory, History and Contemporary Practice.* London: Routledge and Kegan Paul.

Wilmot, P. (1994) (ed.) *Urban Trends 2.* London: Policy Studies Institute.

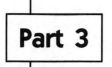

Part 3 | Teaching and learning issues

Adolescence

John Head

There is little doubt that adolescents often receive a bad press, with lurid tales of blackboard jungles in schools, and car theft, drug use and sexual promiscuity outside school. For reasons such as these adolescence has been described as a time of 'storm and stress'. Is this reputation justified?

The first point to note is that there is nothing new in these criticisms. Even in Classical Greece there were complaints about unruly youth failing to respect their elders. In *The Winter's Tale*, Shakespeare wrote, 'I would that there were no age between ten and three-and-twenty, or youth would sleep out the rest.' In the past thirty years in Britain we have experienced rockers and mods, punks, and a whole series of youth cults and fashions which have aroused adult disapproval.

What is the contemporary evidence? It is mixed. On many criteria, for example, physical health, adolescents are a favoured group (Heaven 1996). But there are some problems. Among boys the high crime rates for those in their late teens is disturbing, with over 8 per cent of the eighteen-year-old cohort being convicted or cautioned for an indictable offence (that is an offence sufficiently serious to attract the possibility of a prison sentence). One third of males have such a finding of guilt by the age of thirty. The crime rates for females is much lower, in the range 10 to 20 per cent of that for males, at all ages. In addition, suicide rates among young men aged 15 to 24 more than doubled between 1971 and 1992, from less than 7 per 100,000 of the population to over 15, despite the fact that the overall rate for the general population had gone down in that time. The suicide rate for females aged 15 to 24 remained under 4 per 100,000 throughout this period. Among girls, eating disorders are common, but it is difficult to give a precise estimate of the extent of the problem as only the most severe cases get notified to the authorities. Clearly, it is possible to gather data to support either argument, that adolescents are, or are not, undergoing storm and stress.

Modern psychologists (for example, Coleman and Hendry 1990) tend to argue that each phase of life presents certain characteristic challenges and problems, and that adolescence is not unique, it just presents a particular set of such challenges. That thesis leaves open the question whether the passage through adolescence has become easier or more difficult in recent years.

We can attempt to sort out what these issues might be by considering four major ideas related to adolescence.

Physical development

Adolescence is usually taken to start with puberty. This phase of life not only involves development of the genitalia but several other associated physical changes. Prior to puberty, both boys and girls grow at about the same rate – about 5 cm per annum. Girls experience puberty first and enter a spurt phase when they grow at about 8.5 cm per year. Boys experience puberty later, but their growth spurt is more dramatic (height increase of about 9.5 cm per annum) and it lasts longer. Consequently in about Year 8, girls tend to be bigger than their male contemporaries. Later on the boys overtake them.

These body changes can produce side-effects, such as reduced co-ordination and fatigue (muscular growth occurs before a corresponding growth of the heart and lungs). But there are not only these external changes but also internal ones, arising from the hormonal environment changing. Occasionally boys experience short term problems, e.g. breast enlargement, but it is the girls who suffer most, with the majority of young adolescents reporting considerable distress from menstruation (Prendergast 1992).

Alongside the purely physical effects of puberty there are the psychological effects. The adolescents know that they are now capable of parenthood and hence issues such as one's sexual orientation become important. In the past some psychoanalysts, notably Anna Freud (1937) and Peter Blos (1962), suggested that prior to puberty children enjoyed a latency period, in which they had overcome the problems of childhood and they were able to cope with all the demands that life placed on them. Puberty brought about a new set of problems, physical and psychological, and adolescence was a period of crisis until solutions had been found to these new concerns. Maybe they made this argument too strongly. For many adolescents puberty presents few major problems, but we should be sensitive to the possibility that for some there are real concerns. In Western Europe in the past century the age of puberty has dropped by about three years, and as a result, the period of adolescence has been extended.

The age between

The second major idea comes from sociology. It is argued that with both children and adults we have a clear idea about appropriate roles and functions, but with adolescents the situation is confused. They receive alternate messages telling them to grow up and reminding them that they are not yet adult.

Adolescents tend to envy adults for their perceived freedoms, e.g. to drive a car, to drink, or to stay out late, and they will tend to pester adults to be allowed more freedom for themselves. This battle for independence can strain relationships with parents and teachers. It may not be easy for parents to abandon their role of a protector.

Part of the problem is that adolescents do not always appreciate the constraints placed on adults. If we were totally selfish and did just what we liked we would probably lose all our friends because of our selfish, antisocial behaviour and could even end up in prison. Adolescents may fail to recognise the constraints implied in adult behaviour. They may carry the battle for independence too far, for example taking the rule that they can do what they like within their own bedroom as a licence to play their radio as loudly as they want, regardless of the others in the house.

Probably the wisest course for parents and teachers is to negotiate a progressive position, one in which the adolescent gains increasing freedoms year by year. Certainly, in an 11–18 age range school I would expect the Year 12 and 13 students (sixth formers) to be treated very differently from eleven-year-old pupils.

Sometimes adults may despair but there is evidence that even disadvantaged adolescents, those in residential homes and with experience of abuse, do listen to adults. The youth culture is such that adolescents cannot be seen to be too submissive to adult authority. In school you may find students seemingly hostile in front of their peer group but in reality they are listening and responding to what you are saying.

This period of detachment from adult control can generate anxieties of its own, and it is in early adolescence that boys and girls conform most closely to the norms of their peer group, in respect to such matters as dress and leisure interests (Cotterell 1996; Montemayor et al. 1994). Membership of the group provides security and gives the basis for a recognisable teenage culture and lifestyle. In many respects, membership of the peer group can be a positive experience, leading to the formation of lifelong friendships, but there is a negative side. Teenage groups sometimes develop an ethos which demands that members demonstrate that they are cool by taking risks, including some which involve criminal behaviour. Those who do not conform to the group ethos can be bullied or marginalised.

Cognitive and emotional growth

One of the rewarding aspects of teaching in secondary schools is witnessing the students suddenly 'take off'. Students who recently did the very minimum of work necessary to avoid trouble develop a new enthusiasm for ideas and ideals. They may wish to challenge your beliefs, to ask searching questions, and express commitment to various causes. They want to read books and want to hear your opinion on issues. It might be noted that the commonest age for religious conversion is sixteen.

One model of thinking, that of Jean Piaget, suggests that there is a qualitative difference in thinking occurring in adolescence. Children tend to be concerned with the real immediate world. In adolescence an interest in abstract notions develops. A child will feel unhappy about something tangible, pain, loneliness or hunger. An adolescent may feel unhappy when listening to music or seeing a beautiful sunset. This inexplicable emotional response may be puzzling to the adolescent.

Another aspect is that adolescents are very self-conscious. Children tend to live in their own world and are not too concerned about others. As adolescents decentre (to use the jargon) they may do so in a lopsided way (Elkind 1967). They realise that other people have their own ideas but adolescents feel that they are the focus of these ideas. They believe that they are being observed and judged by others. A more adult stance would be to recognise that other people have their own agenda of interests and concerns, and we probably only feature in a very minor way in most of them.

Gaining a personal identity

The fourth major idea is that adolescents need to gain a sense of identity (Erikson 1950, 1968; Kroger 1996). A child's sense of self is largely determined by others. The social class is that of the parents. Where one lives and goes to school, and how one spends one's leisure time, is determined by others. In becoming adult they have to carve out their own lifestyle, decide on their own career and develop their own sexual and social relationships (Moore and Rosenthal 1993). The three main areas of identity are in respect to career, personal relationships, and having some beliefs which give a sense of purpose and worthwhileness to life.

A successful identity comes from matching a sound sense of oneself, what one is like and what one is good at, with a sound sense of the world, what opportunities exist. It is necessary to have some goals but these need to be realistic. Often adolescents are adrift, switching from a sense of aimlessness to enthusiasm, and back again. This process of identity achievement can only be directly undertaken by the individual concerned, it is something occurring within their mind. We can help, partly by informing students about the world, the range of careers and lifestyles available, and partly by helping them recognise their own qualities and limitations. Possibilities should be debated. We should not force teenagers to rush into making decisions as adolescence should provide space and time for this process of identity acquisition to occur.

Gender differences

Consideration of gender differences is important in itself and also because it reminds us that adolescents are not a uniform homogeneous group. There will be both individual diversity and social diversity, defined by race, class and gender (see Chapters 7 and 8).

It is in adolescence that gender differences become most marked (Wolpe 1988). In part this is due to the earlier maturation of girls. In addition, boys and girls have a very different experience of puberty. For most boys it does not in itself present a problem, in fact it adds to life's pleasures. As noted earlier, for girls puberty introduces physical discomfort. It is believed that one cause of anorexia is an attempt to reverse the effects of puberty. The main problem for boys is in not experiencing puberty. The boy who is a late developer tends to have a low status as he cannot compete effectively in sports or in looking after himself in a fight (Askew and Ross 1988).

Boys and girls tend to approach sexual relationships with different agendas (Lees 1986). For boys, sexual activity is seen to be solely a source of pleasure and is undertaken for selfish reasons. Girls tend to be more socially mature and see sexual experience leading on to the possibility of pregnancy, a prospect which produces mixed feelings (for girls of fourteen it is both what they dread most and look forward to most in life).

These differences in maturity and attitudes towards sexual experience, combined with the effects of belonging to the same sex peer groups in early adolescence, tend to bring about a short term separation or hostility between the sexes. Girls at this age complain of the sexual harassment they receive from boys and that they are in a no-win situation. A girl who consents to sex may be labelled a 'slag' and those who refuse are seen to be frigid. Later in adolescence individuals break away from the same sex group and the seeing of the other gender in terms of stereotypes in order to form stable one-to-one relationships.

Until recently we have tended to see girls underachieving in education, for instance, in 1980 only about 40 per cent of the places in higher education were taken by women. Recently there has been a change. Females are participating more (they are now a majority in higher education) and achieving more (in 1995, 57 per cent of girls gained Grades A–C in the GCSE examinations, only 49 per cent of boys did so).

There are debates about what is seen as a male malaise, but the decline of employment prospects in traditional male areas, such as mining, engineering and military, is widely believed to be a major factor (Winefield *et al.* 1993). Boys can confirm their masculinity by gaining employment in such traditionally male areas, in so doing they gain both income and status. The loss of well over a million jobs in manufacturing since 1980 has been accompanied by increases in opportunities in the service industries and fields such as information technology. Girls have been quicker in moving into these new areas of employment. Boys seem to have lost the incentive to succeed.

What worries adolescents?

I have encountered four main areas of concern. About one third of those surveyed reported a reasonable degree of unhappiness about one of these items: The first is the family, sometimes about a split home, more usually about arguments relating to money and staying out late at night. The second is the school. Complaints are mainly about the disciplinary procedures, which seem unnecessary but complaints about the workload are common too. The third concern is a feeling of lacking an aim in life, in fact in not seeing much purpose in life at all. As already noted, these feelings tend to be labile, and are indicative of the continuing search for a sense of identity. Finally, there is concern about social and sexual relations. There is a conflict between the wish to assert individuality and the wish to be popular with others. In addition there are concerns about sexual orientation and being sexually successful. Within the competitive ethos of the peer group, success with a partner of the other sex confers a high status.

It is difficult to generalise about how one responds to these expressions of unhappiness. Remembering their self-consciousness, it is essential to respect confidence and not do or say anything to embarrass the individual. Ultimately, choices have to be made by the individuals about their own lives. Our role is to listen, to provide factual information if appropriate, and to help the students think through for themselves what it is they really believe in and want to do.

Sometimes the problems will be beyond your competence. You should be able to call upon the school pastoral and PSE (personal and social education) staff to help you. There are also various agencies which deal with specific issues, for example, drug abuse and pregnancy, and it would be sensible to know the names and contact telephone numbers of such agencies.

At the beginning of this chapter the question of whether adolescence is harder nowadays was left unanswered. It is true that society has become more labile in recent years. There is less job security and it is more common for families to break up, with current divorce rates being about one third of marriage rates. Factors like these may make the adult world appear more difficult to enter.

Working with adolescents is challenging, but it can also be most rewarding, and in outlining some of the problems you might encounter I would not wish the difficulties to obscure the sense of achievement, and even the fun, you should enjoy.

References

Askew, S. and Ross, C. (1988) *Boys Don't Cry*. Milton Keynes: Open University Press.

Blos, P. (1962) *On Adolescence*. New York: Free Press.

Coffield, F., Borrill, C. and Marshall, S. (1986) *Growing up at the Margins*. Milton Keynes: Open University Press.

Coleman, J.C. and Hendry, L. (1990) *The Nature of Adolescence*. London: Routledge.

Cotterell, J. (1996) *Social Networks and Social Influences in Adolescence*. London: Routledge.

Elkind, D. (1967) Egocentrism in adolescence. *Child Development*, 38: 1025–34.

Erikson, E.H. (1950) *Childhood and Society*. New York: Norton.

Erikson, E.H. (1968) *Identity, Youth and Crisis*. New York: Norton.

ESRC (1989–92) *16–19 Initiative*. Series of booklets on identity, careers and political beliefs. London: Social Statistics Research Unit of The City University.

Freud, A. (1937) *The Ego and the Mechanisms of Defence*. London: Hogarth Press.

Heaven, P.C.L. (1996) *Adolescent Health*. London: Routledge.

Kroger, J. (1996) *Identity in Adolescence*. London: Routledge.

Lees, S. (1986) *Losing out: Sexuality and Adolescent Girls*. London: Hutchinson.

Montemayor, R., Adams, G.R. and Gullotta, T.P. (1994) *Personal Relationships During Adolescence*. Thousand Oaks: Sage.

Moore, S. and Rosenthal, D. (1993) *Sexuality in Adolescence*. London: Routledge.

Prendergast, S. (1992) *This is the Time to Grow up: Girls' Experience of Menstruation in School*. Cambridge: Health Promotion Trust.

Winefield, A.H., Tiggemann, M., Winefield, H.R. and Goldney, R.D. (1993) *Growing up with Unemployment*. London: Routledge.

Wolpe, A.M. (1988) *Within School Walls*. London: Routledge.

Further reading

Head, J.O. (1988) *Adolescent Development course EP228P*. Milton Keynes: The Open University.

Head, J.O. (1997) *Working with Adolescents*. London: Falmer Press.

Martin Monk

Introduction

As someone new to teaching, you will be concerned with two learners. The first are your students. The second is yourself. Both your students and you share learning in common. As your students learn from you so you learn to teach them. From actions in the present, both you and your students will be learning about how successful you are now, and therefore how successful you might be in the future. Both you and your students will have ideas about how successful you might be now, from things remembered from the past.

> There is one thing that all children learn at school: they learn how good they are at learning at school.

Without doubt, the single most important thing that any child learns at school is where they stand with respect to the attainment of success in the formal educational process. Some children learn that they can be very successful in learning in school. Sadly, others might learn that they do not do well no matter how hard they try. Teachers have a professional responsibility to try to maximise the learning of their pupils. In helping pupils to learn, teachers need to consider how they can help their pupils to enjoy success. For by being successful in their learning, pupils come to know that they can learn. This is the most important lesson of all.

Who do you think you are?

Human beings are self-reflective animals. We are able to use our minds to reflect on our actions, rather than just act. We can mentally model our actions and reflect on them. We develop a mental model of who we are as an individual human being by reflecting on our actions and their outcomes. Out of the successes and failures of our biographies we have an idea of what type of person we are compared with others: what we are good at doing and what we are appallingly bad at doing. Each of us has a view of ourselves, or a self-image.

At the same time we also carry an image of the person we would like to be, or our ideal self. In choosing to act, or not, we can close the gap between our ideal self and our self-image. Success in our chosen actions provides a reward that is not external, in the experimental psychological sense of laboratory rats with food pellets, but internal and subjective. The reward, in that it belongs to us subjectively, directly reinforces our view of ourselves as being a particular type of person with particular skills and talents. Failure challenges our view of ourselves and therefore is distressing.

Much of what we do is what we think is appropriate for us to do to bring about closer congruence between our self-images and our ideal selves. How successful we are in closing the gap between our self-images and our ideal selves, through our actions, adds to our self-esteem. A small gap between one's self-image and ideal self is indicated through high self-esteem. We value ourselves because we can do those things we feel we ought to be able to do.

If part of our self-image is that we are good at mathematics we will try to do well at it. If we think we cannot learn French we will not bother to try. The effort we put into learning depends upon the degree of success we expect to achieve. This can lead to a self-fulfilling prophecy. If part of our self-image is that we are poor at games and sports then when we do not put much effort into playing sports we will probably not be successful. That lack of success can be used as evidence to reinforce the original judgement. Not only does 'nothing succeed like success', but also there is nothing like failure for providing that 'I told you so' rationalisation of our incompetence.

Moral components may be worked into our self-images and ideal-selves but the process itself is amoral. A pupil who is consistently disruptive in class may be closing the gap between his self-image and ideal self as a hell raiser and someone who does not get on at school.

Why are we the people we are?

For young children the sorts of ideal selves that they develop very much depend upon the influence of others about them. Older siblings, parents and what are termed 'significant others' (people with whom the child forms an emotional attachment) can all contribute to the manufacture of the ideal self of the child. The child watches the actions of others and, through observational learning, builds a composite picture of how it is best to behave in the environment in which the child finds itself. This is also amoral. The young child learns to behave in a way that ensures its survival. If lying and stealing are what others around the child do, then there is very little chance that the child itself will do otherwise. The actions of others provide the basic experiences for the manufacture of the ideal self.

Our early self-images can only be constructed out of our actions in social settings. Parents, older siblings and significant others, shape who we think we are by reacting to our actions and rewarding, or punishing, certain behaviour patterns. The 're-actions' of siblings, parents and significant others to the child's actions contribute to the manufacture of the child's self-image. These others, in 're-acting' to our actions, act as 'mirrors' by which we come to know ourselves. C.H. Cooley was the first to introduce the term, the 'looking glass self' which was later worked into a theory of symbolic interactionism by the American social-psychologist George Herbert Mead.

Much of the manufacture of students' self-images has occurred long before the students set foot inside schools. Once in the school the shaping and moulding of self-images continues with a new set of significant other people. In the past, attention has been paid to teachers. Equally as important are classmates and peer groups. The effect of these has also been studied. The symbolic interactionist theory of the self proposes that students do, or do not, work in the classroom according to what they personally think they are, or are not, capable of doing. 'Mirrors' surround them in class through the reactions of their teachers and their peers. These can confirm, or challenge, the students' self-image.

Can we only be the projections and reflections of others?

As children get older they have more experience and are able to form more independent judgements about the nature of themselves. As reflective, imaginative, creatures we can all make a mental model of ourselves that is other than what we may currently think of as our present self-images or ideal selves. As reflexive creatures we can change our actions to make them more congruent with our emerging different self-images and ideal selves. We can re-invent ourselves.

The notion that we can think of ourselves as being different from what other people think we are was taken up by R.D. Laing who developed it into a theory of socio-pathology which focused on the problems experienced in family settings. Laing argued that families suffer socio-psychological breakdown when the actions of its members are no longer aligned with the images that its members have of each other and of themselves. Typically, adolescent rebellion can be redescribed in terms of children attempting to remake their self-images in line with a personally constructed ideal self rather than a projected ideal self provided by the 'distorting mirrors' of parents or significant others. Teenage rebellion in schools can be redescribed in a similar way with teachers taking the place of parents as significant others.

Your students will project onto you the image of you being 'their' teacher. They will expect you to behave in a teacherly way. They will expect you to be helpful and patient when setting out tasks. They will expect you to 'have a laugh' occasionally but provide clear guidelines on acceptable behaviour. They will expect you to be fair. The challenge for the new teacher is to meet that expectation with a suitable performance.

Sometimes, you may find yourself driven to actions that, on reflection, you feel are not the true you. In learning to become your students' teacher you have to abandon some of what you think you are, your self-image, and conform to what others expect of you. Often success comes with the flexibility to act appropriately rather than in a mode that you might feel as your true self.

How can teaching be organised to maximise students' learning?

Symbolic interactionist theory of the growth and development of the self directs attention to a primary consideration of the social nature of the development of learning potential. The position of any one individual within the group(s) of which that individual is a member cannot but influence the development of the individual's self-image, ideal self and self-esteem and learning.

Structural features of an educational system undoubtedly influence the range of learning opportunities that are available to students and thereby the opportunities to judge one's self as being successful. Being selected to go to a highly prestigious school may be rewarding for both parents as much as for the child selected. Being the bottom of a class, in that same selective school, in which competition between pupils is strong, may rapidly erode one's self-esteem. Being in a 'sink-class' in a streamed school may drive one to being a member of an anti-school group. Being the top of that same bottom class may have quite different effects on one's self-image, ideal self and self-esteem.

Although several studies have been carried out on children's self-images under the conditions of selective education and streaming, far fewer have been carried out in non-selective or comprehensive systems. We know that different grouping practices between schools, within schools and within classes all offer different opportunities for children to come to see themselves as different types of learners. But the current state of our detailed knowledge is poor and fragmented. Much of what is claimed to be knowledge is in fact opinion based on personal anecdote and political prejudice. We have little careful and systematic research evidence on how the various grouping arrangements change learning opportunities and outcomes (see Chapter 15 for a discussion of the effects of setting).

Which grouping practice offers most opportunity for students to feel that they can cope with the demands of the learning regime and be successful at it? From the point of view of students' learning the question remains unresolved. Even following further research it is unlikely we will be able to answer this question by endorsing one mode rather than another. It is likely that we will know more about social mobility through educational achievement. We need to know more about how different modes of stratification of the educational system provide quite different opportunities for success in learning by creating different climates within which students' self-esteem as learners develops.

What can teachers do?

Should your teaching experience be in a school that sets or streams you will quickly realise that students judge each other and their own performance.

Their self-images, ideal selves and self-esteem are adjusted accordingly. Even if they are on the 'blue table' all is not gloom and doom. The teacher can, and should, provide students with learning activities at which they will be successful. The teacher can reward that success with praise and encouragement. Positive experiences that are mentioned most often by students in surveys include:

- producing a good piece of work
- being successful
- recognition of that success by others
- working with others
- being able to follow up and develop a personal interest
- having a teacher who appeared to care about you and your work.

Negative experiences that are mentioned most often include:

- being told off
- being shouted at
- not knowing what you are supposed to be doing
- not being able to do what you are supposed to do
- not getting the recognition you deserve.

Being successful has several component features which are reflected in the positive and negative experiences above. The following are worth serious consideration. Good teachers help their students by:

- selecting activities for students that are within the students' capabilities
- giving clear instructions
- monitoring students' progress
- helping students with difficulties with the activity
- shepherding students back onto the activity when they stray
- focusing comments on features of the activity rather than students' behaviour
- praising students for success with the activity
- using praise appropriately rather than casually; you must mean it.

This is all very obvious when it is laid out on a page in front of you. It can be more difficult to achieve in the classroom. Good teachers with long experience organise this instinctively. The new teacher can be equally well prepared through planning. The single most common mistake made by new teachers is in not organising clear, well-focused tasks that the students can work on independently.

Why are activities so important?

You can lead a horse to water but you cannot make it drink. You can take the horse to the fountain; you can provide it with a 'drinking opportunity'. But ultimately it is the horse that must drink. You cannot drink for the horse. We would only expect to produce top athletes by helping them to run, jump and throw. Why do some new teachers abandon this common sense when they go into the classroom?

Learning is carried out by the learner. You do not expect to become a competent teacher solely by reading your way through this text. You do expect to have to try your hand at planning, organising and managing classroom activities for your students. Planning student activity is the key to helping students be successful in their learning.

Athletes build muscles by exercise and practice. Students have to practise skills and rehearse their knowledge. From a neurological point of view, to build the synaptic connections in the neural networks of our brains we have to engage in activity, either mental or physical, to cause the neural networks to process and thereby selectively strengthen different patterns of neural connections.

Why are practice and repetition so important?

The more you do something the more familiar you become with the operation. The more familiar you are with the operation the more likely you are to produce a skilled performance. The more skilled your performance the more likely you will take an interest in improving that skill. The whole thing is one benign spiral. Advice to new teachers must include something on giving their students an opportunity to repeat exercises and thereby, in exercising the students' cognition, manipulations and effect, to improve their performance.

Research into repetition of activities has been the province of psychologists who are often labelled as Behaviourists. The best known of these is B.F. Skinner, an American whose work was of most importance, and influence in education, between the 1940s and 1970s. All standard psychology textbooks carry some reference to Skinner's work, the philosophy of which is sometimes, perjoratively, termed Skinnerism. Skinner adopted a strict laboratory approach to experimental psychology. He picked up the Pavlovian idea of a conditioned reflex and studied how this might be used to account for learning in general. Here are some of the more important outcomes of Behaviourist inspired research into learning.

- The frequency of actions increases when actions are pleasurably rewarded.
- Punishment, through pain, does not extinguish actions as effectively as reward, through pleasure, increases the frequency of actions.
- Increasing stress (through pain) can increase performance, but only up to a limit. Beyond that limit, further increase in stress reduces performance.
- Irregular bouts of practice, repetition and reward accelerate gains more than regular bouts.
- In non-reflective animals (and a lot of human action) that action-reward link is amoral.

Much of what happens in schools involves students practising and repeating while being rewarded with verbal praise, gold stars or high marks, as the teacher balances pleasure and pain – stretching pupils with extension activities, moving on to new activities. The good teacher surprises pupils with irregular bouts of revision and review.

So why do students misbehave in class?

In classrooms children are in constant action, and not just that which the teacher plans, organises and manages. In those actions they are pleasured or pained, rewarded, more or less. The individual student's repertoire of actions develops out of their own biographical details in terms of actions, reward and punishment. They do most often those things which give them most reinforcement and reward. In pathological cases this may be throwing desks through the third-floor window. In cases like this, over-simple, half-baked, behaviourist wisdom is to ignore the desk-throwing and to try to find positive things to reward. Pragmatically, the desk throwing has to be stopped.

New teachers who are familiar with the sanctions operated by the school are more likely to use those sanctions. In operating the sanctions consistently the teacher immediately influences two people. First, they modify the student's view of themselves as students in the learning situation. Secondly, with successful operation of the sanctions, the teacher reinforces their own self-image as a capable teacher. Beyond the two people immediately involved the rest of the class have their selves altered, no matter how minutely, by witnessing the interaction.

But you cannot make a silk purse out of a sow's ear, can you?

Mass public education is a relatively new idea in the history of education. It is only recently that we have attempted to treat all adults as equals in political life. Universal adult suffrage, voting rights for women at 21, did not come in until 1928; that is, within living memory. In social and economic life we are still a long way from being egalitarian. It is therefore not surprising that until the late 1960s the emphasis in educational provision was not on devising programmes of study, schemes of work and learning activities that would help all children to learn more effectively and efficiently. Instead the emphasis was very much on sifting and sorting so as to find the right people for sponsorship and advancement.

Psychological models, in being socially, politically and economically located, work symbiotically to support the grouping and training practices of the society in which they are embedded. In a society that is built on difference, legitimation of that difference is part of the burden carried by psychological theories. From this perspective the rise of the intelligence quotient (IQ) as a means of sifting and sorting pupils for different educational destinations can be seen as entirely appropriate. In such a situation it makes sense to try to match educational opportunity to educability, particularly in a climate of parsimonious resource. Placing pupils along some scale of IQ fixes them, so that they then become a case for suitable treatment, rather than a messy human being who does well on some things and not others and who has good days and bad days. In the decades after the Second World War the measure of a person's IQ came to have the popular, erroneous, interpretation of being fixed. A measure, once made, a decision, once taken, was not troublesome if this viewpoint was adopted.

Whatever happened in the 1960s, 1970s and 1980s, a definite and gradual shift has started to take place in education. Pupils are increasingly seen
as having equal potential and thereby equal value, even though they may
not have equal performance.

So how can pupils have equal potential but different performance?

Our selves are underwritten by a biological substrate over which we have
limited, if any, control. As a newborn infant we are mechanically poorly
co-ordinated for life on the land. Within each of us there is a maturational
plan that unfolds as we grow, develop and mature. Not all of us reach the
same stages at exactly the same split-second timing: there is a spread. This
spread increases as we progress to further stages of development and
maturation (Figure 11.1 shows how we progress through different stages
as we grow older).

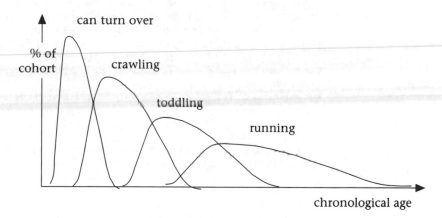

Figure 11.1   Stages in early maturation

We are all equal, in the sense of having the same trajectory through
maturation, but we are different in travelling that pathway at different
speeds. All babies end up as walking and talking toddlers with a trajectory
of the same maturational stages to pass through but different timings of
when things will happen.

We talk about babies 'learning' to walk and 'learning' to talk in a rather
loose way. That looseness allows us to avoid a careful examination of how
the development of walking and talking involve an intimate mix of both
maturational and interactional aspects. The baby learns to walk because
it has the genetic potential to do so. But, that genetic potential cannot be
realised if the baby is bound in swaddling clothes and its muscles are not
allowed to develop. In terms of knowledge and skills, the genetic potential unfolds in the process of interaction with the environment: not
despite the environment.

School learning is interactional rather than genetically controlled maturation, although for younger children there is a maturational component.

For a cohort of same-age students a distribution of performance can be expected on given tasks at any one time. Students will reach levels of attainment, on a time axis, that also shows a similar form of distribution. Such a distribution is more likely to be skewed.

In a mixed performance class students will require different tasks appropriate to their levels of performance. This means the teacher may have to plan for a set of differentiated activities that will allow for students progression. The fact that different students achieve success at different stages of their careers does not mean they cannot achieve success. It just means it may take a little longer to do so. To be successful, students need to feel that they can be successful. It is the teacher's responsibility to make them feel that is possible.

Further reading

Atkinson, R.L., Atkinson, R.C., Smith, E.E. and Bem, D.J. (1993). *Introduction to Psychology*, 11th edn. Orlando: Harcourt Brace Jovanovich.

Borba, M. and Borba, C. (1978) *Self-esteem: A Classroom Affair. Volume 1: 101 Ways to Help Children Like Themselves*. London: Harper Collins.

Borba, M. and Borba, C. (1982) *Self-esteem: A Classroom Affair. Volume 2: More Ways to Help Children Like Themselves*. London: Harper Collins.

Burns, R.B. (1981) *Self-Concept Development and Education*. Eastbourne: Holt, Rinehart and Winston.

Davenport, G.C. (1994) *An Introduction to Child Development*, 2nd edn. London: Collins International.

Hargreaves, D.H. (1975) *Interpersonal Relations and Education*. London: Routledge and Kegan Paul.

Hargreaves, D.H., Hestor, S.K. and Mellor, F.J. (1975) *Deviance in Classrooms*. London: Routledge and Kegan Paul.

Language, thought and learning

Michael Quintrell

It is through language that we learn, and with language that we think. 'Thought is not merely expressed in words, it comes into existence through them' (Vygotsky 1962).

Helen Keller, who lost her sight and hearing in early infancy, describes in a famous passage in her autobiography a moment in her early learning:

> We walked down the path to the well-house, attracted by the fragrance of the honeysuckle with which it was covered. Someone was drawing water and my teacher placed my hand under the spout. As the cool stream gushed over one hand she spelled into the other the word 'water', first slowly, then rapidly. I stood still, my whole attention fixed upon the motions of her fingers. Suddenly I felt a misty consciousness as of something forgotten – a thrill of returning thought; and somehow the mystery of language was revealed to me. I knew then that 'w-a-t-e-r' meant the wonderful cool something that was flowing over my hand . . . I left the well-house eager to learn. Everything had a name and each name gave birth to a new thought.
>
> (Keller 1959)

The teacher plays a significant part here, by providing and repeating the appropriate information to allow her pupil to capture the learning. Keller's success was achieved through collaboration and two-way communication: 'knowledge may itself be inseparable from language; . . . in communicating ideas we come to understand them better' (Mercer 1991: A9).

But learning has not always been seen as a collaborative process. The writings of Jean Piaget, which became influential in the mid-1960s, described learners as lone, problem-solving scientists interacting with the physical world and forming hypotheses as they reflect upon experience (see Donaldson 1978). This notion gives a comparatively small role to the teacher as the facilitator of solo scholarship. The learner is self-motivated and self-directed, progressing through distinct and predictable stages of intellectual development. For example, Piaget asserts that, at a certain stage of their development, children are incapable of expressing ideas which involve an appreciation of the world from another person's viewpoint, making it unproductive for a teacher to attempt with pupils at this stage any exercise requiring empathy.

Creative problem-solving also interested the American psychologist, Jerome Bruner. His early studies of adult learners revealed that people use a range of strategies and processes to make sense of the world. Like Piaget, he emphasised the importance of practical experience for learners as a prerequisite of understanding abstract concepts. But he placed much more emphasis on the part played in the learning process by communication with other people through language. Social interaction, and teaching as an instructional form of it, were to him more important.

Indeed, much developmental psychology since Piaget has emphasised that children are social beings, and that they learn through interaction with others, their peers as well as more capable and knowledgeable people like parents and teachers. Lev Vygotsky, in particular, sees the development of children in terms of co-operatively achieved success, and language is the medium of that co-operation. He describes a process by which the learner extends current understanding into new areas with the help of a more competent person, with the aim of becoming independently capable: 'What a child can do today in co-operation, tomorrow he [*sic*] will be able to do on his own' (Vygotsky 1962).

The learner is then ready to attempt further development, while consolidating independent mastery of recently learnt skills or knowledge. This dynamic process gives a number of important functions to the teacher: arriving at an understanding of the learner's current knowledge, assessing the potential areas for new learning (which Vygotsky calls the 'zone of proximal (or potential) development'), encouraging the learner to be prepared to explore, and supporting while the learner is making mistakes. Once the learner is succeeding independently, the teacher need do little more than praise the achievement and organize the practice and consolidation of it, while planning the next phase of learning, looking for something just beyond the child's independent grasp. This is, of course, much harder than it sounds for thirty mixed-ability children at different stages in their development, and quite impossible without the teacher first having detailed knowledge of the children's current competences and understandings.

In order to describe the teacher's role in the learning process in more detail, Bruner uses the metaphor of 'scaffolding' (see, e.g. Wood 1988: 80; Wood *et al.* 1976). The teacher sets up a supporting structure to protect the tentative, exploratory, mistake-prone learner from damaging failure. This image is attractive to teachers as a description of their work in stimulating and supporting learning while promoting pupil independence. Good teachers:

> are not just people who provide suitable 'learning environments' for individuals, or who present new information to an audience in an interesting and engaging way, but rather co-operative adults who can

scaffold learners' development on their way to independence through activity, questioning, explanation and discussion.

(Mercer 1991: A10)

As the learner becomes self-sustaining in the new learning, the support is progressively removed; this 'handover', as Bruner calls it, is important since the ultimate aim is to produce pupils who are autonomous, not slavishly dependent on their teacher.

These concepts also give an interesting new perspective on pupils' errors; they are not necessarily to be deplored as signs of carelessness, but rather may be welcome signs of pupils' struggling at the frontiers of knowledge and competence, the very thing you most wish to encourage. Mistakes give teachers valuable insights into the meanings pupils are constructing from their lessons, and they can also be the stimulus to, and context of, helpful teacher intervention. Thus a vital task for the teacher is to foster a classroom atmosphere in which it is safe to be exploratory and to hazard ideas, a place where to get things wrong does not result in public humiliation: 'the child should not be made to feel that it does not pay to take risks . . . he [sic] needs the opportunity to experiment with new forms, and do so with security' (DES, 1975: 167). 'Classrooms ought to be the safest place in the world to make a mistake' (Moy and Raleigh 1980).

Language – a corporately held responsibility in schools

Language as a crucial tool for learning is far too important to be left to the English Department alone, though they do have a specialised concern with language which is part of their subject expertise.

In the 1970s, a major report into language in schools (the Bullock Report) argued emphatically that all teachers should take responsibility for pupils' language development, and bring their teaching styles and practices into line with the most effective ways in which children learn in their subject:

> we must convince the teacher of history or of science, for example, that he [sic] has to understand the process by which his pupils take possession of the historical or scientific information that is offered them; and that such an understanding involves his paying particular attention to the part language plays in learning. The pupils' engagement with the subject may rely upon a linguistic process that his teaching procedures actually discourage.

(DES 1975: 188)

All teachers, then, should take responsibility for answering the language needs of pupils in their subject and classes. They should examine their own use of language to see how it is facilitating or impeding their pupils' learning.

In practice, if a subject requires a particular vocabulary of specialist terms to be known and used appropriately by the pupils, then this is the subject specialist teacher's responsibility. The correct spelling of these terms is the teacher's concern, too. If there are specific styles of writing (for example, producing a play script, a discursive essay, or writing up a scientific experiment) which she will be demanding of her classes, then she needs to build into her plans activities which will support the confident achievement of these. Technical language needs to be introduced to pupils gradually; Sheeran and Barnes (1991: 14) caution the teacher that:

> using the special discourse of a school subject should be postponed until the learner has made some progress towards grasping the conceptual framework of the subject. Taking over the discourse mode of an academic subject is more complex than at first appears ... The technical vocabulary is useless unless it is the visible tip of a network of concepts that can be used to generate thinking in other contexts.

But the teacher's task really begins before the pupils enter the room. It is important to know what children bring to the class in the way of understandings about the subject. The teacher's job in any lesson is essentially to engage with the pupils in a process of modifying or extending this knowledge. Arriving at shared understandings is a central task in classrooms; this applies to learning as much as to behaviour (Edwards and Mercer 1987). Effective teaching depends on communication through appropriate, accessible language, so that pupils can make sense of the teacher's telling, explaining and demonstrating. This latter is particularly important; direct experience is very effective in the construction of knowledge and its long-term retention.

Teacher-directed talk

To be consistent with the approach to children's learning summarised above, the teacher needs to know the pupils' knowledge and skills well, choose learning that is within the assisted grasp of the pupils, make accurate judgements about the extent and nature of the support needed, promote a low-risk classroom atmosphere, then organise the teaching into exposition, discussion, discovery, demonstration, experiment and so on in such a way that co-operative, exploratory and supportive talk is possible.

The use of pairing and small group work is endorsed by the National Curriculum Council; the grouping of pupils is identified as a key issue in the implementation of the National Curriculum, which 'requires the development of collaborative skills', (NCC, 1989a: 11). The Non-statutory Guidance for Mathematics (NCC, 1989b: B9) advises: 'Pupils should be encouraged to undertake work in teams, discussing mathematical problems, evaluating ideas and alternative solutions, and jointly finding ways to 'crack' an onerous assignment.' There is a clear requirement here for pupil talk which is not only permitted, but organised and even encouraged by teachers.

Yet it is not easy to achieve successful exploratory talk in a classroom. A beginning teacher, new to a class, will need to establish how used to pair- and group work the pupils are; if they are not much practised in this area, they should be introduced to it in a gradual and structured manner, with clear expectations and negotiated ground rules. Established teachers sometimes feel so hard-pressed to cover the syllabus that they perceive exploratory group talk as a distraction from progress rather than an enhancement of it. This external pressure, whether it derives from parental expectation or concern to produce good examination statistics in published league tables, can lead to the use of rote-learning and the drilling of skills. It is only if clear benefits can be perceived in these terms that more active methods will be used.

And there are, indeed, clear benefits. Classroom talk is active and involving: it allows pupils to bring their own learning into the class; it can help them be exploratory; give substance to half-formed ideas; it encourages them to clarify, reframe and consolidate learning through explaining to others and defending in discussion; it invites them to reflect on learning and review progress. All these factors help to produce more confident and responsible individuals, and more effective team members. There are significant gains for the teacher from this:

> Successful group work allows the teacher to observe and to interact with groups and individuals in a much more varied and complex way than does whole class teaching, and to sustain and develop learning through the hundreds of conversations which take place in the classroom.
>
> (Johnson 1991: A21)

Classroom research shows that pupils respond very positively to skilfully structured discussion:

> Pupils were virtually unanimous in describing the major value of group-work as being, like class discussion, that it widened the pool of available ideas, and through this, enabled pupils to advance their thinking in ways they could not achieve alone.
>
> (Cooper and McIntyre 1996)

Sound advice on practicalities, especially progressing from simple pair-work to a much more varied grouping of pupils, can be found in Howe (1992) and Kemeny (1993); the latter also gives attention to ways of balancing the spoken contributions of boys and girls in class. The training of pupils to use techniques for eliciting more elaborated responses from one another is described in King (1990).

A substantial proportion of pupils' talk in school is, of course, out of class and therefore not consciously organized by a teacher. Research into this indicates that even outside of lessons 'children's talk to each other plays an important part in the learning process' and concludes that it is 'a rich source of learning' (Maybin 1991).

It is appropriate that, on this subject, we should give a rare opportunity to pupils to have the final say:

> If you work in a group, you get everyone's ideas together.

> things that I hadn't even thought of were brought up and that helped me.

> I learn better . . . if I understand it than . . . if somebody else figures it out and they tell me, then it doesn't sink in as well.

> I think a teacher who can talk [and] communicate easily with pupils is a lot better than the teacher that stands there and dictates ... just reads out o' the book and things, it's not interesting.

> you can come out of a lesson and say 'Oh, I've actually done that', instead of like a normal lesson ... where you've just written something down or whatever.
>
> (pupils quoted in Kemeny, 1993: 26–7, 121)

Questioning

Research suggests that on average teachers talk at least twice as much as all the pupils put together (Bellack *et al.* 1966), leaving the pupils to share out at best a third of a lesson between them. Also, 'teachers see talking out of turn and other forms of persistent, low-level disruption as the most frequent and wearing kinds of classroom misbehaviour' (DES 1989: 67). These findings suggest that there is scope both for a reduction in the amount of time that teachers talk at pupils, and also an improvement in the quality and purposefulness of pupil talk in the classroom.

Teachers may spend as much as 30 per cent of their time asking questions (Brown and Edmondson, 1984), and one relatively simple way in which teachers can promote focused pupil talk is to examine carefully the way they question their pupils. Pupil responses enable the teacher to estimate the extent of the pupils' understanding, and the degree to which they have benefited from the lesson. They get a sense of the children's continuing needs and can make appropriate future plans. They also use questions to guide the course of children's learning, and they are not necessarily so successful in this. The teacher may set up an elaborate and even irritating game (at any rate to the children) in which pupils have to try to find out what answer the teacher has in mind. By trial and error, sometimes having their logical but 'incorrect' responses brushed peremptorily aside, the pupils gradually converge on the 'right' answer. Teachers' questions can thus have an undesirable constraining effect on classroom discussion; if they require only short, factual responses, teachers may actually limit the scope and depth of their pupils' thinking.

> The process of education is seen as the pupils accepting the teachers' conceptual world ... In some lessons pupils merely make the same noises as the teacher, as when the teacher indicates clearly the answer required, and demands a choral response of the target word or phrase. The basic IRF structure (initiation, response, feedback) giving the teacher the last word, allows him [*sic*] to recast in his own words any pupil responses. Pupils acknowledge this domination by choosing eliptical responses and by avoiding initiation.
>
> (Sinclair and Coulthard 1975: 130)

Here the teacher's questions are failing to stimulate thought and discussion; rather, by asking direct questions to which there is one answer, the teacher is limiting pupil response to 'making noises'. But teacher questioning does not have to follow this familiar, convergent pattern: 'The learner should be given the chance to solve problems, to conjecture, to quarrel, as these are done at the heart of the discipline' (Bruner 1974).

The art is in engendering exploratory and divergent thinking in children while also ensuring that the class meets statutory National Curriculum targets; these are not necessarily incompatible aims. Much more indirect prompting and open-ended questioning would be required. The teacher might simply make a declarative opening statement and leave the class to react, or even remain silent until the pupils have begun to frame their own questions in response to some topic or problem.

Reading

Teachers need to take a hard critical look at the reading requirements of their subjects, too. Reading is the most difficult way for children to gather information. The Bullock Report (DES 1975) describes an ascending ladder of difficulty thus:

- finding out from observation and first-hand experience
- finding out from someone who will explain and discuss
- finding out by listening to a spoken monologue, for example a radio talk
- finding out by reading.

(DES 1975: 12.7)

Bullock continues:

Subject teachers need to be aware of the processes involved, able to provide the variety of reading material that is appropriate, and willing to see it as their responsibility to help their pupils meet the reading demands of their subject.

(DES 1975: 12.7)

So new teachers should browse through the textbooks in the school's stock-cupboards, and see what they think of the clarity and helpfulness of them. At their worst, textbooks can be obscure and impenetrable, written in technical language which presents a considerable barrier for the pupil, who may well perceive the book to be alien, and fail to understand, let alone enjoy, the subject within. Most of us can remember times during our formal education when our eyes dutifully scanned the lines of a set reading, left to right, top to bottom, while our brains remained inert, or roamed free elsewhere. Such an experience is at best unproductive, at worst dispiriting and destructive.

Complex ideas can be conveyed in serious books without unnecessary obfuscation, and textbooks do not have to be obscure, eye-watering and mind-numbingly boring. Take, for example, the distribution of income in modern Britain. Will Hutton describes it thus:

The average salary in Britain in 1994 was around £19,000 a year – but the average disguises remarkable variation. Two-thirds of wage earners earn the average or below: only a third earn more than this. An imaginary parade of the entire working population dramatises the point. If the population of Britain were divided according to income, if income were made equivalent to height and if the population then marched past for an hour, it would take a full 37 minutes before the first adult of average height was seen. For the first fifteen minutes there would be a parade of dwarves. Stature would increase gradually thereafter, but 57 minutes would have passed before we saw people of twice the average height. Giants of 90 feet or more would appear in the last few seconds, with the last one or two literally miles high.

(Hutton 1995: 193)

This lively and amusing metaphor makes a complicated concept approachable, and helps fix the idea in the learner's mind.

Care needs to be exercised in the choice of reading, and judicious editing and even rewriting by the teacher can sometimes make texts more accessible to pupils. But activities can be designed to help pupils manage texts in the original, even if they are complex in argument and advanced in vocabulary. DARTs – Directed Activities Related to Texts – enable pupils to learn about their subject, but also learn ways of asking questions of texts themselves, so that they can use reading for learning more effectively in future, and gain confidence in the handling of difficult material. If this strategy is used across the curriculum, pupils also begin to gain an understanding of what makes a valuable text in different subjects. (For a full account of DARTs, see Lunzer *et al.* 1984.)

It can be an important learning moment if a carefully chosen text is read aloud well in class. Teachers need to develop their abilities as performers, and it is wise for them to prepare and rehearse, even when they are experienced public readers. Pupils often suffer considerable anxiety about reading aloud to the class, and this can be reduced by asking them in advance and giving them time to practise. A humiliatingly faltering performance by a pupil on whom the task was sprung at the last moment must at all costs be avoided; the text will not come alive for the class, and the pupil's self-esteem will suffer needlessly.

Indiscriminate use of the 'Read Chapter 11 for a test on Friday' approach needs to be checked. In this, the reading is being used more as a mechanism for control, or a device to fill an awkward slot on the homework timetable, rather than as an essential text which pupils will read actively and interrogate for new learning essential for completing a task. Pupils should be given:

positive invitations to read, demonstrations, information, explanations that fit their understandings and texts that engage them if they are to learn what reading is all about. If they are having difficulties, they need more of these not less. Without the insights that accompany success, they do not want to go on.

(Meek, 1990: 146)

Writing

Likewise, writing needs to be driven by a purpose, and this should be made clear to the pupils before they write. The more real the purpose, the more motivating the task. Written work usually also has unspoken 'ground rules' – the rules of interpreting the question that defines the sort of answer that is appropriate – which the teacher expects the pupils to divine from the context, or from habit. Teachers need to think about how many important instructions in their subject areas are unspoken, and give them voice from time to time. Setting written tasks is an opportunity to introduce pupils to the language of the discipline, too.

It is commonly noted that a significant number of pupils perform less well in their writing than they do in oral work, and it is worth considering whether this is partly because the instructions for written activities were insufficiently explicit. As adults, we often use a simple strategy to clarify what is required of us: 'When you said XYZ, did you mean such-and-such?' we ask. This strategy is not common among school pupils; perhaps they lack the confidence to use it.

Harold Rosen has argued that all subjects should look for ways of encouraging pupils to write more expressively, so that their personal interest and involvement can be included and evidenced in their writing: 'The demand for transactional writing in school is ceaseless, but expressive language with all its vitality and richness is the only possible soil from which it can grow' (Barnes 1971: 138). It is productive for a teacher to analyse the types of writing regularly demanded in the specialist subject, and attempt to bring greater variety. These might include: narratives; recounting of events; reports presenting descriptions and information; arguing a point of view and presenting a substantiated case. This last is the most demanding, and the most useful in later life, yet perhaps is less commonly set in school than the others.

Certainly, school writing tasks can be less purposeful and real, more routine, than those performed by adults at work:

> it is easy for pupils to become alienated from the tasks set, for they lack the motivation provided by writing with a real purpose for a real audience, for the teacher is no more than a simulated audience. Writing, too, can often become meaningless and routinized, something they have to do and over which they have little control.
>
> (Sheeran and Barnes 1991: 106)

Pupils can be given a greater sense of control by a teacher who gives the task a real purpose (writing a letter to be posted to a recipient rather than an imaginary, unsent exercise), defines a clear audience (another group of pupils, younger or older), defines the criteria for good writing of this kind, with examples, and organises discussion of the writing once it has been assessed. As pupils become more confident in their handling of this range of written tasks, and clearer about assessment criteria, their sense of ownership of the tasks should increase. They may, in some subject areas, feel able to negotiate specific written tasks with the teacher (an open study at GCSE English Literature, for example).

Whether in talk, reading or writing, pupils' minds need to be actively engaged on the task in hand, forming, transforming and reforming ideas. This implies minimal use of dull, unchallenging routines: teacher monologue, dictated notes, copying from the board, writing out spellings 20 times, tests on undiscussed reading from textbooks. Hamblin (1983), writing about promoting the well-being of school pupils, puts it succinctly: 'Pastoral care is an attack on inert and passive forms of teaching.'

Cross-curricular collaboration and successful innovation

With the progressive introduction of the National Curriculum in the late 1980s, a new and most welcome kind of dialogue was beginning to take place between English teachers and their colleagues in other disciplines. Historians, for example, were asking how to encourage pupils in writing which showed empathy for the situations of various historical figures; Maths teachers were asking urgent questions about the organisation of oral work so that investigations could be conducted effectively in class. Almost overnight, teachers who had never willingly allowed talk in their classrooms were having to promote it, organise and chair discussion, instead of putting talkers into detention.

Developing a school language policy, and achieving consistent practice across all subject departments, are challenging tasks because discussion of language use soon leads to a consideration of fundamental aspects of teachers' professional activity – teaching style, classroom organisation, assessment procedures, attitudes to correctness in speech and writing. Yet such discussions about policy and practice can be a very productive forum for teachers to work together. If a strategy for improving spelling works in one subject area, it figures that it will work elsewhere. Note-taking is a valuable skill which will enhance the effectiveness of learning in most subjects. Arguing a convincing case using carefully selected, appropriate evidence will be valued in many areas of the school. By working out whole-school policies, teachers not only save time and energy, and avoid confusing pupils with conflicting demands, but more importantly give reality to the notion of common responsibility for language which Bullock urged on teachers so forcefully in his conclusions and recommendations:

> 138: In the secondary school, all subject teachers need to be aware of:
> (i) the linguistic processes by which their pupils acquire information and understanding, and the implications for the teacher's own use of language;
> (ii) the reading demands of their own subjects, and ways in which the pupils can be helped to meet them.

> 139: To bring about this understanding every secondary school should develop a policy for language across the curriculum. The responsibility for this policy should be embodied in the organizational structure of the school.
>
> (DES 1975: 529)

Chapter 12 of the Bullock Report, entitled 'Language across the Curriculum', leant official support in England and Wales to a doctrine which was gathering force in Europe, Australasia and North America. In Canada, the Ontario Ministry of Education has been particularly advanced in enacting this policy (see Corson 1987). For a language policy to be truly across the curriculum, major changes are required both in teacher attitudes and teaching methods – it is a document about how children learn, after all, and that is the central concern of education. Many schools in the UK did respond to Bullock by formulating statements of whole-school language policy, and in recent times there has been a further flowering, as schools generate policy documents in preparation for Ofsted inspections.

An excellent example of a language policy statement is 'Language and Learning: the language policy of Forest Gate Community School', prepared by the Language and Learning Working Party, and published in July 1991. Information about the school and the way it generated policy may be found in Hickman and Kimberley (1988) (extracts from the policy statement itself are printed in Open University 1995: 83–9).

Most recent innovations in education have been based on a 'top-down' model; distant experts decide, for example, on subject curricula, and these are imposed from above with the full force of statute. This model has a deskilling effect, and teachers find it hard to get a sense of ownership of the policies thus handed down. By contrast, the Forest Gate document was the work of twelve subject teachers from a wide range of disciplines who formed a working party, established a network of contacts throughout the staff and beyond, and undertook investigations into classroom practice. They believed that expertise about language and learning was not confined to a few specialist teachers, and they had confidence that they and their colleagues could develop both their own knowledge and also policies which were not dead letters or impressive but empty rhetoric, but which would take root in the school and have a long-term impact on teaching and learning styles. Excellent and wide-ranging though this document is, its principal significance lies in the manner in which it came into being – 'bottom-up' innovation which recognised, developed and confirmed staff expertise. Such policies have high credibility with colleagues, and are more likely to be treated seriously and energetically implemented. They can have a major impact on the quality of pupil achievement.

References

Barnes, D. (1971) *Language, the Learner and the School*. Harmondsworth: Penguin.

Bellack, A., Kliebard, H., Hyman, R. and Smith, F. (1966) *The Language of the Classroom*. New York: Teachers' College Press.

Brown, G.A. and Edmondson, R. (1984) Asking questions, in E.C. Wragg (ed.) *Classroom Teaching Skills*. Beckenham: Croom Helm.

Bruner, J.S. (1974) *The Relevance of Education*. Harmondsworth: Penguin.

Bruner, J. (1985) Vygotsky: a historical and conceptual perspective, in J.V. Wertsch (ed.) *Culture, Communication and Cognition: Vygotskian Perspectives*. Cambridge: Cambridge University Press.

Cooper, P. and McIntyre, D. (1996) *Effective Teaching and Learning: Teachers' and Students' Perspectives*. Buckingham: Open University Press.

Corson, D. (1987) *Oral Language Across the Curriculum*. Clevedon: Multilingual Matters Ltd.

Department of Education and Science (DES) (1975) *A Language for Life*. The Bullock Report. London: HMSO.

Department of Education and Science (DES) (1989) *Discipline in Schools*. The Elton Report. London: HMSO.

Donaldson, M. (1978) *Children's Minds*. London: Fontana.

Edwards, D. and Mercer, N. (1987) *Common Knowledge: The Development of Understanding in the Classroom*. London: Methuen.

Hamblin, D. (1983) *Guidance 16–19*. Oxford: Blackwell.

Hickman, J. and Kimberley, K. (eds) (1988) *Teachers, Language and Learning*. London: Routledge.

Howe, A. (1992) *Making Talk Work*. London: Hodder and Stoughton.

Hutton, W. (1995) *The State We're In*. London: Jonathan Cape.

Johnson, J. (1991) Classroom strategies, in Open University P535 Talk and Learning 5–16: an in-service pack on oracy for teachers. Milton Keynes: Open University.

Keller, H. (1959) *The Story of My Life: With Her Letters (1887–1901)*. London: Hodder and Stoughton.

Kemeny, H. (ed.) (1993) *Learning Together Through Talk*. London: Hodder and Stoughton.

King, A. (1990) Enhancing peer interaction and learning in the classroom through reciprocal questioning, *American Education Research Journal*, 27(4): 664–87.

Lunzer, E., Gardner, K., Davies, F. and Greene, T. (1984) *Learning from the Written Word*. London: Oliver and Boyd.

Maybin, J. (1991) Children's informal talk and the construction of meaning, *English in Education*, 25(2): 34–49.

Meek, M. (1990) What do we know about reading that helps us teach?, in R. Carter (ed.) *Knowledge about Language and the Curriculum: The LINC Reader*. London: Hodder and Stoughton.

Mercer, N. (1991) Learning through talk, in Open University A5–A10. Milton Keynes: Open University.

Moy, B. and Raleigh, M. (1980) Comprehension: bringing it back alive, *The English Magazine*, Autumn: 29–37.

National Curriculum Council (1989a) *Curriculum Guidance 1: A Framework for the National Curriculum*. London: National Curriculum Council.

National Curriculum Council (1989b) *Curriculum Guidance 1: A Framework for the Primary Curriculum*. York: NCC.

National Curriculum Council (1989c) *Mathematics: Non-statutory Guidance*. York: NCC.

Open University (1995) *E890, Language and Learning*. Milton Keynes: Open University.

Sheeran, Y. and Barnes, D. (1991) *School Writing: Discovering the Ground Rules*. Buckingham: Open University Press.

Sinclair, J. and Coulthard, R.M. (1975) *Towards an Analysis of Discourse: The English Used by Teacher and Pupils*. London: Oxford University Press.

Vygotsky, L.S. (1962) *Thought and Language*. Cambridge: MIT Press.

Wood, D. (1988) *How Children Think and Learn: The Social Contexts of Cognitive Development*. Oxford: Blackwell.

Wood, D.J., Bruner, J.S. and Ross, G. (1976) The role of tutoring in problem-solving, *Journal of Child Psychology and Psychiatry*, 17: 89–100.

Further reading

On language and learning:

Britton, J. (1987) Vygotsky's contribution to pedagogical theory, *English in Education*, 21(3): 22–6.

Bruner, J. (1985) Vygotsky: a historical and conceptual perspective, in J.V. Wertsch (ed.) *Culture, Communication and Cognition: Vygotskian Perspectives*. Cambridge: Cambridge University Press.

Wood, D. (1988) *How Children Think and Learn: The Social Contexts of Cognitive Development*. Oxford: Blackwell.

On questioning:

Brown, G.A. and Edmondson, R. (1984) Asking questions, in E.C. Wragg (ed.) *Classroom Teaching Skills*. Beckenham: Croom Helm.

On assessment:

Stibbs, A. (1979) Assessing Children's Language: Guidelines for Teachers. London: Ward Lock for NATE.

On talk:

Howe, A. (1992) *Making Talk Work*. London: Hodder and Stoughton.
Norman, K. (ed.) (1992) *Thinking Voices: The work of the National Oracy Project*. London: Hodder and Stoughton.

On reading:

Lunzer, E., Gardner, K., Davies, F. and Greene, T. (1984) *Learning from the Written Word*. London: Oliver and Boyd.

On writing:

Sheeran, Y. and Barnes, D. (1991) *School Writing: Discovering the Ground Rules*. Buckingham: Open University Press.

On cross-curricular policy development:

Hickman, J. and Kimberley, K. (eds) (1988) *Teachers, Language and Learning*. London: Routledge.

13 | Classroom management and organisation

Sheila Macrae

Without the ability to manage a class effectively, any other skills teachers have may be neutralized. It is no good knowing your subject matter, being able to devise interesting activities appropriate to the topic, knowing what sort of questions to ask or being able to give a clear explanation, if you cannot obtain a hearing or organize a group of children.

(Wragg 1993: 1)

In this chapter I explore issues concerning classroom management and organisation. Although I do not claim to have all the answers to problems encountered in the classroom, I offer some theoretical and practical advice. Indeed, 'Class control and management are not topics that yield the precise guidelines possible in certain areas of psychology and of teacher education' (Fontana 1994: v). However it is essential for teachers to develop effective management skills and they 'should be supported in doing so by their schools' (Charlton and David 1993: 221). With practice and reflection in an enabling environment, teachers can become proficient practitioners.

What is classroom management and organisation?

Ask a group of student teachers before their first teaching practice to describe any anxieties they may have, and before long someone will mention discipline or class control. It is the source of greatest unease amongst student teachers.

(Wragg 1981: 4)

The unease felt by new teachers is often felt by much more experienced teachers too. Indeed, many long-serving teachers have resigned from teaching because they found the stress of managing adolescents too much for them. But there are many effective teachers and part of learning to teach involves observing and working with such teachers.

Studies of teacher behaviour (Rutter *et al.* 1979; Wragg 1984) have identified specific skills which are demonstrated by effective teachers and which can be learned and applied by those new to the profession. These skills, it should be stressed, are not an end in themselves; rather they are the basis of effective teaching and learning and there can be a world of difference between knowledge at a theoretical level and a teacher's practical experience.

To implement effective classroom management and organisation on a regular basis is no easy task and no honest teacher will claim otherwise. As with other aspects of education, it depends upon the quality of support and guidance within the school as well as the aptitude of the individual teacher. The work that goes on in the classroom, therefore, does not, and should not, take place in a vacuum. Instead, it can be viewed as one of four layers (the institution, classroom, individual teacher and local community) in the overall structure of the school (Watkins 1995).

The first three layers, that of the institution, the classroom and the individual teacher, play the most important parts but these are impacted upon by the fourth layer identified by the DES (1989), which is the community the school serves. Each layer is dependent upon input from the others and each has its own distinct role which must be understood and supported by the others. It is the successful interweaving of management and organisational strategies at all four layers that maximises a school's well being and enables teachers to teach and students to learn in a supportive, enabling environment.

Whole-school approach

To promote coherence across all four layers it is now widely recognised that a whole-school approach is the most effective (see, for example, DES 1989). Any such policies need to have agreed, connected and workable strategies and should not be inflicted on the school by one section of staff as this can result in decisions remaining at the level of empty rhetoric. Instead, when the views of the whole school community are canvassed and taken seriously, people feel valued and are much more likely to support policies in which they have some investment.

The aim of a whole-school approach is neither to produce a cloned staff nor to take a behaviourist, mechanistic stance but to identify and deal with, in a proactive, systematic, supportive and open way, the sorts of inconsistencies that can lead to confusion or cause problems. For example, under what circumstances are students allowed to leave class during lessons; what are the procedures for taking students on a school visit? To encourage openness and promote support it is important to avoid blame. Similarly, no one benefits from such *schadenfreude* as, 'Well, of course, 9C never gives *me* any trouble'. It is important for teachers to have a forum in which they feel safe to discuss issues without fear of ridicule. Depending on the topic, meetings may be on a one-to-one basis with perhaps a mentor when a teacher may wish to discuss, for example, the basic concern of how to get a class to enter the room without wreaking havoc on the way. Some issues may be more appropriately discussed in a departmental

setting, for example, how to improve the pass rate at GCSE within the constraints of a decreased budget and fewer staff. Yet other topics may best be organized within whole-school INSET when a helpful way of discussing issues is to use hypothetical rather than actual events:

> It is sometimes easier to do this without prejudice, recrimination or blame being attached. For example, take the case of bullying, something that can happen quite suddenly even in the best-run school. If teachers begin by reviewing a case that has actually happened recently in their own school, then the head and teacher concerned may feel defensive, if their actions are under scrutiny, and it may be difficult to discuss policy separately from personalities.
>
> (Wragg 1993: 53)

It is very often the case that school policies are developed in response to problems in a particular area but staff also need to identify where they are successful in order to see if, and how, favourable strategies might be transferred across areas.

For these whole-school guidelines to be effective, the role played by all concerned needs to be made explicit and procedures need to be clear, concise and consistent. Since governors are now responsible for appointing staff and for school policy, their support must be sought. Clearly understood rules and ways of operating apply not only in the classroom but also in the playground, dining area, corridors and cloakrooms and this requires that ancillary staff too are cognisant of aspects of school policies. Parents need to be consulted in order to obtain their views and enlist their support because without it, a school's chances of successfully implementing any policy involving students are lessened.

Although the Elton Report (DES 1989) was concerned mainly with discipline in schools, its recommendations apply equally to wider issues of classroom management and organisation:

> We recommend that headteachers and their senior management teams should take the lead in developing school plans for promoting good behaviour. Such plans should ensure that the school's code of conduct and the values represented in its formal and informal curricula reinforce one another; promote the highest possible degree of consensus about standards of behaviour among staff, students and parents; provide clear guidance to all three groups about these standards and their practical application; and encourage staff to recognise and praise good behaviour as well as dealing with bad behaviour.
>
> (DES 1989: 128)

Successful schools

There are several organisational features which tend to characterise successful schools (see Charlton and David 1990; Cooper 1993; Fontana 1994). These include, school rules which are few, realistic and open to change and development; clear and efficient lines of communication within the school; and decisions which are never arbitrary but are related to the procedures, standards and values that the school is seen to operate and all concerned are seen to support. Successful schools have classrooms which reflect their ethos. Some teachers begin the academic year by encouraging their students to draw up most of their own class rules.

A US study, conducted by Wayson *et al.* (1982) identified 13 character-istics of a successful school. Among these were that the type of leadership role adopted by the headteacher is a major determinant in how the school operates and that this role needs to be balanced by complementary leader-ship qualities in the senior management. In successful schools, teachers believe in what they are doing and in their students' abilities, and both groups see the school as where they come to work together successfully in a student-oriented manner. The ways in which these schools are organ-ised is conducive to hard work and good discipline because proactive, preventive measures are used rather than haphazard responses to prob-lems by the implementation of piecemeal, punitive procedures. The causes of problems are focused on, as opposed to the symptoms and, for the most part, individual teachers deal with the problems they encounter. Specifically, practices are adapted to meet the school's own identified needs and to reflect their particular styles of operation rather than trying to use other institutions' methods and processes. In addition, these schools have well-developed links with both parents and community agencies, are open to comment and criticism from sources within and outside the school and practise well-tried methods rather than new, trendy, insub-stantial procedures.

The role of the teacher

The classroom is a small, dynamic, social arena in which the teacher's and each student's performance is open for all to see. To operate effectively within such a vital environment calls for a special awareness and sensit-ivity from teachers in order that students do not feel threatened and defensive:

> Being constantly exposed to things that you cannot understand (like Maths) or required to attempt actions that you cannot do (like gym) is itself threatening for many people: unable to run away, every moment is fraught with the danger of being exposed, yet again, as incompetent. And this in its turn threatens to bring the public humi-liation that we would do almost anything to avoid.
>
> (Claxton 1984: 215)

Students' problems may not have their roots in school but their effects can be felt there and for those whose social relationships are out-of-sorts learning may be impossible. Although the school may be able to do little or nothing about home problems, a tactful, patient and understanding teacher may go some way towards helping a troubled student to cope in the short term. According to Maslow's (1962) hierarchy of needs, those of a higher level cannot be attended to unless all the lower level needs (the lowest being food, health, and so on) are satisfied. Thus students cannot pay attention to school learning (self-actualisation) if they are concerned with personal relationships (esteem of others):

> How can I care about French and history and all the other things? The teachers go mental because I don't always listen. How can I when I don't even know if my mum'll still be there when I go home – she keeps saying she'll leave. You can't tell anyone because it's like grassing on your own family.
>
> (Student quoted in Macrae 1990: 195)

Although there may be little a school can do about family problems it is important to realise that some 'difficult' behaviour can be explained only with reference to the student's wider social context. For some students school can be a refuge, a temporary respite from distressing home circumstances, 'I hate it when they [teachers] shout – it's like being at home. I only come here for a bit of peace and quiet' (Macrae 1990: 447). Teachers, of course, are not social workers but they are in a better position to accommodate and work with these students when they have some understanding of where the students are coming from both physically and emotionally.

Much of a teacher's time and energy is devoted to maintaining interpersonal, physical and emotional order because, for effective teaching and learning to take place, it is essential that favourable conditions are created and sustained. The way in which a teacher responds to a student on one particular occasion may well have an effect on that student (and indeed others) on subsequent occasions. Therefore, teachers are advised to think carefully before publicly criticising students because such behaviour may well have an adverse effect on their motivation to learn and to contribute in future lessons. Teachers also have to be sensitive to the difference between challenge and threat. When students feel challenged they can be tempted to further efforts; their learning can be encouraged and stimulated. However, there can come a moment when it is all too much and the student 'switches off':

> 'Switching off' means defending, for example, by going unconscious; and defending is not learning. Prodding and pushing are now the last thing that a person wants . . . Though from the outside it appears unjustified, defending is always appropriate, being the natural response to a perceived threat. If teachers do not spot the shift, and they keep on pushing when a learner is threatened, the learner can very quickly be turned off the teacher, the subject, the context (for example, school), learning in general, and eventually himself [sic].
>
> (Claxton 1984: 214)

Based on extensive experience of observing lessons in a variety of secondary schools, Hargreaves (1975) found that most teaching sessions follow a pattern: the entry phase, settling down, the central part where teachers present their main points and set the students tasks, followed by clearing up prior to the exit. Smith and Laslett (1993) describe this pattern as the 'four rules of classroom management': get them in, which has two components: greeting and seating; get on with it, which includes lesson content; get on with them, which means knowing who is who and what is going on; get them out, which has two phases: concluding the lesson and dismissing the class.

Classroom practice can be improved by studying what others do successfully and understanding the principles on which their practice is based. It is most useful for this study to take place in a context of reflection and action across a whole range of teaching skills. In isolation, the ability to manage students, resources, time and space has little meaning. But in context, the value and meaning of strategies and techniques will become apparent.

All this, of course, is not new. At the beginning of the century Dewey (1904), writing about the relationship between educational theory and classroom practice, argued that:

> The would-be teacher has some time or other to face and solve two problems, each extensive and serious enough by itself to demand absorbing and undivided attention. These two problems are:
> 1   Mastery of subject matter from the standpoint of its educational value and use; or, what is the same thing, the mastery of educational principles in their application to that subject matter which is at once the material of instruction and the basis of discipline and control.
> 2   The mastery of the technique of classroom management. This does not mean that the two problems are in any way isolated or independent. On the contrary they are strictly correlative. But the mind of a student [teacher] cannot give equal attention to both at the same time.
>
> (Dewey 1904: 318)

Many student teachers are asked during their Post Graduate Certificate of Education (PGCE) year to observe lesson phases in order to chart what experienced teachers do to move the teaching session from one stage to another in an orderly, effective manner. It is frequently the case that disruption occurs at the point where the lesson moves from one phase to the next. Student teachers are usually asked to focus on 'starts and finishes' the language used, the ways in which experienced teachers respond to early signs of trouble, whether teachers plan for fast workers and slow learners, whether teachers give clear signals of movement from one phase to the next, 'Right, we are going to pack up in five minutes' and what actions teachers take with disruptive students.

It might be advantageous for student teachers and teachers to reflect on and identify the sorts of professional skills they think are necessary for themselves and their colleagues. Wragg (1993) suggests this might take the form of a hierarchical list of dimensions with levels appropriate to beginners and more experienced teachers:

> In class management, for example, a notion like 'organize the handing out and collection of materials' might be a fairly basic matter, involving a teacher thinking about how this can best be organized ...
> On the other hand, 'judging the right language register, appropriate response to and suitable activities for a student bewildered by a new mathematical or scientific concept' clearly exerts a much higher level of intellectual and practical demand.
>
> (Wragg 1993: 57)

Smith and Laslett (1993) describe the four 'Ms' needed for effective classroom organisation: management, mediation, modification and monitoring. The management of lessons includes their organisation and presentation, which requires the ability to analyse the various phases and elements of a lesson, select and deliver appropriate material and reduce sources of friction. Mediation, they argue, is about ways to enhance self-concepts and avoid damaging confrontation in the classroom. Modification is about understanding learning in order to devise programmes for shaping and rewarding behaviour. Monitoring concerns checking the effectiveness of school policies on discipline and pastoral care and how senior management can help colleagues avoid stress and cope with problems in classroom management.

Many transactions that take place are immediate and unpredictable and coping with the idiosyncratic and peculiar demands of classroom life sets school teaching apart as a distinctive professional activity. Essentially, teachers have to create, organise and promote learning in a forum which does not offer ideal conditions, very often with limited resources and in which they must maintain order and be responsive to students' different temperaments, abilities and social relationships. Smith and Laslett (1993) compare teaching with a game of chess in which experienced teachers understand opening moves and their effects on subsequent moves. It can also be argued that learning, both academic and social, follows the same rules.

In the course of a day, teachers are frequently called upon to make rapid, informed judgements which are shaped by a number of factors. These include, among other things, their own values about how students should be treated, their own physical and mental state and their intuition about the current classroom climate. This means that they may react differently to similar sets of circumstances from day to day.

Essentially teachers need to be encouraged to understand and develop different styles of management and organisation according to the work being undertaken as well as the age and ability of the students. Clearly, different strategies would apply according to whether the teaching is aimed at the whole class, a group or an individual. Therefore, although teachers need to be consistent, paradoxically, they also need to be flexible and adaptable and the ways in which they operate with one group may not be appropriate with another. There is no one remedy for every problem and teachers must identify those strategies and techniques which work best for them and fit their own philosophy of teaching. Successful teachers operate a series of bargains and accommodations which are essential to maintain a healthy learning environment. The resolution of these tensions is described by McNamara (1994: 67) as practical pedagogy. 'The teacher's practical pedagogy should be based upon informed choices so that she is aware of the costs and benefits entailed in pursuing one course of action rather than another . . .' These informed choices are part of an arsenal of strategies which teachers build up and can draw upon and the development of these is a career-long task (Chase and Chase 1993). Martin Monk (in Chapter 11) discusses a range of ways that teachers can use to help their students.

As I have indicated, the class teacher's job is largely about maintaining order which does not necessarily mean dealing with discipline problems and disruptions. Rather, it is about allocating attention and 'orchestrating the flow of people, events and materials in a confined space with few resources' (McNamara 1994: 22). Although the focus of maintaining order is not disciplinary, it can be argued that teachers who successfully achieve this, have fewer discipline problems.

Managing behaviour

The sort of misbehaviour teachers deal with most regularly is of a persistent, low-grade nature such as 'talking out of turn', 'calculated idleness or work avoidance', 'hindering other students' and 'making unnecessary (non-verbal) noise' (DES 1989). These repetitive patterns of bad behaviour can result in student under-achievement as well as teacher and student stress. They can also lead to habitual negative responses from teachers, which do nothing to improve the situation and can actually exacerbate it.

As Watkins and Wagner (1987: 9) warn, 'Whether a student's action is seen as a 'breach of discipline' will depend on who does it, where, when, why, to whom, in front of whom and so on'. One teacher's interpretation of deviancy may be another's idea of liveliness and creativity. This is where a whole-school policy is essential so that behaviours can be evaluated and responded to in a socially just and fair manner. One of the first questions to ask of problem behaviour is, 'how can we try to ensure it does not arise?' or 'how do we understand it?' An inability to understand the other side is frequently at the root of classroom dissonance:

> It is all too easy for both sides to set up the other as a cardboard cut-out: a caricature of lawlessness on the one side, of oppression on the other. Neither opponent acts alone. For the adolescent boy angrily confronting his teacher, the endorsement, the admiration of his watching classmates is crucial. To the teacher trying to contain the potential violence, at stake is his [sic] own professional reputation: the approval or the contemptuous pity of his colleagues. Both sides have to win. It has become necessary to fight to the death.
>
> (Salmon 1995: 79)

Watkins (1995) suggests that it is advisable to take a broad problem-solving approach which sees behaviour in terms of the constructive engagement of students. The sort of language used to describe disruptive incidents can carry interesting messages and it is important to remain focused on the behaviour and not the person. Salmon (1995) warns against the 'language of complaint':

> Instead of focusing on the unpleasant effects which a particular action may have for others, it becomes necessary to step into the aggressor's shoes, to try to see what he or she may be attempting to achieve by such behaviour. Rather than seeing hostile behaviour as an in-built problem of particularly difficult individuals, it becomes possible to look for what is essentially at stake for young people who behave in this way. The situation may then be resolved, without

either side 'winning', by means which allow students to keep face, to retain their vital sense of dignity.

(Salmon 1995: 79)

In addition, as Watkins (1995: 3) points out, 'by talking about *patterns* of behaviour, diagnostic thinking can be improved and a better range of interventions considered'.

Schools with well-articulated behaviour policies are likely to deal more confidently with issues of discipline and individual teachers, in the knowledge they will be supported, can feel empowered to try to handle all or most of the routine discipline problems themselves. In a study by Maxwell (1987) it was suggested that there were lower suspension rates in schools that felt empowered to deal with behaviour problems.

The role of the student

On examining student–teacher relationships, Hargreaves (1972) found that students take particular interest in three aspects of teachers' behaviour: their discipline style; their instructional style; and their personal characteristics. Other studies show that students prefer teachers who: are respectful to them; listen to their concerns; consult them; and enhance their self-esteem. According to Morrison and McIntyre (1969) and Nash (1976) students prefer teachers who: maintain a disciplined atmosphere; are cheerful; give interesting lessons; take an interest in students as individuals; and present an amicable learning situation. Students expect to learn and to be taught and those teachers who fail to be friendly, firm and fair in their dealings are frequently 'punished' by students for refusing to be 'proper' teachers. The punishment usually takes the form of bad behaviour as a way of 'getting their own back' but may also take the form of 'bunking off'. In extreme cases students may stop coming to school altogether. For those students who have been long-term absentees or truants it is important that teachers realise their return to school may be very difficult and may be on a very fragile footing (Reid 1987). Teachers would be advised not to make an issue of their return but to welcome them back unobtrusively, aware that academic and social re-integration may be necessary.

School procedures and ways of operating should be made explicit for students in order to encourage them to take responsibility, make decisions, organize themselves and control their own behaviour. By setting high standards for themselves, teachers can encourage students to do likewise (Charlton and David 1993; McManus, 1994). It should be kept in mind, however, that students come from a variety of backgrounds with a wide range of experiences and what is understood by 'high standards' and what is attainable may vary between students and for students at different times in their school career.

Bryk and Driscoll (1988: 89) found that students were better behaved in schools with a well-developed community spirit. Such schools they emphasise, 'attend to the needs of students for affiliation . . . provide a rich spectrum of adult roles [and] engage students personally and challenge them to engage in the life of the school'. Relations between staff and students can be further developed and deepened when they are given the opportunity to see each other in different roles; for example, in a drama production, in organising a school fair, or on a school journey. There is a tendency for both teachers and students to ascribe to each other narrowly prescribed roles and it can be a revelation for both parties to observe different and often unimagined facets of the other, outside the teacher/ student situation.

Conclusion

Although teachers' lessons should challenge the students academically, Bereiter (1972) argued that lesson content is not particularly academically demanding and the organisation of students is a fairly straightforward activity. However, the integration of these activities is far from straight-forward and to orchestrate them into a coherent performance presents teachers with an enormous challenge. It is this notion of practical performance which is central to the teacher's pedagogical expertise: the ability to 'keep the plates spinning' while attempting to promote learning in the dynamic, social arena of the classroom. Good classroom management and organisation liberates teachers from many of the daily hassles and confrontations and enable them to establish the order without which the classroom can become a 'battleground' (Watkins and Wagner 1987).

For teachers to feel comfortable in the classroom it is advisable that they try to develop their own professional philosophy, to think about the sort of teacher they would like to become and decide what they need to do to actualise this aim. They might also like to consider the sorts of relationships they would like to develop with both colleagues and students and identify where compromises might be necessary. These issues are crucial as they relate to the sort of person the teacher is and to reasons for being a teacher. It is the willingness continually to reflect on these concerns that will enable teachers to grow, develop, enjoy and make a success of their teaching.

References

Bereiter, C. (1972) Schools without education, *Harvard Educational Review*, 42(3): 390–413.

Bryk, A.S. and Driscoll, M.E. (1988) *An Empirical Investigation of the School as a Community*. Chicago: University of Chicago School of Education.

Charlton, T. and David, K. (1990) Towards a whole school approach: helping to ensure pupils are fit for the future, *Links*, 3(15): 20–24.

Charlton, T. and David, K. (eds) (1993) *Managing Misbehaviour in Our Schools*. London: HMSO.

Chase, C.M. and Chase J.E. (1993) *Tips From the Trenches*. Lancaster, Pennsylvania: Technomic Publishing Co.

Claxton, G. (1984) *Live and Learn*. London: Harper and Row.

Cooper, P. (1993) *Effective Schools for Disaffected Students: Integration and Segregation*. London: Routledge.

Department of Education and Science (DES) (1981) *Class Management and Control: A Teaching Skills Workbook*. Teacher Education Project. Basingstoke: Macmillan Education.

Department of Education and Science (DES) (1989) *Discipline in Schools*. The Elton Report. London: HMSO.

Dewey, J. (1904) The relation of theory to practice in education, in R.D. Archambault (ed.) (1964) *John Dewey on Education: Selected Writings*. Chicago: University of Chicago Press.

Fontana, D. (1994) *Managing Classroom Behaviour*. Leicester: British Psychological Society.

Galloway, D. (1983) Disruptive students and effective pastoral care, *School Organization*, 3(3): 245–54.

Hargreaves, D. (1972) *Interpersonal Relations and Education*. London: Routledge and Kegan Paul.

Hargreaves, D. (1975) *Interpersonal Relations and Education*. Revised Student edn. London: Routledge and Kegan Paul.

Macrae, S. (1990) Students' perceptions of and reactions to stress in school, unpublished PhD thesis. CNAA.

Maslow, A. (1962) *Toward a Psychology of Being*. Princeton: Van Nostrand.

Maxwell, W.S. (1987) Teachers' attitudes towards disruptive behaviour in secondary schools, *Educational Review*, 39(3): 203–16.

McManus, M. (1993) Managing classes, in B. Moon and A. Shelton-Mayes (eds) *Teaching and Learning in the Secondary School*. London: Routledge.

McNamara, D. (1994) *Classroom Pedagogy and Primary Practice*. London: Routledge.

Morrison, A. and McIntyre, D. (1969) *Teachers and Teaching*. Harmondsworth: Penguin.

Nash, R. (1976) *Teacher Expectations and Pupil Learning*. London: Routledge and Kegan Paul.

Reid, K. (ed.) (1987) *Combating School Absenteeism*. Sevenoaks: Hodder and Stoughton.

Rutter, D., Maughan, B., Mortimore, P. and Ouston, J. (1979) *Fifteen Thousand Hours: Secondary Schools and Their Effects on Children*. London: Open Books.

Salmon, P. (1995) *Psychology in the Classroom*. London: Cassell.

Smith, C.J. and Laslett, R. (1993) *Effective Classroom Management*. London: Routledge.

Watkins, C. (1995) *School Behaviour*. Viewpoint No. 3. London: Institute of Education.

Watkins, C. and Wagner, P. (1987) *School Discipline: A Whole School Approach*. Oxford: Blackwell.

Wayson, W.W., Achilles, C., Pinnell, G.S., Cunningham, L., Carol, L. and Lintz, N. (1982) *Handbook for Developing Schools with Good Discipline*. Bloomington: Phi Delta Kappa Educational Foundation.

Wragg, E.C. (1981) *Class Management and Control: A Teaching Skills Workbook*. Basingstoke: Macmillan Education.

Wragg, E.C. (1984) *Classroom Teaching Skills*. London: Croom Helm.

Wragg, E.C. (1993) *Class Management*. London: Routledge.

Further reading

Blatchford, P. and Sharp, S. (eds) (1994) *Breaktime and the School: Understanding and Changing Playground Behaviour*. London: Routledge.

Claxton, G. (1993) *Being a Teacher: A Positive Approach to Change and Stress*. London: Cassell.

Denscombe, M. (1985) *Classroom Control: A Sociological Perspective*. London: Allen and Unwin.

Furlong, J. and Maynard, T. (1995) *Mentoring Student Teachers: The Growth of Professional Knowledge*. Buckingham: Open University Press.

McGuiness, J. (1993) *Teachers, Pupils and Behaviour: A Managerial Approach*. London: Cassell.

McIntyre, D. and Hagger, H. (1996) *Mentors in Schools*. London: David Fulton.

Provis, M. (1992) *Dealing With Difficulty: A Systems Approach to Problem Behaviour*. London: Hodder and Stoughton.

Putnam, J. and Burke, J.B. (1992) *Organising and Managing Classroom Learning Communities*. New York: McGraw-Hill.

Weinstein, C.S. (1996) *Secondary Classroom Management*. New York: McGraw-Hill.

Wilkin, M. and Sankey, D. (1994) *Collaboration and Transition in Initial Teacher Training*. London: Kogan Page.

14 | Differentiation in theory and practice

Christine Harrison

Introduction

There have been many claims concerning the effect of the introduction of the National Curriculum in England and Wales, but one outcome that deserves recognition is its influence on the educational vocabulary of teachers. While the 1980s was a time when phrases including 'positive achievement', 'mixed ability teaching' and 'graded assessment' were very much in vogue, the 1990s are associated with terms such as 'progression', 'attainment' and 'differentiation'. While aspects of progression and attainment will be considered in this chapter, since they are not only related to, but intertwined within the ideas that will develop, I will focus on a consideration of differentiation and I will consider not only what differentiation is, and how some schools have responded to it, but suggest teaching and learning styles which allow for differentiation to be achieved.

As with many educational terms that have emerged as front-runners in 'teacher-speak', the meaning, interpretation and practices of differentiation differ markedly depending on who is using the term and for what purpose. Ubiquitous use of a term does not denote common understanding and may suggest the contrary. The increase in the use of the term 'differentiation' arises possibly not from interest but from concern, not from knowledge but from misunderstanding. It follows that without a clear understanding of what differentiation involves there is a minimal chance of the development of strategies to strengthen aspects of it within teaching and learning.

It may help, at this point, to try to identify where the problem in understanding what differentiation is occurs. A dictionary definition may be along the lines of: 'to make different; to distinguish; to classify as different.' The mystery lies in what it is that has to be made different, distinguished or classified. It is not about the differences between pupils, these will manifest themselves anyway. It is not about the curriculum offered nor the school that pupils attend, because, in the words of Gillian Shephard, Secretary of State for Education in the mid-1990s, the 'National Curriculum provides a minimum entitlement to education for all children regardless of their background, where they live or which school they go to.' Instead it concerns the ways in which schools provide for the needs of pupils; the difference is in the types of action taken by schools and teachers rather than in the abilities of the pupils or the structure of the system.

Undoubtedly the structure of the National Curriculum, with its attainment targets, statements of attainment and programmes of study, has been one of the major reasons behind this interest in differentiation. However, it is not a new idea within education, but one that has gained more prominence at a time when teachers were implementing a new type of curriculum. In a 1981 DES document, in spite of the term not being used, there was a clear indication that differentiation was an important ingredient within the teaching and learning process:

> It is part of the teacher's professional role to recognise and develop the potential of individual pupils. All pupils should be encouraged throughout their school careers to reach out to the limits of their capabilities. This is a formidable challenge to any school since it means that the school's expectation of every pupil must be related to their individual gifts and talents.

> (DES/WO 1981: 9)

Maximising potential is central to the notion of differentiation. It hinges on creating learning experiences for children that will allow each of them to progress, from the stage that they are currently at, towards where each has the potential to be. It is about identifying what a pupil can do and deciding on the subsequent experience, encouragement, support and advice that will further develop the knowledge, ideas and skills of that pupil. The Warnock Report (DES 1978) emphasised this by stating:

> The purpose of education for all children is the same: the goals are the same. But the help that individual children need in progressing towards them will be different.

The National Council for Educational Technology (NCET) defined differentiation in a pragmatic way as 'the planned process of intervention in the classroom that maximises potential based on individual needs' (Dickinson and Wright 1993). It requires a series of actions by teachers to create and manage strategies that will recognise pupil capabilities and provide for educational development. For some teachers this will require a change in teaching and learning styles, while others will adapt and strengthen their present pedagogy to develop differentiation in their classrooms.

The 1982 Cockcroft Report drew attention to the 'seven-year difference' in mathematical understanding of children entering secondary school and there is every reason to suppose that a similar range exists within other curriculum areas. The task facing teachers in developing a differentiated approach to teaching and learning is neither simple nor easy. There is no miracle 'off the shelf' solution, but there are recognisable ways of differentiating and within each of these a number of strategies that can be identified. By selecting, practising, developing and honing these strategies, teachers can evolve their own systems of differentiation that suit their teaching style and provide for their pupils' needs.

Ways of differentiating

There are three main approaches to differentiation:

- differentiation by task
- differentiation by outcome
- differentiation by support.

These approaches are not exclusive and it is possible that all three approaches may be working concurrently within a classroom.

Other approaches to differentiation exist – the response of some schools and teachers is to try and differentiate by organisation. These schools have dealt with the wide range of pupil needs by organising them into narrower bands of abilities for all their lessons (streaming or banding) or for specific subjects (setting). Within classrooms, some teachers place pupils into working groups of similar ability, so that the range of needs in each group is reduced. However, these systems of organisation are not in themselves a means of differentiating. The range of pupil needs and abilities within one classroom might be reduced by organisational methods but this only limits the range that the teacher needs to respond to. Organisation may reduce the number of strategies that a teacher needs to employ or reduce the preparation time in planning and preparing for a reduced number of needs, but it is not differentiation *per se*.

Differentiation by organisation is simply a mechanism that some schools and teachers use to begin making differentiation a manageable task. It is important to note here that there are a number of teachers, schools and educationists who would consider the sociological implications of setting, streaming and banding intolerable, mainly because they 'label' pupils and limit the expectations of both pupils and teachers (see Chapter 15). Rowntree (1988) discusses this 'self-fulfilling prophecy' by considering that pupils generally have been led to believe that they cannot all achieve a worthwhile level of learning. Those that exhibit that they can learn early on are recognised by both their teachers and peers and continue to progress with their learning. Other pupils, who have not had the opportunity or confidence to demonstrate some competency or other, remain unrecognised in the social context of the classroom and possibly continue unchallenged and perhaps unsuccessful in their learning. It is a complicated issue that teachers and schools need to unravel, evaluate and consider. The concern that I have about differentiation by organisation is that some may believe that this action at the organisational level answers the problem of differentiation, while omitting to focus on the classroom level as the means of differentiated provision.

An analogy of this might be a garden. A variety of plants are grown and while the gardener cannot do a great deal about the inherent characteristics of that generation, she can decide to grow similar types of plants together. However, simply dividing up the garden into different areas and planting each group of plants in a specific area could be disastrous. To grow successfully each plant will have specific requirements: some will prefer shade and others full sunlight, some need a large area to develop their root systems while others spread across the soil surface using their aerial parts, the acidity of the soil may affect them, etc. The gardener, through experience and information gained from books and other gardeners, can plan for the needs of each group of plants and so select where to plant them and how to care and nurture them during their development. By continually checking each plant's progress and growth, she can maintain, intervene or alter its conditions so that the plant can fulfil its potential. If the gardener decides to plant her garden with only four types of plant then there are fewer decisions and actions to be taken than a gardener who might select twenty plant types, but there is still monitoring, planning, preparation and intervention to be done to ensure successful crops. Organisational ploys may render differentiation more manageable in the classroom but it does not solve the task of differentiating for the teacher.

Differentiation by task

This involves offering different activities to individuals or specific groups of children where the learning outcomes may be similar or different. At the simplest level the teacher uses a number of tasks that match the learning needs of each of the pupils. However, the practicalities of lesson planning usually limit the number of tasks to around three and yet the range of needs that reflects the capabilities and past learning experiences of the pupils in the class will undoubtedly warrant a larger number than this. However, three tasks within one lesson are a beginning and, if care is taken to match tasks to students' abilities, aptitudes and interests, then it is possible for the system to work and evolve.

The manner in which the teacher introduces a task to pupils can be used to fine tune the task to individual needs. The choice of stimulus activity, depth of detail, 'clues' given, ways in which links with previous learning are highlighted and, most importantly, which outcomes are stressed can all be used to hone a task to suit an individual or group.

Allowing students choice in tasks will enable them to develop their differing aptitudes and interests. Giving pupils a shared role in the responsibility for their learning fosters good practice for future learning and creates a sense of motivation and trust. This will depend even further on the teacher giving explicit outcomes and instructions to pupils, so that pupils are aware of all the tasks to be undertaken and therefore make a sensible choice. Discretion will obviously need to be used by the teacher to ensure suitable choices are made.

If resources such as worksheets are used within activities, then the selection or production of these might focus on appropriate readability levels, ease of use or good design to ensure accessibility. The appearance of a worksheet must invite a pupil to interact with it, removing any barriers to learning by its clarity, interest and attractiveness. It may be beneficial to replace text-based materials with other sources, such as video or audio tapes, CD-ROMs or concept keyboards. An alternative delivery may stimulate interest and fit in with the preferred learning style of certain pupils. The drawback with a multimedia approach is that the teacher may spend a considerable proportion of the lesson organising distribution, correct use and collection of the materials. However, this can be overcome if a well-managed storage and retrieval system is set up for the pupils and they are given sufficient training and responsibility to use and maintain the system.

In some schools and in some published courses learning modules are designed that cater for different abilities. Within a topic that lasts several weeks teachers map predetermined routes for different ability groups (e.g. average, above average and below average pupils). This is a form of differentiation by task. However, there are drawbacks with such approaches, which teachers must overcome if such schemes are to be effective. This approach may reinforce teacher expectation of individuals and limit the opportunities available for pupil learning. It may also 'label' pupils and create a poor work ethos with some of them. Unless a regular monitoring system is built into the scheme, pupil progress during the topic will not be recognised and mismatches of work with pupil capabilities may occur. The formative assessment role of the teacher is vital in this approach to differentiation, as with other differentiated approaches, because the teacher is the link between the materials and the learner that can mediate and encourage the learning. Published schemes may save teachers preparation time in terms of devising activities but still require them to judge the appropriateness of each activity, to adapt activities where necessary to allow access or extend pupil learning and also to match the challenges of an activity with the capabilities of individual pupils. The most worrying aspect of implementing a prescribed system, such as a published scheme, is that it may cause some teachers to shift the responsibility for differentiation from their own planning and delivery to that of the published scheme.

Differentiation by outcome

This involves organising an activity from which several outcomes may emerge. Such activities are often called 'open-ended', but it is important that the teacher anticipates and identifies learning routes that particular pupils might take within the activity so that the necessary support can be given. It may be that the knowledge or skills developed in the activity are common to all pupils but the activity allows for different products. This will cater for students' differing aptitudes and interests and preferred learning styles, particularly if the products can be created within different media.

Differentiation, within an activity that starts from a common point, may develop the learning so that there are differences in the knowledge or skills which are acquired by individuals. This often requires an exploration of what ideas and skills pupils bring to the learning situation by such techniques as brainstorming or concept maps, or simply encouraging pupils to ask questions about some stimulus material that reflects their ideas, knowledge and background interests. From this starting point, different ideas can be developed within the planned activity and the final products and outcomes matched with pupil capabilities.

It is important to ensure that all pupils achieve at the highest level they are capable of when working on a task where the outcomes are differentiated. Pupils will be more likely to compare their product with others in the class if the task seems, on the surface, a common one, and such comparison can be demotivating for some pupils. The way in which progress is recognised for each pupil may be an essential factor in overcoming such problems. In helping pupils recognise what they have learned, how they have progressed over recent weeks and in negotiating targets for future learning situations, an anxiety-free and supportive learning environment can be established. Such an atmosphere would benefit any mode of differentiation but is especially important when differentiating by outcome as this system can expose the capabilities of pupils to a wider audience than differentiation by task.

Differentiation by support

This form of differentiation is probably the most important and yet least recognised of the three described here. Teachers know that some pupils require more help than others to complete a set task and, in giving or organising this help, teachers are differentiating by support. It exists as a variety of strategies, which I have grouped as resources, group work and interventions.

Within a task, pupils may need help getting started, staying on task or completing specific parts of it. Poor readers can be helped by providing audio-taped versions of the worksheet. Alternatively, hint sheets, planning sheets or study guides may cue pupils in to what they should do. The use of icons on worksheets, spelling lists or keywords can also be helpful for some pupils.

Vygotsky (1978), a psychologist whose work underpins a number of recent educational projects and research ideas, believed that human development is 'intrinsically social and educational' and that 'children undergo profound changes in their understanding by engaging in joint activity and conversation with other people'. Groupwork not only overcomes the problems shy pupils have in one-to-one conversations, but presents a forum in which all pupils can voice their ideas. The language and analogies used allow pupils to reveal to themselves and others their thoughts and ideas, and also to compare these with the views of other learners. Group work can provide a supportive background that benefits all the learners within the group. However, there is more to group work than a number of pupils sitting around a table or the teacher arranging who should go in which group. The Oracle project, which looked at interactions in primary classrooms, found that the majority of pupils worked as individuals within groups and so the effect of grouping did not benefit their learning. Getting children to work collaboratively and creating group identity are essential prerequisites to group work.

Support by intervention requires the teacher to observe individuals or groups of pupils engaged in activities and, from the responses or actions witnessed to enter into an interaction with the pupils to direct the learning forwards. It is an on-the-spot assessment of where the learning has reached and then a decision about which direction it should now take. It is a difficult task to perform, because the teacher must judge carefully when to intervene, so that words and actions do not hinder the flow of ideas between group members. The teacher must create time to do this because it performs two essential services; it provides a direct feedback message system on pupil progress and also shapes the learning programme for the pupils to ensure a close match with their capabilities. In order to do this, the teacher must reduce the 'housekeeping' role that activity-based learning sometimes relegates teachers to. The organisation and management of resources need to be carefully planned to give the teacher time to interact with pupils during the lessons.

Differentiation in action

The following three scenarios are descriptions of differentiation in action, within different types of classroom. They are fictitious to some extent, but include good examples of differentiated practice that I have witnessed in schools. While the problems and solutions for differentiation may differ between subjects, I am convinced that the messages, hints and ideas that they generate are not domain-specific, and as such, transferable or adaptable to all subject areas.

The mathematics classroom

Kim's department uses an individualised scheme called SMILE to provide for the needs of pupils in mathematics. SMILE has a plethora of workcards, and the teacher regularly negotiates packages of one or two weeks' work with individual pupils. Kim spent most of her first year of teaching sat at her desk, with a line of pupils waiting for their books to be marked or for Kim to tell them what to do next. Some pupils rarely spoke to the teacher but worked on at a steady, though not necessarily determined pace, while others were constantly demanding the teacher's attention. Kim had the resources for differentiated learning, but not the teaching and learning style to make it effective.

In order to overcome these problems, she introduced a learning contract, at the start of each topic of work, in which she negotiated with pupils what work they were going to do, how long they anticipated each part of the work should take and how they were going to carry it out. She also asked each pupil to select a weekly target for improving some aspect of their learning, which was also included in the contract. The contracts were drawn up and signed by both the pupil and Kim and pupils were encouraged to show and discuss their contracts with a mentor, who might be another pupil, a relative or form tutor. While, initially, the introduction of the contract procedures took up valuable class time, the pupils eventually became more expert in deciding what they were capable of achieving and in reflecting on their progress and previous learning, so that contract setting became a fast and efficient task. The contracts also engendered a sense of responsibility for their own learning among the members of the class and a more co-operative and collaborative work ethos. It also freed Kim to move around the class more, enabling her to interact better with the pupils, by witnessing the activities as they occurred, rather than in the product they formed.

Kim made use of the differentiation potential of the SMILE scheme by making the pupils focus on their own learning strategies and capabilities. In carefully negotiating appropriate work and routine, she encouraged pupils to be more receptive to the learning experience and fostered a willingness to learn and respond to the experience. As a consequence of this, she created time within her classroom where she could begin to assess formatively and also, in helping individuals, to differentiate by support.

The science classroom

Rahana's department produced a detailed work scheme of the topic she was to teach. It had a number of activities, each with National Curriculum references and comprehensive apparatus and resources lists, and some of the activities had worksheets to support them.

Rahana started her lesson using an idea taken from some of those developed by Bentley and Watts (1992). She placed a drawing on the overhead projector of an astronaut on the moon who had just let go of a spanner and asked the class to think what would happen to the spanner next. After a few minutes, she asked for suggestions and three possibilities were suggested by pupils:

- the spanner will remain where it is
- the spanner will fall (slowly) to the moon's surface
- the spanner will float upwards into space.

Rahana then asked the pupils to raise their hands for the one of these possibilities they believed correct. She then separated the class into three different groups, using the criteria of similar preconceptions to decide the appropriate grouping. Each group then had a different task to carry out, before returning to the astronaut drawing, and deciding whether their initial idea was upheld with the new evidence acquired from completing their activity.

One activity was based on a short video film and worksheet, which the pupils took away to the resource corner and watched using the remote control to stop or review sections of film that seemed interesting or important to the work they had been asked to do. The main ideas in the video discussed the effects of gravity and the pupils were required to answer a number of questions from information in the film and then to write a paragraph explaining what gravity is and where it can be experienced.

Another activity was worksheet-based and required pupils to discuss, in groups, events in a diary, supposedly written by a space scientist living in the future on a moon station. Pupils had to list all the events on the moon that were linked with the moon's gravity and explain how these would be experienced differently on Earth.

The third activity was textbook-based. Pupils read and discussed in pairs a section from the text, which dealt with the difference between mass and weight, and then answered some questions and calculations on this topic from the book.

Rahana spent the first five minutes or so following the lesson introduction with the pupils attempting the diary activity, listening and helping each group list the first few ideas. She then moved to the video group and asked them to review for her how far they had got with the questions on the worksheet and any sequences on the video that they found surprising. This took around ten minutes, and Rahana then spent a further ten minutes discussing with pairs from the textbook group what they had found from their reading.

This lesson demonstrates differentiation on many different levels. The teacher started with a stimulus activity that revealed something of pupils current understanding of the work. She then geared the activity to build on their current understanding by providing three different tasks to direct their future learning. Her classroom organisation and management meant that pupils were quickly and efficiently engaged in their appropriate tasks, leaving the teacher the freedom to move from group to group and differentiate by support. At the end of the lesson, she created an opportunity for both the pupils and the teacher to judge whether the learning had been developed by reviewing the final products and returning to the initial stimulus activity.

For homework, the pupils were asked to think of a sport that would be played more easily on the moon than on Earth. This is an example of a piece of work that is differentiated by outcome. The pupils all tackle the same task but their level of understanding and their motivation mediate the outcome.

The English classroom

Steven introduced an assignment on poetry by reading three short poems by different styles of poet and asked pupils to state what they liked or disliked about each poem. He then divided the class into groups of four and gave each ten cards that had statements concerning the nature of poetry. Each group was asked to discuss and select three statements that they either agreed with or felt were interesting. They then had to find a poem that they considered best illustrated the chosen statements. They were told to use the teacher as a resource for guidance and to look through the numerous poetry books which had been organised in four different areas in the classroom.

As each poem was selected, the group had to explain to the teacher what had led them to decide both on the statement and the choice of poem. Steven moved round the groups, checking on the progress pupils were making and encouraging pupils to remain on task. He started with a group who had been restless during the stimulus activity and who, by their body language, were initially disinterested in the task. He managed to answer questions from one group, while observing other groups working, so was able to judge which groups were in need of direction and help. This work was developed, in subsequent lessons, to produce a class display on the 'Essence of Poetry', and also as the stimulus material for pupils writing their own poetry.

In this lesson, the teacher again begins with considering and sharing pupils' interests and ideas and by the use of prepared cards allows pupils some choice in the direction that their learning will take. The differentiation is undoubtedly by outcome, but in the selection of one statement rather than another, and in the degree of guidance and direction given to each group by the teacher, the learning routes are both different and supported as they develop. The organisation of the books into four areas gave the pupils space to work and so further supported the work.

The teacher also showed how he valued the work that was produced by creating a wall display that was subsequently used as a further learning stimulus. This motivates pupils and allows them to see some of the markers in their progress as they complete one learning stage and use it to set off on the next.

Final thoughts

Pupils will be more successful learners in a differentiated learning environment where there is structure in the planning, support in the implementation and regular evaluative procedures. The National Curriculum sets out the educational entitlement for all pupils, but it is the teacher in the classroom who will plan, cater and provide for the needs of pupils and ensure that they reach their potential.

The classroom scenarios show three approaches to differentiation and what has not been considered is why these should be different from one another. It may be related to individual preferences with regard to teaching style or to the structures and constraints of a particular domain. Indeed, the problems and solutions to differentiation in the English classroom may be markedly different to those encountered in science, which again will differ in mathematics, classics or history. However, the difference in differentiated approach may also be governed by the features of the learning group rather than that of the teacher or the subject.

References

Bentley, D. and Watts, M. (1992) *Communicating in School Science: Groups, Tasks and Problem Solving 5–16*. London: Falmer Press.

Department of Education and Science (DES) (1978) *Special Educational Needs: Report of the Committee of Enquiry into the Education of Handicapped Children and Young People* (The Warnock Report). London: HMSO.

Department of Education and Science/Welsh Office (DES/WO) (1981) *The School Curriculum*. London: HMSO.

Dickinson, C. and Wright, J. (1993) *Differentiation: A Practical Handbook of Classroom Strategies*. London: NCET.

Rowntree, D. (1988) The side-effects of assessment, in R. Dale, R. Fergusson and A. Robinson (eds) *Frameworks for Teaching*. London: Hodder and Stoughton.

Sotto, E. (1994) *When Teaching Becomes Learning: A Theory and Practice of Teaching*. London: Cassell Education.

Vygotsky, L. (1978) *Mind in Society: The Development of Higher Psychological Processes*. London: Harvard University Press.

Further reading

Hart, S. (ed.) (1996) *Differentiation and the Secondary Curriculum*. London: Routledge.

Postlethwaite, K. (1993) *Differentiated Science Teaching*. Buckingham: Open University Press.

Quicke, J. (1995) Differentiation: a contested concept, *Cambridge Journal of Education*, 25(2): 213–24.

Waterhouse, P. (1990a) *Classroom Management*. Stafford: Network Educational Press.

Waterhouse, P. (1990b) *Flexible Learning: An Outline*. Stafford: Network Educational Press.

| 15 | Setting, streaming and mixed ability teaching |

Jo Boaler

Introduction

Should students be grouped and taught in classes according to their perceived 'ability' or not? This has been one of the most controversial issues in education since the 1960s. One reason for the controversy is that the complex issues that surround setting, streaming and mixed ability teaching are invariably value-laden. Decisions about student grouping are of immense importance to the education of students and this importance extends beyond the development of subject understanding. For these, and other reasons, research into the experiences of students in streamed, setted and mixed ability groups is extremely valuable. In this chapter I will give an overview of the research that has been conducted in this field, in the UK, the USA and beyond. I will use this research to consider the impact of setting and mixed ability teaching on the way in which students learn and the way in which they develop their perceptions of self within the schooling system.

The UK context

Grouping practices vary between schools and between different subjects, but probably the most common form of grouping in UK secondary schools is *setting*. Setting is the term used to refer to the grouping of students of similar attainment in the same subject class, what Sørensen (1970) has termed a narrow scope system. This has largely taken over from the prevalent practice of *streaming* in which students of similar attainment are grouped into one class for all of their subjects – what Sørensen termed a wide scope system. An alternative to either of these practices is the teaching of students in mixed ability groups in which students of different abilities are taught alongside each other. In any one secondary school it is likely that there will be a variety of forms of grouping represented across the different subject areas and across the different year groups. In primary schools mixed ability teaching is by far the most widely used form of grouping, although increasing numbers of primary schools are now starting to teach students in setted or streamed groups.

History of ability grouping

In the 1950s almost all schools were streamed and students were differentiated within, as well as between, schools. Jackson (1964) conducted a survey of junior schools and found that 96 per cent used streaming and 74 per cent had placed children into ability groups by the time they were 7 years old. Jackson's study also identified some of the negative effects of streaming, including the tendency of teachers to underestimate the potential of working-class children, and the tendency for low stream groups to be given less experienced and less qualified teachers. Jackson's report contributed towards an increasing public awareness of the inadequacies of streamed systems. In 1967, the Plowden Report (a major report on primary schools) recommended the abolition of all forms of ability grouping (Bourne and Moon 1994).

The idea that setting and streaming created and maintained inequalities prompted many different schools to move towards mixed-ability teaching. In the 1970s and 1980s support grew for mixed ability teaching based largely upon an increased awareness of, and concern for, the inequalities inherent within the educational system. However, the 1990s have witnessed a reversal of this thinking with a number of schools reconsidering their policies on mixed-ability teaching.

Research has shown that some teachers regard the National Curriculum as incompatible with mixed-ability teaching (Gewirtz et al. 1993). The creation of an educational 'marketplace', which effectively required schools to compete for students, meant that schools became even more concerned than before to create images that were popular with local parents (Ball et al. 1994):

> Mixed ability is also on our agenda. We're reviewing it at the moment . . . The National Curriculum has made us review it really. I think it may well have an offshoot though, it may make us attractive to parents . . . The staff are finding it more and more difficult, you see, resources have been cut, there's no doubt about it. With the National Curriculum coming in there are more and more subjects which are saying, 'coping with that ability range within the classroom, without the kind of support you need is very difficult.'
>
> (Headteacher, quoted in Gewirtz et al. 1993: 243)

The development of an educational 'marketplace' and the introduction of a National Curriculum both meant that the early 1990s saw significant numbers of secondary school subject departments returning to policies of setting by ability. Primary schools received more overt pressure to group their students according to ability with reports from the National Curriculum Council and the Department for Education both encouraging schools to introduce or re-introduce setting.

Reasons for and against ability grouping

The main reason given for the use of setting has generally been that teachers can adapt their pace, style and content to particular ability groups. This is believed to create greater homogeneity among students and enable more whole-class teaching. There is also a widespread notion among the education community that setting increases attainment, particularly for high ability students (Ball 1981a; Dar and Resh 1986). This is a particularly relevant argument given that secondary schools are now ranked according to their GCSE results. On the other side of the fence, those who oppose setting generally do so because they are concerned that it creates inequality. Many proponents of mixed ability teaching also believe that there are significant advantages in giving students the opportunity to progress at different rates using differentiated learning materials (see Chapter 14 for a discussion of differentiated learning materials).

In one of the most significant studies of mixed-ability and streamed teaching conducted in the UK, Ball (1981a) found that different subject teachers were divided over their preferences for ability grouping and that they formed their decisions in relation to a number of ideologies. The proponents of mixed-ability teaching represented what he termed an 'idealist perspective'. They viewed mixed-ability teaching as an important part of comprehensive education that offered students a greater degree of equality of opportunity. At the other extreme he identified a group of teachers as belonging to the 'academic perspective'. This group were concerned about maintaining academic excellence and they viewed mixed ability as a threat to this concern. The third and largest group of teachers he placed within the 'disciplinary perspective'. These teachers were in favour of mixed ability teaching because they believed that the abolition of streams would reform the social atmosphere of the school and eliminate 'troublesome low stream anti-school classes' (Ball 1981b: 162). These three categories provide a useful summary of some of the issues and concerns that UK researchers have found influence decisions about mixed ability and setting or streaming in schools.

Slavin (1990: 473) also summarised these issues well:

In essence, the argument in favour of ability grouping is that it will allow teachers to adapt instruction to the needs of a diverse student body and give them an opportunity to provide more difficult material to high achievers and more support to low achievers. The challenge and stimulation of other high achievers are believed to be beneficial to high achievers. Arguments opposed to ability grouping focus primarily on the perceived damage to low achievers, who receive a slower pace and lower quality of instruction, have teachers who are less experienced or able and who do not want to teach low-track classes, face low expectations for performance and have few behavioural models.

The debates about setting and mixed-ability teaching have important implications, not only for the way in which students learn and develop, but for the ideological conflicts and resolutions which affect teachers in schools. But what does research have to say about these issues? Does it support the notions that setting creates inequality or that setting diminishes or enhances attainment for certain students? In the next section I will consider the way in which research findings support, contradict and, more generally, inform these various notions.

The outcomes of setting and streaming

Focus on equality

Most of the research that has been conducted in the UK into setting, streaming and mixed-ability teaching has focused upon issues of inequality and on the effects of ability groupings upon students' development of image and self-worth. Many of these studies have been of an in-depth, qualitative nature in which students have been observed, interviewed and analysed over long periods of time. The first of these to have a major impact on the educational community was conducted by Brian Jackson (1964). He found that children whose fathers were in professional jobs had a lower chance of being placed in a low stream than children, with a similar IQ, whose fathers were in unskilled jobs. He also found that teachers were likely to underestimate working-class children and place these children in low streams.

Another highly influential study was undertaken by Stephen Ball. He conducted an ethnographic account of a school (which he called *Beachside Comprehensive*) that was moving from streaming to mixed-ability teaching in the 1970s (Ball 1981a). Ball also found that students were allocated to the different streams, partly on the basis of their social class. Tomlinson has commented that:

> Although ability is supposedly the major criterion for placement in subject and examination levels, ability is an ambiguous concept and school conceptions of ability can be affected by perceptions that pupils are members of particular social or ethnic groups and by the behaviour of individual pupils. Factors related to class, gender, ethnicity, and behaviour can be shown to affect the placement of pupils at option time, even those of similar ability.
>
> (Tomlinson 1987: 106)

Ball concluded from his study that ability groupings do not allow the ideals of comprehensive education to be fulfilled, because although children from different social classes enter and share the same building, they are not given equal access to opportunities and they are inhibited from mixing with each other. Ball (1981a), Hargreaves (1967) and Lacey (1970) all found that placing students into high and low streams also created a polarisation of students into 'pro' and 'anti'-school factions. Thus, students who ended up in high sets or streams became 'pro-school' whereas those who ended up in low sets or streams became 'anti-school' and suffered all of the disadvantages associated with this. In a more recent study, Abraham (1995) set out to investigate whether the polarisation of pupils according to their social class occurred as a result of setting as well as streaming. He investigated a setted comprehensive school and found that students were also polarised into pro and anti-school factions, based partly upon their social class, in response to the groups they were setted into within the school.

The various studies that have been conducted in the UK have been relatively conclusive in demonstrating that setting and streaming create and perpetuate social class divisions among students. They have also shown that students of similar ability may be placed in different sets or streams according to their social class, their gender or their ethnic origin. This, they suggest, is part of the reason that low sets and streams in schools are often made up of disproportionate numbers of students who are black, working-class, male and who have behavioural problems. The studies have also shown that the experience of being placed in a low set or stream can create anti-school feelings that derive from diminished perceptions of self-image and worth. Indeed, it was in response to some of these studies that many schools abandoned setting and streaming in the 1970s and 1980s.

Focus on attainment

Most of the studies that have been conducted in the UK have focused primarily upon issues of equality (Abraham 1994). This has meant that they have concentrated more upon the students' developing perceptions of place within the wider school system, than upon the students' development of subject understandings. In contrast, research in the USA has provided a wealth of empirical evidence concerning the relative achievement of students in academic, general and vocational 'tracks'. Slavin (1990) has produced an important review of the most significant of these investigations, from the USA and elsewhere. Slavin included in this analysis every research study conducted in the field as long as it fulfilled criteria related to relevance and methodological adequacy. His review included the results of six randomised experiments, nine matched experiments and 14 correlational studies that compared ability grouping to 'heterogeneous' groupings. Across the 29 studies reported Slavin found the effects of ability grouping on achievement to be essentially zero for students of all levels and all subjects (the median effect size was +0.01 for high achievers, −0.08 for average achievers and −0.02 for low achievers, effects of this size are indistinguishable from zero). Four British studies were included in Slavin's analysis: these found no differences in achievement between streamed and unstreamed classes.

An important piece of research conducted in Israel consisted of four longitudinal studies that considered mathematical attainment and student grouping (Linchevski 1995a; b). In one of the studies Linchevski compared the eventual attainment of students in 12 setted schools with their expected attainment, based upon entry scores. This showed that ability grouping had no effect on attainment in ten of the schools and a small negative effect in the other two. A second study examined the thinking and performance of similar-ability students who were at the border of different ability bands and assigned to different groups. This showed that the students of similar ability assigned to different groups varied in attainment, with the students assigned to higher groups attaining more than students of a similar ability assigned to lower groups. Linchevski concluded from this that 'the achievements of students close to the cut off points are largely dependent on their being arbitrarily assigned to a lower or higher group level' (Linchevski 1995a: 11). Another of her studies compared the achievements of two groups of students at the same school assigned either to setted or mixed-ability groups. This showed that the average scores of the most able students placed in setted groups were slightly, but not significantly, higher than the able students placed in mixed-ability groups. However, the scores of students in the two lower setted groups were significantly lower than similar-ability students in the mixed-ability classes. Linchevski found that low ability students in the mixed-ability classes coped well with tests because they were used to high demands and expectations.

In other studies which have found differences in achievement between homogeneous and heterogeneous groupings these have tended to replicate Linchevski's finding with some small, statistically insignificant increases for students in high tracks gained at the expense of large, statistically *significant* losses, for students in low tracks (Hoffer 1992; Kerchoff 1986).

In a recent UK research study, Boaler (1997a, b) combined aspects of the UK and US studies reported by performing an in-depth study of students over a long period of time that focused upon the students' attainment, in addition to their beliefs and values. This revealed some surprising results. The research included case studies of two cohorts of students, matched in terms of ability, gender and socio-economic status. One of the cohorts was taught mathematics in a mixed ability environment, the other in a highly differentiated, setted environment. This showed that a significant number of *high ability* students were disadvantaged by setting arrangements, more specifically by their placement in the 'top set'. These top set students developed negative attitudes and demonstrated considerable under-achievement in class-based assessments and GCSE examinations. The students related their negative responses to the pressure, high expectations and fast-paced lessons they experienced. In a comparison of the high ability students taught in the setted groups with the high ability students taught in mixed ability groups, the students with the highest eventual achievement were those taught in mixed ability groups (Boaler 1997a, b). One of the important differences between this study and many of the US studies was that it considered individuals, rather than average scores reported across groups. It was this focus upon individuals that revealed that only *some* students were suited to a top set environment, many students reacted against it and under-achieved because of it, particularly the highest ability girls in the groups.

Conclusions

There is a widespread belief, within and outside the UK education community, that setting is an advantageous way of grouping students

– particularly high-ability students. In a recent Ofsted survey, 94 per cent of schools were found to use setting in the upper secondary years for mathematics (*The Guardian* 1996). The support for setting generally derives from a view that setting and streaming confer academic advantages. These are believed to outweigh the potential disadvantages for 'low ability' students as well as any discriminatory practices affecting disadvantaged groups of students of a particular ethnic group, class or gender. However there is little, if any, research that supports the notion that setting enhances achievement for students. In the second international mathematics survey of eight countries (Burstein 1993) it was found that the countries that had the most setting were those with the lowest achievement, and the countries with the least setting had the highest achievement. Indeed, in bringing together the different research studies on ability grouping it is difficult to draw any positive conclusions about the effects of setting and streaming. In a discussion of research in this area, Bourne and Moon (1994: 30) note that a number of major research reports fail to 'show any particular advantage, in terms of academic attainment' for streamed classes. When advantages have been reported in research studies, small gains have centred upon high ability students and these have been matched by large losses for low ability students. Many other studies have reported neither gains nor losses, for low or *high* ability students. Research has also shown, fairly conclusively, that implicit and explicit prejudices result in decisions being made about the grouping of students according to their ethnic group, social class or gender. These decisions probably contribute towards long-term under-achievement and disaffection.

One of the reasons that students in setted and streamed groups do not achieve more than students in mixed ability groups, as many think they should, may be that teachers often do not acknowledge the mixed-ability nature of setted groups. One of the general aims of setting is to reduce the spread of ability within the classroom. This often results in teachers believing that all of the students in an ability group can be taught at the same pace, using the same style and method. Teachers tend to teach towards a 'reference group' (Dahllöf 1971) in each class, at a pace to which all students are assumed to be able to adjust. This model has serious drawbacks for students who deviate from the 'reference group'. In mixed-ability classes, teachers accept that there is a wide range of ability and their lessons cater for the individual needs of learners. Thus, in mixed-ability classes teachers often prepare differentiated materials or use individualised materials and schemes which, inevitably allow learners to have more freedom to work in their own ways, which are likely to be more consonant with their own learning styles (see Chapter 14 for a discussion of differentiation).

However, one advantage of setting and streaming is that many teachers are more comfortable with it. Teachers of subjects like mathematics and languages, in particular, often have strong beliefs about the hierarchical nature of their subjects which they think preclude the use of differentiated materials with mixed-ability classes. However, even teachers of these subjects have devised successful mixed-ability approaches, such as the SMILE mathematics scheme and materials developed by individual mathematics departments (Boaler 1993, 1997a). Unfortunately, many of the schools and teachers that favour setting do not acknowledge the personal nature of their preference but reflect upon notions of academic attainment that, research suggests, are misguided.

The consequences of setting and streaming decisions are great. Indeed, the set or stream that students are placed into, at a very young age, will almost certainly dictate the opportunities they receive for the rest of their lives. It is now widely acknowledged in educational and psychological research that students do not have a fixed 'ability' that is determinable at an early age. However, the placing of students in academic groups often results in the fixing of their potential achievement. Slavin (1990) makes an important point in his analysis of research in this area. He notes that as mixed-ability teaching is known to reduce the chances of discrimination, the burden of proof that ability grouping is preferable must lie with those who claim that it raises achievement. Despite the wide range of research studies in this area, this proof has not been forthcoming.

References

Abraham, J. (1994) Positivism, structurationism and the differentiation–polarisation theory: a reconsideration of Shilling's novelty and primacy thesis, *British Journal of Sociology of Education*, 15(2): 231–41.

Abraham, J. (1995) *Divide and School: Gender and Class Dynamics in Comprehensive Education*. London: Falmer Press.

Ball, S.J. (1981a) *Beachside Comprehensive*. Cambridge: Cambridge University Press.

Ball, S.J. (1981b) The teaching nexus: a case of mixed ability, in L. Barton and S. Walker (eds) *School, Teachers and Teaching*. Lewes: Falmer Press.

Ball, S.J., Bowe, R. and Gewirtz, S. (1994) Competitive schooling: values, ethics and cultural engineering, *Journal of Curriculum and Supervision*, 9(4): 350–67.

Boaler, J. (1993) Encouraging the transfer of 'school' mathematics to the 'real world' through the integration of process and content, context and culture, *Educational Studies in Mathematics*, 25(4): 341–73.

Boaler, J. (1997a) *Experiencing School Mathematics: Teaching Styles, Sex and Setting*. Buckingham: Open University Press.

Boaler, J. (1997b) When even the winners are losers: evaluating the experience of 'top set' students, *Journal of Curriculum Studies*, 29(2): 165–82.

Bourne, J. and Moon, B. (1994) A question of ability?, in B. Moon and A. Mayes (eds) *Teaching and Learning in the Secondary School*. London: Routledge.

Burstein, L. (1993) *The IEA Study of Mathematics III: Student Growth and Classroom Processes*. Oxford: Pergamon Press.

Dahllöf, U. (1971) *Ability Grouping, Content Validity and Curriculum Process Analysis*. New York: Teachers' College Press.

Dar, Y. and Resh, N. (1986) *Classroom Composition and Pupil Achievement*. New York: Gordon and Breach.

Gewirtz, S., Ball, S.J. and Bowe, R. (1993) Values and ethics in the education market place: the case of Northwark Park, *International Studies in Sociology of Education*, 3(2): 233–54.

The Guardian (1996) Blair rejects mixed ability teaching, *The Guardian*, 8 June.

Hargreaves, D. (1967) *Social Relations in a Secondary School*. London: Routledge and Kegan Paul.

Hoffer, T.B. (1992) Middle school ability grouping and student achievement in science and mathematics, *Educational Evaluation and Policy Analysis*, 14(3): 205–27.

Jackson, B. (1964) *Streaming: An Education System in Miniature*. London: Routledge and Kegan Paul.

Kerchoff, A.C. (1986) Effects of ability grouping in British secondary schools, *American Sociological Review*, 51(6): 842–58.

Lacey, C. (1970) *Hightown Grammar*. Manchester: Manchester University Press.

Linchevski, L. (1995a) Tell me who your classmates are and I'll tell you what you are learning: mixed ability versus ability-grouping in mathematics classes. Paper presented at a mathematics education seminar held at King's College London.

Linchevski, L. (1995b) Tell me who your classmates are and I'll tell you what you learn, *Psychology of Mathematics Education* (PME) XIX(3): 240–47.

Slavin, R.E. (1990) Achievement effects of ability grouping in secondary schools: a best evidence synthesis, *Review of Educational Research*, 60(3): 471–99.

Sørensen, Å.B. (1970) Organisational differentiation of students and their educational opportunity, *Sociology of Education*, 43(4): 355–76.

Tomlinson, S. (1987) Curriculum option choices in multi-ethnic schools, in B. Troyna (ed.) *Racial Inequality in Education*. London: Tavistock.

16

Assessing pupils

Bob Fairbrother

Introduction

You will not be able to teach without assessing your pupils to find out how they are progressing. Assessment means any method, whether a formal examination or an informal observation, of obtaining information about their performance. This chapter concentrates on the assessment of pupils' knowledge and understanding – what Bloom (1956) calls the cognitive domain. It omits the affective domain (Krathwohl *et al.* 1956), which is concerned with the attitudes of pupils. I use 'attainment' in an absolute sense and 'achievement' in a relative sense. So, the same attainment can be a high achievement for a low-ability pupil, but a low achievement for a high-ability pupil.

Your major concerns will be to find out how to assess your pupils as an integral part of your teaching, and how to obtain the information which enables you to make reports on your pupils. It is important, however, to know and understand some of the basic principles involved. This chapter provides these in five interrelated parts:

1 the purposes of assessment
2 assessment and the curriculum
3 the validity and reliability of assessments
4 making judgements – norm referencing and criterion referencing
5 reporting and using the results of assessment.

The purposes of assessment

The Task Group on Assessment and Testing (DES 1988) identified four purposes of assessing pupils in school:

- formative
- diagnostic
- summative
- evaluative

A brief summary of these is given below. Other authors such as Rowntree (1977) and Mathews (1985) cover similar points but with different emphases.

Formative purpose

Assessment for this purpose is used to help guide pupils' progress. The results of assessment are used by teachers to adapt teaching to the needs of pupils as their learning progresses. It is important to involve pupils in this process and for some details of how this can be done see Fairbrother *et al.* (1993; 1995).

Diagnostic purpose

The emphasis of assessment for this purpose is on identifying where pupils are going wrong or having difficulties so that something can be done about it.

Summative purpose

This involves a summing up at some end point. The main end points are at the end of a year and at the end of a key stage, with the GCSE at the end of Key Stage 4 probably the most significant.

Evaluative purpose

This uses the assessment of pupils to give some information about the performance of a teacher, a department, a school, and so on. The Parents' Charter (DFE 1994) says parents should get all the information they need to keep track of their child's progress, to find out how the school is being run, and to compare all local schools.

Links between formative and summative

There is a tendency for summative assessment to displace formative assessment (see Black, H.D. 1986). In a detailed review of research evidence, Black, P.J. (1993) found that much of the so-called formative assessment done in schools is, in effect, repeated summative assessment.

One cause of this is the continual changes to the National Curriculum making teachers uncertain about what they are supposed to be doing. The move to greater public accountability has meant that teachers feel their professional judgement is under threat and they will have to justify any decisions they make. Thus they believe the safest strategy is to go for the collection of hard evidence, namely formal test results. Assessment for formative purposes becomes less and less important. As Paul Black (1993: 84) says:

> The one feature directly relevant here is the lack of public and polit-ical confidence in teacher assessments, combined with a lack of will to invest in the development of training, standardising or moderat-ing procedures which could provide the basis for such confidence. Coupled with this is a degree of confidence in external tests which is informed by nostalgia and custom and ignorant of evidence of their limited reliability, let alone their invalidity. In such an atmosphere, teachers' formative assessment is unlikely to receive attention, let alone support.

Assessment and learning

Formative assessment which guides pupils' progress must involve the pupils. HMI have identified 'unduly limited opportunities for self-assessment by pupils' and 'a lack of clearly defined assessment criteria, capable of being understood by pupils'. Wood (1991: 78) adds to this: 'Given that self-assessment is difficult for most pupils anyway, the need for clear, intelli-gible assessment criteria is paramount. This is as true for teachers as for students.'

Many schools have rewritten the National Curriculum criteria so that pupils can understand them and try to make use of them. However, they have to be taught to do this. Several case studies in Fairbrother *et al.* (1995) describe different ways in which this has been done successfully in some schools.

Assessment and the curriculum

The development of assessment has paralleled the development of the curriculum. Some of the changes which have taken place, particularly those relating to assessment, are discussed in more detail below.

Change and political influence

Paul Black, one-time Deputy Chair of the National Curriculum Council writes lucidly about the recent history of assessment policy in England and Wales (see Chapter 6 and Black 1994). A good, in-depth study, based on interviews with key actors in the National Curriculum policy-making process is given in Ball (1990). Snippets from some of the interviews in Ball's book show how the government has taken a greater interest in, and control of, the curriculum. There are several references to the concern of government to reduce the influence of teacher assessment. A much more personal account is given in Graham and Tytler (1993). It is clear in the accounts of both Ball and Graham that politicians are driven by an agenda which is probably more to do with retaining power, political ideology and finance than with achieving excellence in education. A valuable and 'sideways' look at most of the recent changes is given in National Commission on Education (1993).

Records of Achievement

Records of Achievement (RoA) are intended to be for all pupils and to be maintained beyond school into further and higher education and employment. Pupil self-assessment together with teacher–pupil discussion is an important element in RoA and can help to create a feeling of purpose in the record and of ownership by the pupil. (See Broadfoot 1986a, b; 1992; Broadfoot *et al.* 1990).

A case study of RoAs at work in a school is given in Pole (1993). A big problem for teachers is finding the time to consult with pupils and colleagues in order to keep the record up to date. Pupils have difficulty making their own contribution to the record; they are influenced in what they say by their perceptions of what teachers will find acceptable. James (1990) discusses the issue of power and authority, draws attention to 'a confusion of purposes, processes, concepts and principles', and highlights a fundamental dichotomy: on the one hand, processes aspire to be formative, developmental and confidential; on the other hand, they have a summative element and claim public currency.

The GCSE

The background to the establishment of the GCSE appears in many publications (e.g. Butterfield 1990; Judge 1984; Montgomery 1978; Nuttall 1985). The debate which took place reflects the larger problem of what is meant by an education for everyone up to the age of 16.

Discrimination and differentiation

An important task of public examinations is to discriminate between pupils so that reliable decisions can be made about the award of grades. Differentiation is about enabling pupils to show what they know, understand and can do. To achieve this with the wide range of ability covered by the GCSE has meant the development of alternative papers which give access to different ranges of grades.

Standards

Many people see the GCSE and A level as the guardians of standards. Those working for the Examination Boards want to treat candidates fairly so that they can say that all candidates producing the same standard of work have been given the same grade. The GCSE and GCE examination boards are concerned about:

- standards in the same subject in the same Board from one year to the next;
- standards in the same subject in different Boards;
- standards in different subjects in the same Board.

Comparability of standards

You can read about comparability of standards in Nuttall *et al.* (1974) and Forrest and Shoesmith (1985). Further discussion and an account of the attempts made by local authorities and schools to monitor standards are given in Gipps (1990).

The government have approved National Targets for foundation learning which include the aim that by 1997, 80 per cent of young people should obtain five A–C grades in the GCSE (see NACETT 1994 and National Commission on Education 1993).

The eight levels used in the National Curriculum do not go beyond Key Stage 3, letter grades are retained for the GCSE at the end of Key Stage 4 (Dearing 1993). This makes it difficult to relate standards between these key stages.

The National Curriculum

The statutory *Orders* for your own subject are essential reading, for example DFE 1995a, b, c. You should also read about the arguments for the revisions which have taken place. The most recent of these are the reports (Dearing 1993; 1994) made by Sir Ron Dearing, then chairman of the School Curriculum and Assessment Authority.

The assessment *Orders* are issued each year, and give the assessment arrangements for each relevant subject at the end of each key stage. Detailed guidance for the conduct of the tests given at the end of each key stage are issued separately each year and will be in schools.

The validity of assessments

You assess someone for a purpose, and an assessment is valid if the results enable the purpose to be achieved. There are many different kinds of validity, all of which are associated with different purposes. An assessment which is valid for one purpose may not be valid for another.

Face validity

Examination papers have face validity if you can relate the papers to the subject by looking at them. The questions should be recognisable as belonging to the subject.

Content validity

Content validity is concerned with the extent to which the test reflects what has been taught. There are two aspects to this:

1 *Coverage* involves inclusion in the test of those things which have been taught, and the exclusion of things which have not been taught.
2 *Balance* is concerned with the relative importance of the different parts of the subject and the emphasis which has been given in the teaching.

Good coverage and balance is difficult in the time available for an examination. Sampling has to take place, and the extent to which the examiners cover the syllabus over the years can influence teaching. Something which is rarely covered in the examination will be seen to be of little importance and may be omitted from the teaching.

Construct validity

Constructs are abstract qualities such as intelligence and understanding. A construct requires some definition, description and exemplification so that we can measure it. Showing understanding, for example, involves doing a variety of things which, when grouped together, enable some judgement to be made about performance in the construct.

Construct validity becomes important as we try to assess the ability of pupils to understand, reflect (on writing), be sensitive (to the different styles of vocabulary), recognise, show awareness, hypothesise, interpret, analyse, and so on. The elusive nature of these constructs (or processes as they are often called) is a source of difficulty when trying to bring together different bits of evidence in order to assess pupils (see Wiliam 1993a, b for a deeper discussion).

Criterion-related validity

This measures the relationship between the scores on a test and the achievement of some other criterion, such as the results of another test or performance in a job. There are two kinds of criterion-related validity:

1 *Concurrent*, in which the test results are compared with another measure of the same thing at the same time.
2 *Predictive*, in which the test results are compared with another criterion in the future, e.g. success in a job or at university. 16+ examinations are often used as predictors of performance in jobs and at A level.

The reliability of assessments

Reliability is concerned with the repeatability of results. There are three main sources of unreliability: the tests themselves, the pupils who take the tests, and the markers of the tests.

The tests (the measure)

When measuring the attainment of pupils, there is no single agreed measure. The GCSE examinations used this year are not the same as those used last year and will be different from those used next year. This means the same pupil could get different results in different years. Also, as Gauld (1980) found, pupils may interpret questions in a way which is different from what the examiner wanted or expected and so give answers which are not what the examiner is looking for.

The pupils

Pupils' knowledge and understanding change from day to day. Forgetfulness, headaches, arguments with a friend, the temperature of the examination room, can all affect what a pupil does in a test. If they took the test on a different day, they would get different results.

The markers

Even the most experienced examiners can vary in their interpretation of marking instructions so that the same standard of work is given different marks. Similarly, oral questions in an informal interchange with a pupil can be badly phrased and misinterpreted, and a teacher can be careless in the marking of homework or classwork for a variety of reasons ranging from overwork to laziness.

Interpreting reliability

If a pupil's knowledge and understanding of the subject changes from time to time then, even if the test itself is very reliable, you will get different scores which reflect these changes. You need to be assured of the reliability of a test so that you can interpret different scores for a pupil from one occasion to the next as true changes in the pupil's attainment and not as vagaries caused by the test.

Improving reliability

Ways of improving reliability are discussed in Tuckman (1988). One way is to ask several questions about the same thing, pupils then get several chances to show their knowledge and understanding. This increases the length of a test but increases the reliability also. The assessment of your teaching practice performance involves several lessons with different classes. A judgement based on just one lesson would not be sufficiently reliable.

Reliability is increased by having more than one person mark a pupil's work. The amount of time available and how much rests on the result (high stakes and low stakes) will govern the extent to which this is done.

The GCSE boards use moderation procedures to try to ensure comparability of standards between different schools. Different boards use somewhat different procedures but they all have to follow the *Mandatory Code of Practice* (SCAA 1995).

Individual subject departments in schools should do their own standardising sessions in which the work of pupils (classwork, homework and test results) is assessed by several teachers so as to put it on the same scale. A short but good discussion of some of the main issues in the moderation of National Curriculum assessment at Key Stage 3 is given by Cowling (1994).

Bias and fairness

Examination Boards try to include examples and contexts which represent the range of candidates who take the examinations. Wood (1991) discusses these and mentions particularly the apparently strong bias in favour of boys caused by the use of multiple-choice items in an examination and the bias in favour of girls caused by the use of essay questions.

Some teachers argue that it is unfair to reward a lazy but bright pupil the same as an industrious but dull pupil even though both have the same attainment. In reports to parents many schools say something about effort as well as about attainment.

Validity and manageability

Increasing the length and variety of a test increases its validity and reliability on the one hand but decreases its manageability.

Validity vs. reliability

In general, for an examination to be valid it must also be reliable. There is, however, often a tension between validity and reliability. By reducing uncertainty of marking and ambiguity in the questions and the answers, a multiple-choice test consisting of very simple questions of fact is highly reliable. However, it is of limited validity for assessing attainment in the subject because there is so much which multiple-choice items cannot assess. Attempts to increase the validity of the test by increasing the variety of questions inevitably result in reduced reliability particularly because of increased difficulties in marking.

High validity is obtained if you assess pupils by asking them to do what you want them to do. So, if you teach pupils French verbs so that they can converse in French, you assess the pupils by asking them to speak French, not by asking them to give the first-person singular of the present tense of the verb 'to be'.

Backwash

Examinations influence the kind of teaching and learning which takes place and must be seen as one of the purposes of assessment, intentional or otherwise. Publication of National Curriculum test results puts pressure on teachers to teach to the tests. If the tests can only measure a limited amount of what pupils should know, understand and do, then the teaching and learning will be similarly confined. As Paul Black (1993) explains:

> High stakes testing can dominate classroom work and so distort teaching that the conditions for good formative assessment do not exist. Teachers believe that preparing pupils for a specific test by narrow concentration on its demands and procedures will enhance their success. There is research evidence to support this belief (e.g. Becher 1990 and the meta-analysis by Lundeberg and Fox 1991).

Making judgements: norm referencing and criterion referencing

Norm-referencing

Norm referencing puts pupils in rank order, and pre-determined proportions are placed in the various grades. For norm referencing to work properly the assessment must discriminate between pupils. If there are big differences between candidates, then unreliability in the examination is not so important and it is easy to allocate grades reliably. You do not need to have a very reliable measure to distinguish between a competitor who does a high jump of 2 metres and one who clears 1.5 metres, but you do if the difference between them is only 0.5 cm.

Criterion referencing

Criterion referencing awards grades on the basis of the quality of the performance of a pupil irrespective of the performance of other pupils. It should be clear what is being assessed so that pupils can be judged against this, and not against each other.

Writing examinations

The GCSE examinations are more criterion-referenced than the old O level and CSE. New criteria have now been drawn up to match the National Curriculum, and you should look at the criteria, syllabuses and examination papers for your own subject.

Facility values

Learning objectives are capable of broad interpretations and the associated questions can be made easy or hard. If a test is too hard or too easy, then scores are bunched together; examiners wish to avoid this and so reject items with either high facilities or low facilities. However, a question on something important which is taught well could have a high

F value, and strict adherence to the rule could result in it not being assessed. If eventually omitted from the examination, the backwash effect could lead to important things not being taught at all.

Marking

A strict criterion-referenced approach to marking is one which makes yes/no decisions about each objective. Early versions of the key stage tests adopted this approach and ran into many difficulties particularly in bringing together all the yes/no decisions to decide what level a pupil had attained. In addition, most teachers unnecessarily adopted a similar approach to their teacher assessment and ended up ticking hundreds of boxes.

The mark schemes used by GCSE and key stage test examiners set out specific things to look for but it is usually possible to get a range of marks for a question. In the interests of manageability, however, many questions or parts of questions have simple short answers for which there are only one or two marks. You should look critically at the questions in your own subject and see what they are like.

Marking classwork and homework

When setting and marking classwork and homework, do you adopt a criterion-referenced approach or do you adopt a norm-referenced approach? Consider this quotation from Rowntree (1977: 53):

> The maximum 20 is given only to God, 19 to his saints, 18 to the professor's professor, 17 to the professor himself – and so the student of French composition can't be expected to score more than 16!

A criterion-referenced approach enables all pupils to get high marks (or low marks) depending on their attainment of the criteria. However, criteria have to be built into your teaching as learning outcomes. Also the pupils should know the criteria by which they are being judged.

Awarding grades

The examination boards have always used a mixture of norm referencing and criterion referencing in making decisions about the award of grades. If they applied a norm-referenced system, it would have to be the same norms for every subject, because to have different norms would be unfair. All subjects would then have the same percentage of candidates in each grade. Statistics produced by examining boards each year show that this is not the case. The reason for this is that the awarders are guided by both criteria and norms when making decisions about the award of grades. The use of criteria involves looking at the standard of work of the candidates (looking at samples of scripts) and using their collective judgement, guided by the grade descriptions issued by the School Curriculum and Assessment

Authority (SCAA), to decide upon the band of marks for each grade. The use of norms involves comparing the percentages of candidates in each grade this year with the percentages in earlier years. With large-entry subjects involving many thousands of candidates it is most unlikely that the overall standard of the candidates will change a great deal from one year to the next, and hence it is reasonable to expect similar grade distributions in different years. In small-entry subjects it is more difficult to use norms because the standard of the candidates can change, and the percentages of candidates in the different grades can fluctuate quite widely from year to year. This is a common experience in schools where one year of pupils can be significantly better or worse than the previous year. If there is a large number of schools entering for an examination, a good year in your school is balanced by a poor year in another school.

Grade descriptions and grade criteria

Both the GCSE and the National Curriculum use grade or level descriptions rather than grade criteria. Level descriptions:

> describe the types and range of performance which pupils working at a particular level should characteristically demonstrate. In deciding on a pupil's level of attainment at the end of a key stage, teachers should judge which level description best fits the pupil's performance.
>
> (DFE 1995: 49)

Domain referencing

The descriptions outline a domain of performance for each level, and require a greater use of teachers' professional judgement when deciding a pupil's level of attainment. To be able to use this domain referencing system, teachers need to have confidence in what they are doing, and to understand that issues of reliability discussed above make it inevitable that different teachers will sometimes make different judgements (Read Montgomery (1978: 73–7) for a discussion of pass, fail and grading decisions).

Reporting and using the results of assessment

There are some broad principles about reporting the results of assessment, and there are some statutory requirements issued by the Government which set out the minimum requirements which must be followed.

Why and who?

It is important to be clear about the audiences and purposes of reporting. These are directly linked to the purposes of assessment which were discussed earlier. The information, style and frequency of reporting is likely to be different for different purposes and audiences. Information about performance in subjects on the curriculum is almost always reported. Personal information and extra-curricula information are not always reported.

Grading

Pass/fail reporting involves an implicit decision made by the examiner about whether the performance is 'acceptable' or not. Graduated reporting (e.g. letter or numerical grades) which makes no indication of passing and failing leaves the decision about acceptability to the user of the results.

Passing and failing

A GCSE examination in your subject is not a test of competence. An employer may wish to use it as such, and some employers may want a higher level of attainment than others. In this case the examiner is not in a position to make decisions about competency and must leave it to the user of the results. Under these circumstances it makes sense to report different grades of result rather than pass and fail. It would be difficult to sustain the argument that a pupil has failed to make some progress in 11 years of compulsory education, and so a pass/fail judgement at the end seems inappropriate.

Records and reports

Records are uninterpreted statements of evidence whereas reports interpret the evidence before presenting it. Teachers and schools tend to keep records and issue reports. An examination mark or National Curriculum level which is sent to a parent is a report, although it may not be very informative on its own.

Records are usually detailed and indicate progression. Frequently, a shorthand is used which can only be understood properly by those who are making the record. Typical records which you keep will include the marks given to pupils for homework and classwork, notes of late handing in of work and of absences, and comments of various kinds to remind you of specific things about individuals. Part of your record might be the comments you write in the pupils' books, but this is an uncertain record since it may not be available when you need it.

Evidence

The evidence for producing a report may be permanent, for instance work which can be shown to someone if necessary, or it may be ephemeral, for example the words and actions of pupils which only you will have heard or seen. A report should use both permanent evidence and ephemeral evidence, and you should be prepared to use your judgement about the ephemeral evidence.

Profiles

Profiles are multidimensional methods of presenting information. Generally they contain the following:

- a list of items, categories or headings in the profile;
- an indication of the level and/or nature of performance;
- some indication of the evidence.

Probably the simplest profile is a list of grades awarded for different subjects in an examination. More complex profiles would give more information within each subject and also information about personal attitudes, participation in out-of-school activities, and so on. Often there will be an input from the pupil.

References

Ball, S.J. (1990) *Politics and Policy Making in Education: Explorations in Policy Sociology.* London: Routledge.

Becher, B.A. (1990) Coaching for the Scholastic Aptitude Test: further synthesis and appraisal, *Review of Educational Research*, 60(3): 373–4117.

Black, H.D. (1986) Assessment for learning, in D. Nuttall (ed.) *Assessing Educational Achievement.* London: Falmer Press.

Black, P.J. (1993) Formative and summative assessment by teachers, *Studies in Science Education*, 21: 49–97.

Black, P.J. (1994) Performance assessment and accountability: the experience in England and Wales, *Educational Evaluation and Policy Analysis*, 16(2): 191–203.

Bloom, B.S. (ed.) (1956) *Taxonomy of Educational Objectives: Handbook 1 Cognitive Domain.* London: Longman.

Broadfoot, P. (ed.) (1986a) *Profiles and Records of Achievement.* London: Holt, Rinehart and Winston.

Broadfoot, P. (1986b) Records of achievement: achieving a record?, *Studies in Educational Evaluation*, 12: 313–23.

Broadfoot, P. (1992) Multilateral evaluation: a case study of the national evaluation of records of achievement (PRAISE) project, *British Educational Research Journal*, 18(3): 245–60.

Broadfoot, P., James, M., McMeeking, S., Nuttall, D. and Stierer, B. (1990) Records of achievement: report of the national evaluation of pilot schemes, in T. Horton (ed.) *Assessment Debates.* London: Hodder and Stoughton/The Open University.

Butterfield, S. (1990) The development of secondary assessment and examinations, in R. Riding and S. Butterfield, *Assessment and Examination in the Secondary School.* New York: Routledge.

Cowling, L. (1994) Issues in moderation of national curriculum assessment at Key Stage 3, *Education in Science*, (158): 22–3.

Dearing, R. (1993) *The National Curriculum and its Assessment: Interim Report.* London: NCC/SEAC.

Dearing, R. (1994) *The National Curriculum and its Assessment: Final Report.* London: School Curriculum and Assessment Authority.

Department for Education (DFE) (1994) *Our Children's Education: The Updated Parent's Charter.* London: Department for Education.

Department for Education (DFE) (1995a) *English in the National Curriculum*. London: HMSO.

Department for Education (DFE) (1995b) *Mathematics in the National Curriculum*. London: HMSO.

Department for Education (DFE) (1995c) *Science in the National Curriculum*. London: HMSO.

Department of Education and Science (DES) (1988) *National Curriculum: Task Group on Assessment and Testing: A Report*. London: Department of Education and Science and Welsh Office.

Fairbrother, B., Black, P. and Gill, P. (eds) (1993) *Teacher Assessment of Pupils: Active Support*. London: Centre for Educational Studies, King's College.

Fairbrother, B., Black, P. and Gill, P. (eds) (1995) *Teachers Assessing Pupils: Lessons from Science Classrooms*. Hatfield: Association for Science Education and King's College London.

Forrest, G.M. and Shoesmith, D.J. (1985) *A Second Review of GCE Comparability Studies*. Manchester: Joint Matriculation Board.

Gauld, C.F. (1980) Subject oriented test construction, *Research in Science Education*, 10: 77–82.

Gipps, C. (1990) The debate over standards and the uses of testing, in B. Moon, J. Isaac and J. Powney (eds) *Judging Standards and Effectiveness in Education*. London: Hodder and Stoughton.

Graham, D. and Tytler, W.D. (1993) *A Lesson For Us All*. London: Routledge.

James, M. (1990) Negotiation and dialogue in student assessment and teacher appraisal, in T. Horton (ed.) *Assessment Debates*. London: Hodder and Stoughton/The Open University.

Judge, H. (1984) *A Generation of Schooling*. Oxford: Oxford University Press.

Krathwohl, D.R., Bloom, B.S. and Masia, B.B. (ed.) (1956) *Taxonomy of Educational Objectives: Handbook 11 Affective Domain*. London: Longman.

Lundeberg, M.A. and Fox, P.W. (1991) Do laboratory findings on test expectancy generalise to classroom outcomes? *Review of Educational Research*, 61(1): 94–106.

Mathews, J.C. (1985) *Examinations*. London: Allen and Unwin.

Montgomery, R. (1978) *A New Examination of Examinations*. London: Routledge and Kegan Paul.

NACETT (1994) *Summary Report on Progress*. London: National Advisory Council for Education and Training Targets.

National Commission on Education (1993) *Learning to Succeed: Report of the Paul Hamlyn Foundation*. London: Heinemann.

NCVQ (1993) *NCVQ Information Note 3*. London: National Council for Vocational Qualifications.

Nuttall, D. (1985) Doomsday of a new dawn? The prospects for a common system of examining at 16+, in P. Raggatt and G. Weiner (eds) *Curriculum and Assessment: Some Policy Issues*. Oxford: Pergamon Press/The Open University.

Nuttall, D.L., Backhouse, J.K. and Willmott, A.S. (1974) *Comparability of Standards Between Subjects*. London: Evans/Methuen.

Pole, C.J. (1993) Assessing and Recording Achievement. Buckingham: Open University Press.

Popham, W.J. (1993) The instructional consequences of criterion-related clarity. Conference paper, Annual Meeting of the American Educational Research Association, Atlanta, 12–15 April.

Rowntree, D. (1977) *Assessing Students: How Shall We Know Them?* London: Harper and Row.

SCAA (1995) *GCSE Mandatory Code of Practice*. London: HMSO.

SCAA (1996) *Review of Qualifications for 16–19 Year Olds, Summary Report*. London: School Curriculum and Assessment Authority.

Tuckman, B.W. (1988) *Testing for Teachers*. San Diego: Harcourt Brace Jovanovich.

Wiliam, D. (1993a) A look at some principles, in B. Fairbrother, P. Black and P. Gill (eds) *TAPAS. Teacher Assessment of Pupils: Active Support.* London: Centre for Educational Studies, King's College.

Wiliam, D. (1993b) Validity, dependability and reliability in National Curriculum assessment, *The Curriculum Journal,* 4(3): 335–50.

Wood, R. (1991) *Assessment and Testing: A Survey of Research.* Cambridge: Cambridge University Press.

Part 4 | Whole curriculum issues

17

Educating the spirit

Chris Wright

Introduction

What constitutes a valid spirituality within an educational context? If you were asked to define the term 'spiritual development' at an interview what would you say? Do you consider it possible to define the term 'spiritual development' in such a way that it is acceptable to both people with a religious and people with a non-religious perspective on life? What contribution do acts of collective worship make to the spiritual development of pupils? The 1988 Education Reform Act (discussed in more detail in Chapter 2) clearly emphasised that all teachers are responsible for the spiritual development of pupils. It is not just the role of the religious education (RE) teacher. The 1992 Education (Schools) Act emphasises that inspection of provision for the spiritual development of pupils must be carried out at regular intervals. But what exactly do we mean when we talk about the 'spiritual development' of pupils? This chapter will consider three concerns of spiritual development; principles which may underlie a schools' policy on spiritual development; how different subject areas can contribute to the spiritual development of pupils; and how the spiritual development of pupils can be inspected.

The spiritual dimension and the 1988 Education Reform Act

The spiritual dimension of life is of interest to many. In an article in *Psychology Today*, Eugene Taylor reported that 25 per cent of the titles on the *New York Times* bestseller list were on spiritual subjects and that one of them has been there for over ten years (Taylor 1994). The law makes it clear that the spiritual dimension of life is important. The preamble to the 1988 Education Reform Act includes the statement that the National Curriculum:

for a maintained school satisfies the requirements of this section if it is a balanced and broadly based curriculum which – (a) promotes the spiritual, moral, cultural, mental and physical development of pupils at the school and of society; and (b) prepares such pupils for the opportunities, responsibilities and experiences of adult life.

(Great Britain 1988)

In this approach to spiritual, moral, social and cultural development it echoes the 1944 Education Act. These four types of development are commonly referred to as SMSC.

It is clear from the Act that there is an assumption of a link between what happens in school and what happens in society. In a sense the school is a microcosm of society. In relation to the spiritual dimension of the curriculum it should, first, promote the spiritual development of pupils, but secondly, also contribute to the spiritual development of society. Thirdly, the reason that the curriculum should do this is to prepare 'pupils for the opportunities, responsibilities and experiences of adult life'. In this sense, the curriculum is partly seen as transmitting the spiritual values of the society in which it is found. While the transmission of spiritual values is seen to be important in the Act there is, however, no consensus on what these values are. The first part of this chapter will therefore concentrate on exploring what we might mean by talking about promoting the 'spiritual development' of pupils.

The inspectorate has helped us in fleshing out what the term 'spiritual development' might mean when it states:

Effective provision for spiritual development depends on a curriculum and approaches to teaching which embody clear values and provides opportunities for pupils to gain understanding by developing a sense of curiosity through reflection on their own and other people's lives and beliefs, their environment and the human condition . . . To the extent that spiritual insights imply an awareness of how pupils relate to others, there is a strong link to both moral and social development.

(Ofsted 1995a: 89)

Both the ERA and the *Guidance on the Inspection of Secondary Schools* make it clear that 'spiritual' is more than a synonym for 'religious' and as such is not covered merely by the statutory provisions for religious education. In the Act itself the spiritual development of pupils is mentioned separately from the provision of religious education. The spiritual development of the pupil can therefore not be left to one or two periods of religious education per week plus the statutory (though rarely observed) daily act of collective worship. Instead, by placing the term 'spiritual development' at the beginning of the Act legislators were attempting to highlight spiritual development as a priority to be addressed throughout the education process.

The term 'spiritual' is broader than 'religious' and thus has a greater functional use: 'the term "spiritual" could be one of the few terms left which someone who dislikes religion can use to describe that area of human experience traditionally called religion' (Hay 1982: 128). A past president of the British Humanist Association recognised that all of us have a spiritual dimension while denying a transcendent element when he wrote:

> The spiritual life is part of our biological life. It is the 'highest' part of it, but yet part of it. The spiritual life is part of the human essence . . . It is part of the real self, of one's identity, of one's inner core . . .
>
> (Hemming 1969)

The separate mention of spiritual development is also a recognition of the religious diversity in society at large (Sutherland 1993). In a culturally rich and multi-faith society, people will root the spiritual development of human beings within a number of religious and non-religious traditions. Religious education may have as one of its aims to promote the spiritual development of pupils, and indeed this may be one of its outcomes. However, the spiritual development of pupils is the responsibility of the whole school and its curriculum. In a pluralistic society any workable definition of the term 'spiritual development' must take into account the fact that for some non-religious people (including staff and pupils) the term 'religious' may have no meaning while for some religious people (again, both staff and pupils) there may be no recognisable distinction between the religious and secular – all of life is understood within a religious framework and spirituality is regarded as an essential part of their whole worldview.

Defining the spiritual

One of the major difficulties in discussing the spiritual dimension is that there is no consensus on the authoritative definition of the word 'spiritual', either in society at large or more narrowly within an educational context. The word 'spiritual' is used in a great variety of ways and contexts. Here are a few recent definitions:

> Spirituality means deep values, deep questions and deep feelings.
>
> (O'Donnell 1992: 5)

> anything which might be regarded as a source of inspiration to a person's life.
>
> (Mott-Thornton 1996: 7)

> The spiritual dimension is to do with the individual's stance in life, the inner world where feeling, imagination, mind and heart combine with values and commitments of belief and action.
>
> (Bradford Inspection and Consultancy Services 1990: 1)

> It is most helpful to interpret 'spiritual education' as education of the human spirit, that is, education which is directed towards the development of fundamental human characteristics and capacities such as love, peace, wonder, joy, imagination, hope, forgiveness, integrity, sensitivity, creativity, aspiration, idealism, the search for meaning, values and commitment and the capacity to respond to the challenges of change, hardship, danger, suffering and despair.
>
> (Halstead 1996: 2)

Spirituality concerns the essence, the inner realities of things – realities which, by definition, are often hidden.

(Gent 1989: 10)

By the word spiritual . . . there is a great deal to explore: ideas of the transcendental, of symbol, or of form, silence, reflection, as well as words.

(Young, cited in Bradford 1995: 57)

Spirituality should be understood as a process of transformation and growth, something dynamic which is part and parcel of the full human development of the individual and society.

(King 1985: 135)

Part of the difficulty of arriving at a consensus on the meaning of the word is the fact that by its very nature spirituality:

draws attention to what is invisible but not illusory . . . to what is non-rational but not meaningless. There will be no final logical clarity here, no rational demonstration or accurate conceptualization.

(Webster 1993b: 357)

However, all these definitions fall under two broad umbrellas which may be helpful for those working in schools: understanding ourselves and understanding the world.

The spiritual dimension is concerned with how people understand themselves

One of our major projects in life is to understand ourselves, as individuals and in relation to others. One definition of education is to enable 'people to write their own biographies' (as quoted in Bradford Inspection and Consultancy Services 1990: 2). 'A search for a full understanding of what human beings are is one foundation of the education of the spirit' (Sutherland 1993: 9). People are moral agents, capable of both good and evil, with a capacity for creative achievement.

This first category points to the fact that human beings have the capacity to rise above their animal nature, to transcend such animal functions as eating, excreting and procreating. The spiritual dimension is about reflective self-awareness, and an exploration of some of the ultimate questions in life: 'Where do I come from?', 'Who am I?', 'Where am I going?', 'What is the purpose of life?'. It also includes, according to the *Framework for Inspection*, 'valuing a non-material dimension to life and intimations of an enduring reality'. What is meant by this may be glimpsed in the following story:

A miser hid his gold at the foot of a tree in his garden. Every week he would dig it up and look at it for hours. One day a thief dug up the gold and made off with it. When the miser next came to gaze upon his treasure, all he found was an empty hole. The man began to howl with grief so his neighbours came running out to find out what the trouble was. When they found out, one of them asked, 'Did you use any of the gold?' 'No,' said the miser. 'I only looked at it every week.' 'Well, then,' said the neighbour, 'for all the good the gold did you, you might just as well come every week and gaze upon the hole.' It is not by our money but by our capacity for enjoyment that we are rich or poor. To strive for wealth and have no capacity for an appreciation of life outside that of possessions is 'to be like the bald man who struggles to collect combs'.

(Mello 1989: 20)

Halstead draws our attention to the 'danger that a de-spiritualised education might seek to . . . break down children's natural sensitivity to the inner world and imprison them in an impoverished, non-human materialism'. John Hull pictures this danger graphically as the triumph of Mammon as the 'omnipresent and omnipotent creator of human destiny' (Halstead 1996: 40). 'The education of the human spirit is precisely what is needed to help children to avoid the passive acceptance of the sovereignty of Mammon and to help them to recapture their imagination, perception and delight and grow towards autonomy and integrity' (Halstead 1996: 3). Spiritual development is therefore concerned partly in how people acquire personal beliefs and values, and how people come to answer some of the ultimate questions in life.

The spiritual dimension is concerned with how people understand the world in which they live

People live in an awe-inspiring world, the details of which we can see under the microscope and the majesty of which we see through a telescope. Sutherland draws our attention to an appropriate response to the world when he writes: 'The core of this which is absolutely crucial for the education of the spirit is the capacity to look attentively' (Sutherland 1993: 11). This need for attentiveness and appreciation 'sometimes even at the simplest everyday things' (SCAA 1996) is exemplified in the following story:

'When will I be Enlightened?'
'When you see,' the Master said.
'See what?'
'Trees and flowers and moon and stars.'
'But I see these every day.'
'No. What you see is paper trees, paper flowers, paper moons and paper stars. For you live not in reality but in your words and thoughts.' And for good measure, he added gently, 'You live a paper life, alas, and will die a paper death.'

(Mello 1985: 37)

The world's principal religions and philosophies have much to say about both of these spiritual concerns. It is therefore the pupil's educational right to learn what they have to say about the nature and source of the spiritual. However, it is important to note that when 'spiritual development' carries any religious connotations great care must be taken between adopting an ethical, as opposed to unethical, position on promoting it. It would be unethical for schools, other than church schools, to foster in their pupils religious beliefs. This would run the risk of overriding pupil autonomy. However, it could be considered ethical for schools to promote spiritual truths which are embodied in the various world religions so long as no attempt was made to indoctrinate pupils into the world religions themselves. The world's religions are united in emphasising spiritual attributes and in the search that human beings have for a sense of meaning and purpose in life. Religions are also united in relating this search for meaning with ultimate reality or God. It can be argued that schools are denying their pupils their educational entitlement if they fail to put them in contact with this rich religious heritage. Whatever definition of the spiritual schools accept, it is important that they are clear what they are talking about if the term is not to be hijacked by particular party interests who would like to promote their own specific brand.

Appropriate conditions for spiritual development

Schools, as institutions, need to provide appropriate conditions for the promotion of spiritual development:

> Just as such biological development requires appropriate conditions – to do with such things as climate and soil in the case of plants – so, the (Ofsted) report claims, the personal development of pupils demands a favourable 'climate and soil' . . . provided and promoted by the school.
>
> (White 1994: 370)

People are becoming aware that every institution or social structure (be it a school, business, etc.) has its own unique corporate personality, its own ethos and ambience (Bradford 1995: 55). Businesses speak of 'corporate cultures'. Businesses and schools are formulating their 'Mission Statement' in which they clarify their goals and ideals. 'We are beginning to recognise that you cannot change an institution without dealing with its unseen but palpably real spirituality' (Wink 1994: 18).

Schools do not have to be conscious about their unseen spirituality for it to be real. However, if they are not conscious of their spirituality it may be that they are unconsciously passing on the predominant spirit of the age.

> There are already indications that if schools rest content with attempting to develop knowledge and skills only and do not attend to the varied spiritual needs and nature of pupils purposefully, then their pupils are likely to become prey to the spirit of the age which is often only to do with consumerism, personal, political and economic exploitation and an impoverishment of what it can mean to be or become human.
>
> (Bradford Inspection and Consultancy Services 1990)

At a time when current educational jargon is littered with concepts such as league tables and Ofsted inspections it is easy for education to become compartmentalised into subject areas, as is captured by the following tale:

One spring afternoon when Sam Keen was six or seven years old he saw a Summer Warbler building its nest. He was sitting in school doing his writing exercises. Fascinated by this activity he just watched and neglected his school work. Mrs Jones, his teacher, kept him behind after school to finish his letters. Later he understood that her theory of education said, in effect: 'The quest for wisdom, for identity, for ecstasy, like Summer Warblers, must remain outside the classroom.' She was wrong. It must not.

(Webster 1993a: 362)

An education without attention to the spiritual and moral is not education, it is simply training.

(Wood 1995: 5)

A principal of a school in the USA recognised this when he sent the following letter, written by a Jewish concentration camp survivor, to his teachers on the first day of term:

Dear Teacher,
I am a survivor of a concentration camp.
My eyes saw what no man should witness:
Gas chambers built by learned engineers
Children poisoned by educated physicians,
Infants killed by trained nurses,
Women and babies shot and burned by high school and college graduates.

So I am suspicious of education.
My request is – help your students become human.
Your efforts must never produce learned monsters, skilled psychopaths, educated Eichmanns.
Reading, writing, arithmetic are important only if they serve to make our children more human.

(Lovelace 1993: 139)

Part of what it means to be human, as opposed to merely animal, is to be a spiritual being, and the promotion of the spiritual development of pupils happens both within the subject matter and within the relationships and pedagogical styles which are adopted in schools, a point recognised by Ofsted: 'A major part is also played by the relationships that are established in a school . . . Judgements should be based on evidence from the whole curriculum and the day-to-day life of the school, *including the examples set by adults*' (Ofsted 1995a: 89, my italics). Webster draws attention to the fact that the spiritual dynamic is especially evident in the relationships teachers have with pupils and the methodologies they adopt, what is elsewhere referred to as the general ethos and climate of the school. The centrality in education of the relationship between teachers and pupils is testified to by the general experience of many pupils who will remember their relationships with teachers long after they have forgotten the subject matter of lessons. At the heart of education is the meeting of persons, which meeting can raise 'the mystery of both . . . the teaching relationship can be a means of hallowing being' (Webster 1993b:

132). As the letter from the concentration camp survivor testifies, teachers should be more than mere transmitters of information. Instead, they relate with their pupils as one human being to another; they provide role models, however unwittingly, of what it means to be human. This is no small task to be undertaken lightly.

The methodologies which teachers adopt in their teaching can contribute greatly to promoting the spiritual development of pupils. Lessons which are not merely transmitting facts and skills but are full of exploration and problem-solving testify to the fact that much of life is an ongoing exploration, which causes people to marvel. 'Behind such methods stand teachers who can marvel in living, who continue to engage in reflective reasoning and whose lives are wonder journeys, parts of which are made with their young people' (Webster 1993b: 133). Elsewhere he writes, 'Unless they [teachers] have asked what kind of a story their's is, it will be difficult to help others recognize "a timelessness within time" in their stories' (Webster 1993a: 360). At the heart of this exchange and journey are teachers who transmit their love of their subject and of life in general.

School policies

Many schools are choosing to write a policy statement on SMSC. When developing the policy, three key issues are paramount. These are the need to consult, the provision of a rationale to support the proposed framework and a strategy to put policy into practice. Since the spiritual development of pupils is something in which all should be able to participate, all need to be consulted and an agreed approach reached. A clear rationale will be seen in having aims and objectives which are communicated to all participants. All parties should understand the intentions of spiritual development from the outset. The policy should be practical and should match rhetoric and reality. It should inform good practice and be viewed as a working document.

The following is an example of one school that has included the following statements in its policy document on promoting the spiritual development of pupils:

- Encouraging pupils to recognise the exciting possibilities of the great questions of existence.
- Encouraging pupils to express their thoughts on the major questions relating to existence.
- The consideration of the meaning of Commitment, Motivation, Truth and Revelation in relation to religious belief and the life of the individual.
- Helping pupils to eliminate their own prejudices towards the consideration of a spiritual dimension to existence.
- Encouraging pupils to express their thoughts on their place as human beings in relation to the world, either from a religious or secular perspective.
- Encouraging pupils to value the possibility of elements of human existence which are not provable.

- Giving pupils the opportunity to examine the variety of ways in which different cultures seek a spiritual dimension to life.
- Giving pupils the opportunity to examine their own emotions in relation to the world around them.
- Attempting to encourage pupils to develop some sense of the meaning of life which can act as a foundation to be developed and modified through later life.

(Francis 1995)

The contribution of individual subjects

The *Annual Report* of Her Majesty's Chief Inspector (HMCI) for 1994–95 indicated that a lot of work still needed to be done in many schools in order to promote the spiritual development of pupils:

> Most, if not all, of the National Curriculum subjects should contribute to pupils' spiritual development. In practice, this potential is exploited only rarely. Too little time is allowed for reflection on issues which pupils could relate to themselves and their life in the wider community.

(Ofsted 1995b)

Opportunities for spiritual development need to be clearly identified to the pupils, otherwise there is a good chance that they may not notice then and have opportunities to reflect upon them. As one inspector comments, pupils are often 'enthusiastic to search both "beneath and above the surface of things"' (Rose 1995: 8).

The following are a few suggestions on how some individual subject areas can promote the spiritual development of pupils.

Science

When, for example, pupils use microscopes and telescopes they are drawn to ask questions about those things which fall beyond their normal sight. Study of the lives of scientists themselves point to a transcendence which inspires them. Some of the great scientists have said that their best ideas have come to them in flashes of inspiration. For example, Pasteur's discovery of the cause of anthrax and Einstein's intuition which led to the theory of relativity came in moments of illumination.

Creative arts and literature

These subjects are ideal for promoting reflection and creativity. Many writers in literature explore spiritual themes, and their literature has often been the vehicle for discussing questions of life and death. Great artists, musicians and poets talk about being inspired. The poet John Betjeman, in an interview on television, said 'I regard myself as not writing my own verse, but as a sieve, through which things come; sometimes a thing presses down, and you've got to do it.' Their work testifies to longings and visions which lie beyond the grasp of human intellect.

History

When considering historical events is it not possible to explore the motivations behind peoples' actions, the spiritual values and beliefs which have affected their attitudes and behaviour? In recent years, history has certainly taken more account of how ordinary people lived through great events and came to terms with them. Pupils can be encouraged to question their own emotions regarding the ways things were and currently are. Furthermore, through the study of concepts such as change and continuity in history, pupils are drawn into considering how people's worldviews have changed.

Religious education

The *Inspection Schedule* points to the 'significant contribution' which religious education can make to a pupil's spiritual development:

> Inspectors might consider, for example, whether pupils are encouraged to: consider life's fundamental questions and how religious teaching can relate to them; respond to such questions with reference to the teachings and practices of religions as well as from their own experience and viewpoint; and reflect on their own beliefs or values in the light of what they are studying in religious education.
>
> (Ofsted 1995a: 90)

This clearly echoes the aims of religious education as stated in the Model Syllabuses proposed by the School Curriculum and Assessment Authority (SCAA 1994: 4)

> How can the subject(s) you are studying contribute to the spiritual development of pupils? What beliefs, values, attitudes and behaviour does your subject encourage?
>
> In what sense can the methodology you employ to teach your subject help to promote the spiritual development of pupils?

Inspecting the spiritual

On the basis of what has already been said about the nature of spiritual development it will be obvious that the inspection of how a school is promoting it will not be a straightforward matter. When Professor Stewart Sutherland was HM Chief Inspector of Schools he gave an address in which he talked about the implications of inspecting the spiritual dimension of pupils' education. He recalled an apocryphal story from the world of the arts, in which a distinguished symphony orchestra was experiencing significant financial difficulties. A firm of consultants was employed to diagnose the problem and suggest a way forward. The orchestra was visited during one of their rehearsals and the following report was submitted:

> My first visit to an orchestra rehearsal has provided early but con-
> clusive evidence of significant weaknesses in management in the
> running of the orchestra.
>
> In the first place overmanning has reached dangerous levels: whereas
> in well-run quartets (see our book *The Financing of the Arts in the
> 1990s*, chapter 2, *The Cost-effectiveness of the Piano-less Quartet*) one
> violin is quite adequate for the elaboration of the violin part, this par-
> ticular orchestra had a First and a Second violin, each of whom was
> shadowed by at least nine other violinists. I regret to report, that the
> same was true of the violas and cello, and that there were no less than
> eight double-basses. This set a very poor example to the brass and
> wind sections of the orchestra, where there were also clear examples
> of over-manning.
>
> There were also many examples of lack of decisiveness in senior
> management. Most blatantly, the opening theme of the symphony
> was played not just once, but four times. On each occasion there were
> variations which suggested to your consultants that the management
> were incapable of forming clear corporate strategies and sticking to
> them. Hence the inefficient and repetitive rerunning of variations on
> old themes at a time in the rehearsal cycle so close to final performance.
>
> If all of the above symptomatic weaknesses are confronted as a
> matter of urgency, then perhaps the composer of the piece, a man
> called Schubert, might have time to finish the symphony before it is
> performed on the seventh of next month.
>
> (Sutherland 1993)

Although this story is apocryphal it helps us to reflect that maybe when we are asking people to inspect the world of the arts and the spiritual some of the normal performance indicators are not appropriate tools. Similarly, it may help to make a distinction between what schools are doing to provide pupils with the opportunities to explore beliefs, values and ultimate questions – through its curriculum, ethos and extra-curriculum – and actually inspecting the process of spiritual development of pupils.

When inspectors evaluate what schools are doing to promote the spiritual development of their pupils they look at the range and quality of the schools' provision to encourage such development:

- through the values and attitudes the school identifies, upholds and fosters. The *Inspection Schedule* states that 'Effective provision for spiritual development depends on a curriculum and approaches to teaching which embody clear values' (Ofsted 1995a: 89) which are expressed through a school's aims and are evident in practice.
- through religious education, acts of collective worship and other assemblies. The *Inspection Schedule* states that 'Evaluation should focus on whether acts of worship are well planned and encourage pupils to explore questions about meaning and purpose, values and beliefs' (Ofsted 1995a: 90).
- through extra-curricular activities;

- through the general ethos and climate of the school. 'Effective provision for spiritual development . . . relies on teachers receiving and valuing pupils' ideas' (Ofsted 1995a: 89).
- Relationships will be open and consistent; 'pupils will be confident and treat each other with mutual respect . . . [the school's ethos] values imagination, inspiration and contemplation, and encourages pupils to ask questions about meaning and purpose' (Ofsted 1993: 15–16).

They also consider how pupils are responding to this provision. This is where the difficulty lies, as the above story of the orchestra makes clear. Is it ethically appropriate, or even pragmatically possible, for schools to assess the inner spiritual life of its pupils? Whereas it might be possible to inspect the development, for example, of such historical skills as understanding, analysis of data and empathy, how does one go about assessing the spiritual health of pupils, where we are talking about attitudes, beliefs and values? Recently, Ofsted has shifted its emphasis away from the assessment of children's spiritual development to assessment of how the school is promoting this development (Woods and Woods 1996: 4). It could be questioned whether this is merely to side-step the difficulties of trying to assess children's spiritual development.

There is a cognitive content in exploring attitudes, beliefs and values. When looking at what a school is doing to make provision for the spiritual development of pupils, inspectors may evaluate pupils' knowledge and understanding of how world faiths answer spiritual questions through their beliefs and practices. They may consider pupils' understanding of different ways of understanding the universe, scientific, religious and historical. They can also evaluate to what extent pupils understand how other people have answered life's existential questions, for example, how other people have confronted suffering and death, and found meaning.

There is a further difficulty: there needs to be discussion of what it means to talk about 'development' in relation to the spiritual. The concept of linear movement is too simplistic; the spiritual development of any person is by nature a long-term process, and does not lend itself to 'snapshot' evaluation. It is characterised by highs and lows, progression and regression and individuals may function at a number of levels over a period of time, as is testified to by the lives of many famous spiritual writers. Furthermore, spiritual development may not be observable until one can see the development of a life retrospectively.

References

Bradford Inspection and Consultancy Services (1990) *The Spiritual Area of Experience: A Framework for Development*. Bradford: BICS.

Bradford, J. (1995) *Caring for the Whole Child*. London: The Children's Society.

Francis, H. (1995) *Religious Education Department Policy on SMSC*. Oxfordshire: Didcot Girl's School.

Gent, B. (1989) *School Worship: Perspectives, Principles and Practice*. Derby: CEM.

Great Britain (1988) *Education Reform Act*. London: HMSO.

Halstead, J.M. (1996) Editorial, *SPES*, 4: 1–3.

Hay, D. (1982) *Exploring Inner Space*. London: Penguin.

Hemming, J. (1969). 'Individual Morality', Nelson citing A.H. Maslow, 'The Good Life of the Self-actualising Person', *Humanist*, 27: 4.

King, U. (1985) 'Spirituality in Secular Society: Recovering a Lost Dimension', *British Journal of Religious Education*, 7(3) 136–39.

Lovelace, A. (1993) *The Practical Assembly Guide*. Oxford: Heinemann.

Mello, A. de (1985) *One Minute Wisdom*. New York: Doubleday Image.

Mello, A. de (1989) *The Heart of the Enlightened*. Glasgow: Collins.

Mott-Thornton, K. (1996) 'Experience, Critical Realism and the Schooling of Spirituality', in R. Best (ed.) *Education, Spirituality and the Whole Child*. London: Cassell.

O'Donnell, K. (1992) *I Wonder*. London: Hodder and Stoughton.

Office for Standards in Education (Ofsted) (1993) *Handbook for the Inspection of Schools*. London: HMSO.

Office for Standards in Education (Ofsted) (1995a) *Guidance on the Inspection of Secondary Schools*. London: HMSO.

Office for Standards in Education (Ofsted) (1995b). *The Annual Report of the HMCI for 1994–1995*. London: HMSO.

Rose, J. (1995) 'School Provision for Pupils' Spiritual and Moral Development', *SPES*, 2: 7–8.

School Curriculum and Assessment Authority (SCAA) (1994) *Model Syllabuses for Religious Education: Model 1*. London: SCAA.

School Curriculum and Assessment Authority (SCAA) (1996) *Review of Qualifications for 16–19 Year Olds: Summary Report*. London: SCAA.

Sutherland, S. (1993) 'Educating the Spirit?' Public lecture St George's Chapel, Windsor, 4 June.

Taylor, E. (1994) 'Desperately Seeking Spirituality', *Psychology Today*, 27(6): 54–68.

Webster, D. (1993a) 'A Spiritual Dimension for Education?' in L. Francis and D. Lankshear (eds) *Christian Perspectives for Education*. Leominster: Gracewing.

Webster, D. (1993b) 'Being Aflame: Spirituality in County and Church Schools', in L. Francis and D. Lankshear (eds) *Christian Perspectives for Education*. Gracewing.

White, J. (1994) 'Instead of Ofsted: A Critical Discussion of Ofsted on Spiritual, Moral, Social and Cultural Development', *Cambridge Journal of Education*, 24, 3.

Wink, W. (1994) *Beat the System*. London: Third Way.

Wood, T. (1995) 'The Spiritual Dimension', *SPES*, 2: 4–5.

Woods, P. and Woods, G. (1996) 'The Promotion of Spiritual Development: Ofsted Inspections of Non-denominational Primary Schools', *SPES*, 4: 4–12.

Further reading

Best, R. (ed.) (1996) *Education, Spirituality and the Whole Child*. London: Cassell.

Bradford, J. (1995) *Caring for the Whole Child: A Holistic Approach to Spirituality*. London: The Children's Society.

SCAA (1995) *Spiritual and Moral Development Discussion*. SCAA Discussion Paper Number 3. London: SCAA.

SCAA (1996) *Education for Adult Life: The Spiritual and Moral Development of Young People*. SCAA Discussion Paper No 6.

SPES, A magazine for the study of Spiritual, Moral and Cultural Values in Education, The RIMSCUE Centre, Faculty of Arts and Education, University of Plymouth.

The CHARIS Project produces classroom resources for teachers who want to teach their subjects in a way which more effectively integrates the spiritual and moral dimensions. Already published: *Charis Deutsch, Charis Francais, Charis English, Charis Mathematics*, Stapleford House Education Centre, Wesley Place, Stapleford, Nottingham NG9 8DP.

18

Teaching for health: health education and health promotion in schools

Faith Hill

Introduction

Health education is generally thought to be a 'good thing'. The National Curriculum Council describes it as 'an essential part of every pupil's curriculum' (NCC 1990) and the Department of Health expects schools to play a major role in working towards the *Health of the Nation* (DOH 1992). As a newly qualified teacher, whatever your subject, you will be expected to teach health education through the informal curriculum and through your role as a tutor. You will also have responsibility for health related topics within your curriculum area. This chapter will help you to consider your role within health education, providing an opportunity to reflect on some of the more controversial aspects and offering some general background and guidance to teaching health related subjects. First, it is necessary to be clear what we mean by 'health'.

Health is . . .

Health is a general term with many different meanings. If you ask any group of teachers what 'health' means to them, you will get a wide range of responses. For some, it refers to the absence of disease and for others it is concerned with more positive attributes, such as personal fitness or total well-being. The most often quoted definition is from the Constitution of the World Health Organization (WHO 1946): 'Health is a state of complete physical, mental and social well-being, and not merely the absence of disease or infirmity.' This is an important definition for teachers because it places the emphasis on the quality rather than on the length of life. Young people are rarely interested in living to be 'old'! It is also an important definition because it highlights the multidimensional nature of health. Health educators and health promoters think of health not as a single commodity but as a rich and interrelated tapestry, involving mental, physical, spiritual and emotional aspects, and concerning groups, communities and the environment as well as individuals. What does 'health' mean to you?

Models of health education

Having looked at what we mean by health, we can move on to considering what constitutes health education. There are a number of different models or approaches to health education. The first is often described as a 'bio-medical model' and is based very largely on medical approaches to health and illness. It is concerned with instructing individuals on how to live their lives in such a way as to avoid becoming ill. It is often criticised for being too authoritarian and 'top-down' in its approach, and for ignoring all the complex issues involved in making real life choices about health issues. In schools, this model has been linked with 'Just Say No' campaigns and with the 'Shock Horror' approach which seeks to prevent pupils behaving in certain ways by presenting gruesome and sometimes one-sided information. Most research suggests that this approach proves counter-productive in the long term.

The second model of health education is known as the 'educational model' as it is based on the traditional principles of liberal education. It suggests that schools should provide young people with the facts about health and leave the decisions to them. This approach has its attractions to schools. It fits with a philosophy of personal freedom and rational decision-making. Teachers can ignore controversial, moral and ethical issues. It is easily accommodated within traditional teaching methods and can be assessed like any other subject.

However, the educational approach has a number of problems. First, health is such a complex matter that the issues often cannot be presented as straightforward 'facts'. Many important areas of health are highly controversial and young people need opportunities to consider a range of values and opinions as well as support in identifying and clarifying their own positions. They also need more than factual information to enable them to make and carry out healthy decisions. They need a range of skills, including decision-making, interpersonal, and those concerned with self-awareness, managing emotions and handling stress. Research has shown that for young people to adopt healthy lifestyles they also need a positive sense of self-esteem. Approaches to health education that address these concerns, emphasising the importance and interdependence of work on knowledge, skills and attitudes, are often described as falling within the 'empowerment model'. This model is most popular with professional health educators and underpins many of the projects designed for schools by the Health Education Authority (see below).

The final model of health education is the 'radical model'. This approach recognises that poverty, poor housing and unemployment are major causes of ill-health. It is concerned with the many factors that affect health which are beyond the control of the individual. This includes the physical environment at both local and global levels. The 'radical model' also addresses the effects on health of advertising, business interests and legislation. This model of health education stresses the importance of collective action to promote health. It is the most 'political' of the models and, so far, plays only a small role in health education in schools.

As a teacher, each time you are asked to teach a health related topic you will have to choose between these different models. Which approach do you think you would be most comfortable with, and which would be most useful for your students? How could you combine different approaches?

Health promoting schools

A new approach to health education is being co-ordinated by the European Network of Health Promoting Schools (ENHPS). The Health Education Authority is supporting a number of schools in England that are taking part in the ENHPS initiative. The idea is to develop schools as centres promoting the health and well-being of pupils, staff, parents and the local community. The approach takes a holistic view of the nature of health, including mental, spiritual and physical well-being. It also recognises the importance of the school environment, physical and social, in contributing to the health and well-being of pupils and staff.

The initiative builds on the whole school approach to health education which recognises that the messages young people receive about health are not confined to the formal, health education curriculum. Much health education occurs in informal ways, for example, through extra-curricular activities and chance discussions in the playground. It also occurs through the hidden curriculum. For example, the quality and nature of interpersonal relationships within a school will not only give young people messages about how to relate to others but will also influence their sense of personal worth and self-esteem. Unfortunately, many of the messages that young people receive through the formal curriculum may be rapidly diluted by the ethos of the whole school. You will commonly find young people being taught about personal hygiene in schools with very inadequate toilet facilities. Nutrition education is rarely reflected by the choice provided in school canteens, and smoking education is often undermined by the fog of smoke surrounding the staff room!

To be truly effective, the whole school approach and the health promoting school initiative require radical changes in the way most schools are run and financed. However, some schools are moving in this direction and it is perhaps useful to think in terms of schools being more or less health promoting. In practice, you will come across many schools that are far from health promoting. As a newly qualified teacher, you will need to consider the type of school you wish to work in and how far you personally want to adopt a health-promoting role.

Curriculum issues

As was mentioned above, health education is defined as a cross-curricular theme by the National Curriculum Council and, although not a statutory subject in its own right, it is seen as playing an important part in contributing to the statutory duty on schools to:

> provide a broad and balanced curriculum which:
> (a) promotes the spiritual, moral, cultural, mental and physical development of pupils at the school and of society;
> (b) prepares pupils for the opportunities, responsibilities and experiences of adult life.
>
> (NCC 1990)

Government guidelines are offered to schools in a key document entitled *Curriculum Guidance 5: Health Education* (NCC 1990). This gives general guidance on health education in the curriculum and also spells out nine key areas of study to be included at each of the four key stages:

- substance use and misuse
- sex education
- family life education
- safety
- health-related exercise
- food and nutrition
- personal hygiene
- environmental aspects of health education
- psychological aspects of health education

(NCC 1990)

For each area, more details are given for each of the key stages. For example, at Key Stage 3, in the area of the psychological aspects of health education, pupils should:

- know how labelling and stereotyping can have a negative effect on mental health;
- be able to receive praise and encouragement in order to promote the self-esteem and self-confidence essential to mental health;
- understand the emotional changes which take place during puberty; understand differences in maturation and have a positive self-image.

(NCC 1990)

From this one example it can be seen that the document supports the 'empowerment' approach and is concerned with skills and attitudes as well as the acquisition of knowledge.

The reason for revisiting each area at every key stage is to build upon and develop the work that pupils have already covered. It is very important to start with the needs and maturity of young people and to ensure that curriculum planning takes into account their developmental stage and previous learning. For example, sex education is included at each key stage because there are different aspects that need to be introduced as the young people grow towards adulthood. This process of programme planning to enable increasing complexity is referred to as a spiral curriculum and is crucial to effective health education.

Planning a spiral curriculum for health education as a cross-curricular theme is a daunting prospect and many schools faced with an already overloaded curriculum fall short of the ideals described in *Curriculum Guidance 5*. As a subject teacher you need to be aware of the areas that come within your discipline and how these are linked in a developmental way. You also need to be familiar with the relevant work that is going on in other subjects and in other areas of the curriculum such as PSE (personal and social education), PSHE (personal, social and health education) or other tutorial programmes. As a tutor you need to be aware of subject specific health education within the school and be able to identify the links with the pastoral curriculum.

Sex education

There is not space here to examine each of the nine areas of the curriculum in detail but it is important to say something about sex education because of its unique position within the curriculum. Many student teachers and, indeed, many experienced teachers are reticent to teach about sex and sexuality. However, in many ways, teaching sex education is no different from teaching in any other sensitive area of the curriculum (see below).

Sex education differs from the other eight areas in its statutory position within the school curriculum. This has been set out in legislation by the 1993 Education Act and is explained in the DFE document, Circular number 5/94, *Education Act 1993: Sex Education in Schools* (DFE 1994). In relation to all maintained secondary schools in England, the main points are:

- Only the biological aspects of human sexual behaviour are to be taught within the National Curriculum, and HIV, AIDS and other sexually transmitted diseases are specifically excluded.
- Other aspects of sex education, including education about HIV and AIDS, are to be taught within a separate sex education programme, which must be offered to all registered pupils.
- The governors of the school are responsible for the content and organisation of the sex education programme, and must maintain a written policy document on sex education within the school.
- Parents have a right to withdraw their children from all or part of the sex education programme, other than the biological aspects taught within the National Curriculum.

It is clear from this that parents may take pupils out of sex education lessons but, in fact, very few parents are taking this option. However, it does mean that schools must organise the curriculum in such a way as to allow for the possibility. Teachers need to be aware of the restrictions imposed by the Act and to ensure that they stay within the school policy.

You should ask to see the policy document and any other guidelines used in the school, and should ask for clarification on any points that are unclear to you. One point that new teachers often ask about relates to Section 28 of the Local Government Act 1988 which prohibits local authorities from promoting homosexuality. Circular 5/94 makes it clear that this does not apply to teachers or governing bodies acting on their own behalf (DFE 1994: 19).

Classroom strategies

the teaching methods used are as important as the content of the lessons . . . the participation of pupils is essential . . . Much of the teaching in health education will be based on the active involvement of pupils.

You may or may not agree with this quote, but it is important to consider interactive teaching methods when planning health education. It may surprise you that the quote is not rhetoric from a 'trendy' educationalist, but from *Curriculum Guidance 5* (NCC 1990: 7). The importance of teaching methods is stressed over and over again in health education texts. This is partly because of the interdependence of knowledge, skills and attitudes discussed earlier. It is also because of the sensitive nature of much health education. So, when planning health education strategies where should you start?

As with any other area of the curriculum, you should begin by clarifying your aims, objectives and learning outcomes. Then, the most important issue to consider is sensitivity. Whatever health education topic you are covering, there will be aspects that may be particularly sensitive to one or more of your pupils. This may be obvious with topics such as sexuality, where pupils may have been abused or be facing difficult personal decisions. It is also true of less controversial topics. Nutrition, for example, can bring up concerns about body image, anorexia, mealtimes without family members because of bereavement or divorce, religious beliefs and a host of other potentially sensitive issues. However good a teacher you are, you can never hope to know all the personal concerns of all your pupils, so you should handle all health education topics with care. That means taking time to consider possible reactions to the work; being alert to signs of embarrassment or distress; being clear about your role and the extent to which you can offer support in and beyond the classroom; and knowing where to refer pupils for help when necessary.

In order to prepare your class for handling sensitive issues and to enable them to participate in group activities, it is important to establish a safe learning environment. This means actively building a climate of trust and empathy, where each individual feels involved and valued by the group. Most of the materials mentioned at the end of the chapter offer activities for establishing a positive classroom climate. These include ice-breakers, relationship and group building tasks and problem solving activities. Of all these activities, the most crucial to health education is the development of groundrules. You should encourage every class to negotiate and agree groundrules, and these should be monitored and reviewed regularly by the whole group.

Having established a good working environment, you will be able to try out a wide range of teaching methods suitable to health education. These include formal information giving, audio-visual and other presentations, visits and the involvement of visitors. They also include interactive group methods, such as small-group discussions, games, simulations and role-plays. Schools are also experimenting with peer-group learning techniques and drama presentations for some areas of health education. All of these methods can be useful and, by varying your approach, you can help to stimulate the pupils' interest and ensure they have some fun! It is then important to *process* the lesson, drawing out and reinforcing the learning from whatever method you have been using.

Support for health education

One really good piece of news for anyone starting to teach health education is that there is a wide range of support available. This comes partly in the form of teaching packs and other classroom materials that can save you a great deal of time in preparing lessons. Many of them have been funded by the Health Education Authority and have been very carefully piloted in schools before publication. Some of the most recent and useful materials are listed at the end of the chapter under Further Reading, and these are full of interesting ideas for lesson planning and details on how to prepare yourself to teach in this area. Some have hand-outs for you to photocopy.

A word of warning, however. There is a vast amount of material on the market and not all of it is useful or appropriate for use in schools. This is particularly true of many videos that have been made for health education over the last few years. You should always check the source of the materials and whether they are presenting a biased or inaccurate view. You should also consider whether materials will be appropriate for your groups in terms of age, sex, ethnicity, culture, school guidelines, and so on. Always preview videos and familiarise yourself fully with other materials.

Support is also available in the form of individuals and agencies that will visit schools to help with health education programmes. This can range from the local GP addressing an assembly through to drama groups running sessions on HIV and AIDS. Visitors can make a very positive contribution but are always far more effective when the pupils are actively involved in the visit. It is also important to be clear why you are involving outsiders, how they are contributing to the overall programme and whether they have the skills to interact well with young people. Visitors have been traditionally involved in sex education and all school sex education policies should state the school's position on this.

The most valuable support that you are likely to come across will be your local Health Education or Health Promotion Unit (their address will be in the telephone directory). Funded by the local health authority, the unit will have at least one person responsible for health education and promotion with young people who will be able to advise you on programme planning, available materials and local concerns. The units are unlikely to offer direct work with pupils but can often offer a variety of training for staff, parents and governors. The units also have materials available on loan and may well be able to organise free delivery of up-to-date resources to your school.

Conclusion

Health education and heath promotion are important to the development of all pupils, and inevitably involve all teachers and most whole school issues. Teaching particular health topics can be very challenging and demands careful planning and sensitive handling. Teachers have to choose from a number of different approaches and have to satisfy the demands of national legislation and school guidelines. However, there is a lot of support available and working in such a significant area of the curriculum can be very rewarding. Teaching for health can make a real difference to the lives of young people.

References

Department for Education (DFE) (1994) *Education Act 1993: Sex Education in Schools.* Circular 5/94. London: Department for Education.

Department of Health (DOH) (1992) *The Health of the Nation.* London: Department of Health/HMSO.

National Curriculum Council (NCC) (1990) *Curriculum Guidance 5. Health Education.* York: National Curriculum Council.

World Health Organization (WHO) (1946) *Constitution.* New York: World Health Organization.

Further reading

Anderson, J. (1994a) *Introducing Health Skills for Life. Health Education and PSE Materials for Key Stage 3.* London: Nelson.

Anderson, J. (1994b) *Introducing Health Skills for Life. Health Education and PSE Materials for Key Stage 4.* London: Nelson.

Clarity Collective (1989) *Taught not Caught. Strategies for Sex Education.* Wisbech: Learning Development Aids.

Department for Education (DFE) (1995) *Drug Prevention and Schools.* Circular 4/95. London: Department for Education.

Emmett, V. (1994) The future of health education, *Health Education*, (3): 13–17.

Gray, G. and Hill, F. (1990–1992) *What is Health?* (Series of seven booklets on health topics). Oxford: Oxford University Press.

Gray, G. and Hill, F. (1994) *Health Education for 16–19s.* Health Action Pack. London: Health Education Authority.

Health Education Authority (HEA) (1991) *Health and Self.* London: Health Education Authority.

Heaven, P.C.L. (1996) *Adolescent Health. The Role of Individual Difference.* London: Routledge.

Henry, L., Shucksmith, J. and Philip, K. (1995) *Educating for Health. School and Community Approaches with Adolescents*. London: Cassell.

Lions and TACADE (1995) *Skills for Life – a Whole School Approach to Personal and Social Development for 11–16-year-olds*. Manchester: TACADE.

Stears, D. and Clift, S. (1995) Health, sex and drug education: rhetoric and realities, in J. Ahier and A. Ross (eds) *The Social Subjects Within the Curriculum*. London: Falmer Press.

Deryn Watson

Never in education has so much interest, investment and sheer hype been associated with any subject as has been the case with information technology (IT). From the late 1970s there has been substantial central and local government investment, supplemented by funds from parent/teacher associations (PTAs) and other sources, to put computers into every school. Following a series of initiatives, targeted on hardware acquisition, software development and inservice teacher training, information technology was identified as a component of the National Curriculum in 1989, a new subject area in its own right, with skills and competencies to be delivered and assessed (DES 1990). To achieve this, schools have been exhorted to develop a whole school policy for the use of IT. One perspective on the development of IT in education is that it has been an enormously successful and dynamic time. A biennial series of statistical bulletins shows that the number of computers in schools and the number of teachers who report using them has increased regularly since 1988 (DES 1989; DFE 1991; 1993; 1995). An alternative perspective, which I propose here, is that this period has been characterised by a confusion of purpose and lack of clarity of objectives.

In essence the use of computers in education has created some fundamental dilemmas. The overriding problem is a dichotomy of purpose. Is IT a subject in its own right, with a knowledge and skill base; or is IT a tool to be used mainly for the learning of other subjects? Official policy and curriculum documents suggest both (HMI 1989; DES 1990; DFE 1995), yet few schools are able to achieve either to their own, or Ofsteds, satisfaction. Indeed research indicates that IT use in schools is not commonplace, and that there are still a number of barriers to the incorporation of IT into the syllabus (Watson 1993; Gardner *et al.* 1992, Watson and Tinsley 1995).

Associated with a confusion over purpose are issues related to hardware availability and access, and teachers' perceptions of the relationship between using computers and their pedagogic intentions. In essence many teachers may espouse the use of the computer to assist learning, and indeed use IT for their own personal work, but in reality few use it with classes on a regular basis. Using IT on a day-to-day basis, for pupils and for teachers, is still the exception not the norm.

Dichotomy of purpose

Pedagogic vs vocational rationales

As early as the mid-1970s Richard Hooper, director of the first national government initiative, stated that there was a distinct difference between teaching people *with* computers, and teaching people *about* computers (Hooper and Toye 1975). During the 1980s, there was a proliferation of courses in computer science and computer studies for pupils at both 14 and 16+. Teaching about the computer, its architecture, systems design and programming, gained attention, and made increasing demands upon the availability of the hardware. In contrast, the publication of a series of reports from subject associations, commissioned by the DES, highlighted the role of Information Technology for each subject area. The reports universally espoused the value of Computer Assisted Learning (CAL) for their discipline.

But this distinction has become increasingly blurred, until the role of the computer as a learning resource has become subsumed by a notion of 'information technology' skills and competencies. Today, computers are used in schools mainly for two main groups – blocks of year 7, 8 and 9 classes doing 'information skills' courses, learning to use a word processor or spreadsheet, and blocks of Business Information Skills (BIS) or Computer Studies GCSE examination classes. The relationship between these classes and the use of the computer to assist the learning of subjects, such as biology or geography, is tenuous. It is as if pupils are taught to drive a car theoretically, with six-week blocks of lessons, to use steering wheels, gears and brakes, but rarely actually take a vehicle onto the road for the purpose of travelling from A to B. How has this come about?

In part this is a reflection of an increasingly vocational agenda – IT is perceived as part of an equation that associates economic growth with modern technology (see Chapter 20 for a discussion of the vocational role of education). This places greater emphasis on the skills base than on a more fundamental pedagogic purpose (Hawkridge 1990). The blurring of the distinction between learning *about* (vocational) and *with* (pedagogic) has been reflected in three documents that lie at the core of current national perspectives of IT that now influence schools.

Information technology from 5–16

This HMI booklet, one of the 'Curriculum Matters' series, presents the dual perception as it 'sets out to help schools devise a coherent strategy for making effective use of IT, both in the enrichment of existing subjects and in learning about the technology itself'. Under the aims, it states clearly that:

> Although IT is only one of a host of important factors affecting society and schools today, it is unusual among current agencies of change in that it impinges directly on the learner at all ages; on the nature and content of study; and therefore on the curriculum and the teacher.
>
> (HMI 1989: 2)

It continues by laying out a clear framework of purpose for the use of IT in schools:

> Through the use of IT in the curriculum, schools will also be helping pupils become knowledgeable about the nature of information, comfortable with the new technology and able to exploit its potential. The aims of working with IT are:
>
> (i) to enrich and extend learning throughout the curriculum, using the technology to support collaborative learning, independent study and re-working of initial ideas as well as to enable pupils to work at a more demanding level by obviating some routine tasks;
> (ii) to help young people acquire confidence and pleasure using IT, become familiar with some everyday applications and be able to evaluate the technology's potential and limitations;
> (iii) to encourage the flexibility and openness of mind necessary to adjust to, and take advantage of, the ever-quickening pace of technological change, while being alert to the ethical implications and consequences for individuals and society;
> (iv) to harness the power of technology to help pupils with special educational needs or physical handicaps to increase their independence and develop their interests and abilities;
> (v) to help interested pupils undertake detailed study of computing and to design IT systems for solving problems.
>
> (HMI 1989: 2–3)

There are two distinct approaches incorporated here, with a pedagogic role at first being followed by vocational and somewhat technocentric aspects. These aims are supported by a detailed list of objectives and translated into specific issues that can be addressed. Geography for instance is described as 'one useful model of how IT concepts can be related to activities in various subject studies'. The aims are then converted into 'IT concepts and objectives', listed as communicating, data handling, modelling, and so on. These, by the end of the document, have become central, and a subject such as geography is demoted to being merely a context for delivery. Thus IT concepts and skills are defined as separate from CAL for subject-based learning.

Information technology in the National Curriculum

The dichotomy noted above continues in the National Curriculum Technology document (DES 1990); teachers are exhorted to use the computer in both roles, but at different stages one message appears to be more important than the other.

IT is defined thus:

> Pupils should be able to use information technology to:
> - communicate and handle information;
> - design, develop, explore and evaluate models of real or imaginary situations;
> - measure and control physical variables and movement.
>
> They should also be able to make informed judgements about the application and importance of information technology, and its effect on the quality of life.
>
> (DES 1990: 43)

These are in effect a condensed form of the IT concepts that the HMI document discussed above identified. The related programmes of study are then defined:

> In each key stage pupils should develop information technology capabilities through a range of curriculum activities which will:
> - develop confidence and satisfaction in the use of information technology;
> - broaden pupils' understanding of the effects of the use of information technology;
> - encourage the flexibility needed to take advantage of future developments in information technology;
> - enable pupils to become familiar with the computer keyboard;
> - encourage the development of perseverance;
> - enable pupils to take greater responsibility for their own learning, and provide opportunities for them to decide when it is appropriate to use information technology in their work.
>
> (DES 1990: 51)

Although related to the HMI aims, the vocational aspects are dominant and increasingly technocentric. It is difficult to relate many of these capabilities to a subject centred curriculum learning purpose. In the Teachers' Notes on IT in the National Curriculum (NCC 1991) IT is referred to as a tool in the curriculum with 'a number of functions'.

The Dearing changes

By 1994 it had become apparent that the attempt to maintain the dual role of IT as a tool to deliver the curriculum and as a subject with a conceptual and skills basis in its own right was under substantial strain. Following the Dearing review (see Chapter 2), IT became separated from the subject Technology (DFE 1995):

> IT capability is characterised by an ability to use effectively IT tools and information sources to analyse, process and present information, and to model, measure and control external events. This involves:

- using information sources and IT tools to solve problems;
- using IT tools and information sources, such as computer systems and software packages to support learning in a variety of contexts;
- understanding the implications of IT for working life and society. Pupils should be given opportunities, where appropriate, to develop and apply their IT capability in their study of National Curriculum subjects.

(DFE 1995: 1)

So after the familiar list of IT concepts and skills, the role of a tool to support subject based learning has been reduced to a mere recommendation.

This shift away from supporting subject based learning has been supported in other ways. The heavy investment during the 1970s and 1980s in the development of curriculum focused software has virtually ceased, with schools encouraged to use commercially based IT packages, a move that was criticised by the Parliamentary Office of Science and Technology (POST 1991) for both the reduction and inconsistency of a pedagogic agenda. Elsewhere, this has been referred to as the 'commodification' of education. Thus it would appear that the pedagogic notion of CAL has been made more diffuse by the increasingly vocational notion of separate concepts and skills of information technology. It is, I believe, this which has made for problems of understanding of the role of IT within schools, and for specific subjects.

The reality in schools

Reconciling the conflict

Most secondary schools have appointed IT co-ordinators with the brief to define an IT policy and to implement it. This involves tackling hardware and software resourcing, network maintenance and management, staff INSET, and reconciling the different perceptions of how, where and why IT should be used. Nor have the co-ordinators been able to start with a level playing field. Some schools have been active in CAL for many years, resulting in local patterns of use and resourcing highly dependent upon the interests and enthusiasms of particular staff. Because of the dictates of the National Curriculum, as outlined above, it is inevitable that the current overriding priority is ensuring that pupils are given opportunities to develop and apply IT skills progressively as they move through the school. But two central issues devolve from this: who is to provide the teaching for these IT skills and where will it happen?

The delivery of a regular IT skills course is hampered by the availability of hardware and the fact that pupils are often learning these skills in isolation. It is sad to see pupils use a spreadsheet without a genuine need to explore and model a relationship in the data they are manipulating. They need to learn 'IT skills' with a real task in mind and practice them regularly so that they become familiar and obvious skills to exercise and tools to use. This suggests that they should use these skills regularly in the normal subject-based classroom.

A number of IT co-ordinators in schools have focused on analysing the component parts of the IT curriculum and then negotiating or persuading different subject departments to deliver them. A familiar pattern is for history or geography to take on databases, English for word-processing, and science or mathematics for modelling. This apparently logical approach has hit a number of snags. First, a number of subject departments may indicate a theoretical willingness to take part, but in reality they find their existing timetable is already squashed with competing curriculum demands. Secondly, a number of staff have been reluctant IT users themselves, and have balked at taking on an IT teaching load. Even for confident IT users there have been problems. Where geography teachers may choose to use a database to encourage pupils to pose and test hypotheses about a topic, for example population growth, at the same time they are now being asked to teach about data retrieval and ensure that a specific and measurable IT capability is delivered. Such teachers using IT have added complexity and potential conflict of purpose in what is otherwise a clearly geographically focused agenda.

A further problem with this approach is that there is a danger of formalising IT delivery as being the responsibility of only some subjects. All the IT resources are focused on these, leaving isolated others which may want to use IT to assist learning in, for instance, art or foreign languages. There is little doubt that this approach is failing. The first survey of IT use in schools (DES 1989) showed that although half the teachers in secondary schools had been on initial awareness training, less than 25 per cent reported that they made significant use of computers, except for those teaching computer and business studies, and on average less than 10 per cent reported that IT made a substantial contribution to teaching and learning. The latest statistical bulletin (DFE 1995), still shows less than 10 per cent of teachers (apart from those of computer and business studies) reported IT making a substantial contribution to teaching and learning; little change in six years of policy, investment and training.

An alternative approach has been the development of the IT skill courses mentioned before, leading on to either BIS or computer studies GCSE classes. The IT co-ordinator and other staff are responsible for ensuring that all pupils attend these courses and so the statutory IT component is assured. But this means that all the focus of attention and resource is on the skills – that is, on the vocational aspect. Some schools have complicated and imaginative procedures in place to attempt to locate these skills classes within real subject needs – joint work schemes are produced, and often team teaching with a subject specialist and the IT specialist working together with the class. But in essence this approach equates IT lessons with English lessons; English as a subject is taught and there are also language across the curriculum initiatives, though the latter are rarely successful.

Neither policy is ideal, and their inadequacies explain the substantial criticisms of IT delivery by inspectors (Ofsted 1995). This highlights the problems that both approaches create. Underlying these approaches however are the related issues of resourcing and teachers' perceptions of the potential of IT for their subject. The reality of IT use in schools is more a reflection of these two concerns than the result of a co-ordinated implementation of whole school policy.

Computers and rooms

Computers originally arrived in schools as stand-alone microcomputers, and were often located in the classroom of an enthusiastic teacher. Provision rapidly expanded until there was a bookable computer room, which may or may not have been networked. There is evidence to suggest that the advent of networked rooms contributed to a decline in the amount of CAL in a school (Wellington 1988). Today there are usually in schools a couple of computer rooms, with other clusters of machines in subject specialist areas.

For many years the type and configuration of the hardware has been a dominant issue in the field, attracting heated arguments between the relative merits of rival machines. But talk of MS-DOS, speed of processing, multimedia, and now Internet access capabilities has for a long time caused IT to be synonymous with technical matters, and with the associated power base for those 'in the know' and who 'understand these things'. This has been both overtly and covertly damaging. Decisions about purchase and computer room layout have too frequently been made on the basis of technical specification, rather than also considering the nature and use of the educational software and applications available. More importantly, this has helped to falsely generate a sense of techno-phobia, a sense of not being part of the inner circle of those who know about and can use 'the machines'. This phobia, which teachers do not display in other fields where machines are involved, has developed into a subtle myth. There is increasing evidence that the myth is not actually about using the computer, but how to manage their use in the classroom situation. Many teachers own and use computers for their own work, but never use them in their classrooms.

The nub of the matter is of course that they are not using them in their classrooms – they are having to book a timetabled fixed resource and move the class there for a limited time (Watson 1990). It is ironic that limited time may be available for the very open-ended, exploratory work which demands flexibility. It is not the resource itself, but the restricted access to it, with all the related problems of pressure for everything to work correctly in the precious 50 minutes when you are in the room, that causes the problem. And the amount of time available for CAL users to book the rooms has been severely limited by the increase in the blocks of IT skills classes.

Schools do not have enough hardware to allow them to plan sensibly for coherent progression in IT skills used appropriately within curriculum settings. Learning with computers has severely declined in this climate. Schools are still relying on highly trained academic staff to act as both technicians for increasingly ageing hardware and to be co-ordinators of IT policy. This is clearly absurd. In the current resourcing and curriculum climate, schools are attempting to devise and implement IT policies that cannot be realistically delivered. Until there is a ratio of 1.5 machines to every pupil, and every teacher has a personal computer, it is unrealistic for schools to be asked to deliver a balanced IT curriculum. It is certainly impossible to do justice to the very real and important conceptual issues about the nature of information and communication handling, and their role in society, in the light of technological capability.

In the meantime, targeted provision for specific groups, and encouraging and building on existing pockets of use and excellence can be the only way forward. Interestingly, in two research studies carried out during the early 1990s, ImpacT (Watson 1993) and PLAIT (Morrison *et al.* 1993), little discernible difference in effect was established between classes with widely different resourcing. It was the use to which the computers were put, and in particular the amount of process-oriented material used, that appeared to have an impact on learning.

The subject teacher's perspective

Teachers wishing to explore the potential of IT for their subject have to invest much time exploring software and applications, often in isolation, and gain confidence in use within a classroom environment. They may need to move their class considerable distances to a timetabled computer laboratory. Success depends upon the considerable individual effort and enthusiasm that is required; success may be in the form of increased discussion and interest about the topic. Learning gains may not be as tangible and amenable to evaluation as the use of other resources. Evidence from research (Albalat and Ruiz 1995; Olson 1990; Veen 1995; Watson 1993) from classrooms in Spain, Canada, the Netherlands and England suggests that teachers who succeed tend to be those who can clearly relate the use of IT to their pedagogic strategy for their own subject.

It is the keen IT users who manage, despite considerable organisational difficulties, to obtain access to resources and who are flexible in their approach to its use. In particular it is these teachers who recognise and enjoy the pedagogic potential of IT because it relates to their own philosophical underpinnings about teaching and the nature of their subject. They are at home with CAL; they 'teach geography (or history, biology, art . . .) with computers' rather than 'deliver IT'.

But careful reading of the DFE statistics shows that such users make up only 10 per cent of the teaching population. This is supported by evidence that most students on initial teacher training courses, whether BEd or PGCE, do not find much exemplar use of IT in their tutoring schools (Dunn and Ridgeway 1991; Mellar and Jackson 1992). Since these teachers are the 10 per cent who do regularly use IT in their classes, it seems important to build IT policies around their success.

The computer as a learning resource

In order to illustrate the style of pedagogic use that these 10 per cent achieve, I report below from research on one teacher's use with one class that was part of the case study work of a larger national project (Watson 1993).

Background information

Fenners School is a large co-educational comprehensive school, with about 1300 pupils on roll, situated in a commuter village in the West Country.

The research was undertaken between 1989 and 1991 as part of a large national research project. The class is a Year 11 geography GCSE class, of five girls and 13 boys. Their teacher, Bob, had taught them in Year 10 also, and was the Head of Geography in the school. He had been using computer software in his geography classes for some years. He arranged for the class to move into the computer room (16 networked RM Nimbuses) about two weeks before the lesson.

The class was studying development (the notion of development indices and the definition of a 'less developed country'). The country used as a basis for the work was Tanzania. I observed the class use the data interrogation package PC-GLOBE. I am explaining the circumstances in detail in order to illustrate the nature of the change brought about through the use of software. It was a rare occasion in which I could get a comparative perspective on how the same teacher had taught the same topic before, but without the use of software.

Previous approach

The geography department had been teaching the GCSE syllabus for some while and had a well-established sequence of related lessons, using a wide stock of class worksheets developed over a substantial period of time. Previously, pupils had been presented with three sheets of information on Tanzania and the UK. The first covered basic data such as area, population, population breakdown into density, birth and death rates, gross national product and percentage literacy; economic data including agricultural production, livestock and industry; and trade, identified as imports and exports with the UK. The other two sheets consisted of maps of population distribution, land use, main towns and railways, relief, rainfall and distribution of the tsetse fly. No specific instructions for use were included with these worksheets of data. I was told that the pupils had been asked first to analyse the population data, and then to draw up a composite picture of Tanzania and consider its stage of development.

Following the arrival that autumn of PC-GLOBE, a geography-specific worldwide country database, the geography department drew up a new worksheet to incorporate this database. In essence the pupils were asked to perform the same tasks but given the whole database to use. An important feature of this change is that it was curriculum led. The teachers were attracted to the potential of this database as it would support work they had already undertaken.

A more open learning task

Comparison between the old and new worksheets enable three points to be highlighted.

1 The data available in the old exercise was the only data which the pupils had before them, thus limiting their perception of relevant data to that chosen by the teacher. In the new exercise the pupils were

encouraged to search the database for themselves, and to consider what data was most appropriate. That is they became active in the exploration and selection of relevant data.

2 Pupils were encouraged to compare Tanzania with other African countries as well as any others of their choice. In the old exercise the only other data was for the UK. Thus what was a crude comparison between a developed and less developed nation had become an exploration of the range of development that might be found in different countries.

3 The pupils were encouraged to test a hypothesis using the data: 'Your main task is to provide evidence to answer the question "Is Tanzania a LDC (less developed or third world country)?" To do this you should investigate comparisons between Tanzania and the rest of Africa, that is, Tanzania and selected countries of your choice.'

Thus the pupils were given a focused task for them to pursue using variables of their choice and countries of their choice. The new worksheet now focused on the pupils' responsibility to explore and define for themselves. It widened and deepened the basis for the pupils' enquiry.

Probing the knowledge base

The lesson using the software was described beforehand by the teacher as one when the pupils would:

collectively interrogate PC-GLOBE. This is an open lesson, that is I have not done any prior teaching (on the topic) so they are starting from cold . . . I have chosen to do it like this so that it is an enquiry exercise.

The pupils went directly to the computer room and they selected where to sit – one group of three, four pairs and the rest singles at the machines. The teacher introduced the lesson as:

Your job is to find sufficient information. After reading the instructions for getting on to the machines and the software, you need to get the info for the next lesson. A lot of this is about you deciding on your enquiry.

Within minutes the class had settled into searching for data; most pupils explored population growth and imports/exports. One pair of boys began to explore health indicators; first, the number of doctors per population and then the numbers of dentists. They were startled to discover that there was a significant difference between the health provision in Kenya and Tanzania, and a long discussion took place as they revised their ideas in the light of this evidence.

During this time the teacher was moving around the class responding to questions about how to work through the menus to set up the enquiry they wanted, but also on the data they were finding. The pupils worked on this task for the whole of the 55-minute period. The level of noise was quite high but tolerated by the teacher. Pupils were sitting forward around the computers and often pointing to results on the screen as they came up. Occasionally one of the pupils would draw in the teacher with

'Look at this then Sir.' I could not see any particular group that was not involved although in a class of 18 I cannot be certain. The overall impression however was of 'talk-on-task'.

Later in the day the teacher reported that he was quite pleased with the lesson. He indicated that this was a very mixed ability class and he found it frustrating when he put things on paper 'as they don't read it. In the computer room some don't look at notes and want it all to come from the screen. In this lesson it was better [than before] for what it made the kids do ... it's all about them generating the question and me responding – not me doing the prompting. The worksheet doesn't tell them what questions to generate.'

In the follow-up lesson the pupils were asked to focus on development, not just in relation to Tanzania, but in general terms. What did we mean by development and can development be measured? They were presented with a list of ten countries; working in pairs they had to rank them in order of development. Looking at a large number of indicators for development, they had to decide the six best indicators of how developed a country was. Their choices ranged across 14 different indicators. The use of the database appeared to have extended the pupils' understanding of the complexity of relationships between geographical indicators.

Implications

What can a new teacher do? It is clear that the problems with a national curriculum and IT school policies that are dominated by the delivery of vocationally-oriented IT skills courses will be as alienating for new teachers as they appear to be for those already in post. Success in schools at the moment appears to hinge on those teachers who become convinced that using certain pieces of software can support their pedagogy and enhance the learning for their pupils. Once they are convinced, they ensure they can use the resource system to ensure access. Subject association journals provide software reviews and advice as they do for other teaching and learning resources. So the solution lies in your subject pedagogy, not in the IT world.

It is encouraging that students on initial teacher training have consistently prioritised two key questions about using IT in class – 'the ways IT could be used in teaching' and 'managing the use of the computer in the classroom' (Lienard 1995; Mellar and Jackson 1992). These are sound questions and relate to the issues discussed above. The potential role of IT in classrooms is enormous. The chances of realising this are fraught because of a lack of clarity of purpose upon which to base policy and practice. Yet without a clear philosophical understanding driving forward and underpinning the role of IT, it will continue to be a much lauded but infrequently used innovation.

References

Albalat, J.Q. and Ruiz, F. (1995) Interpreting internal school influences on the educational integration of IT, in D. Watson and D. Tinsley (eds) *Integrating Information Technology into Education*. London: Chapman and Hall.

Department of Education and Science (DES) (1990) *Technology in the National Curriculum*. London: HMSO.

Department of Education and Science/Department for Education (DES/DFE) (1989 to 1995) *Survey of Information Technology in Schools*: Statistical Bulletins. London: DES/DFE.

Department for Education (DFE) (1995) *Information Technology in the National Curriculum*. London: DFE.

Dunn, S and Ridgeway, J. (1991) Computer use during primary school teaching practice: a survey, *Journal of Computer Assisted Learning*, 4: 66–70.

Gardner, J., Morrison, H., Jarman, R., Reilly, C. and McNally, H. (1992) *Pupils' Learning and Access to Information Technology*. Belfast: Queen's University of Belfast.

Hawkridge, D. (1990) Who needs computers in schools, and why?, in M. Kibby (ed.), *Computer Assisted Learning: Selected Proceedings from the CAL '89 Symposium*. Oxford: Pergamon.

HMI (1989) *Information Technology from 5 to 16*. London: HMSO.

Hooper, R. and Toye, I. (eds) (1975) *Computer Assisted Learning in the United Kingdom: Some Case Studies*. London: Council for Educational Technology.

Lienard, B. (1995) Pre-course IT skills of teacher trainees: a longitudinal study. *Journal of Computer Assisted Learning*, 11: 110–20.

Mellar, H. and Jackson, A. (1992) IT in post-graduate teacher training. *Journal of Computer Assisted Learning*, 8: 231–43.

Morrison, H., Gardner, J., Reilly, C. and McNally, H. (1993) The impact of portable computers on pupils' attitudes to study, *Journal of Computer Assisted Learning*, 9: 130–41.

NCC (1991) *Information Technology in the National Curriculum: Teachers' Notes*. York: NCC.

Office for Standards in Education (Ofsted) (1995) *Information Technology: A Review of Inspection Findings, 1993/94*. London: HMSO.

Olson, J. (1990) Trojan horse or teacher's pet? *International Journal of Educational Research*, 17: 77–84.

POST (1991) *Technologies for Teaching: The Use of Technologies for Teaching and Learning in Primary and Secondary Schools*. London: Parliamentary Office of Science and Technology.

Veen, W. (1995) Factors affecting the use of computers in the classroom: four case studies, in D. Watson and D. Tinsley (eds) *Integrating Information Technology into Education*. London: Chapman and Hall.

Watson, D.M. (1990) The classroom vs. the computer room. *Computers and Education*, 15: 33–7.

Watson, D.M. (ed.) (1993) *The ImpacT Report: An Evaluation of the Impact of Information Technology on Children's Achievements in Primary and Secondary Schools*. London: King's College London.

Watson, D. and Tinsley, D. (eds) (1995) *Integrating Information Technology into Education*. London: Chapman and Hall.

Wellington, J.J. (1988) Computer education in secondary schools: an electronic survey, *Journal of Computer Assisted Learning*, 4: 22–33.

Vocational education in schools

Peter Gill

Introduction

PGCE and BEd courses prepare people for the vocation of teaching. Does that mean that they are vocational courses? And, if so, how are they different from academic courses? Of all the areas of education to undergo change in recent years, vocational education is the one where the changes are still coming thick and fast. Anything written about vocational education is likely to be out of date as soon as it is written – so beware!

Vocational education traditionally was undertaken in the workplace. Indeed, apprenticeship training has a much longer history than academic schooling. Over the centuries many of the craft areas set up their own guilds named after their own jealously guarded skill or profession, such as haberdashers or goldsmiths. Some of these guilds came to be very wealthy and powerful and moved far away from their roots but many more continued to be the lead bodies and set rules and standards to safeguard their position in society.

The development of awarding bodies to examine trainees in the skills defined by the lead bodies led to a degree of rationalisation. One of the largest awarding bodies is the City and Guilds of London Institute (usually referred to as 'City and Guilds' or CGLI). CGLI certificates are still of key importance in many areas and jobs advertised in trade journals frequently quote the City and Guilds qualification required. The Royal Society of Arts (RSA) is another awarding body, but one which tends to specialise in commercial skills such as typing. Both RSA and City and Guilds qualifications are generally earned by attending full or part-time courses in further education (FE) colleges.

In addition to qualifications which accredit the ability to perform certain tasks or the possession of particular skills there are others designed for workers in commerce or industry who need some theoretical knowledge to underpin their work. School laboratory technicians would be examples and they may study typically one day per week at an FE college for qualifications awarded by the Business and Technical Education Council (BTEC). Until recently the main difference between BTEC and the other two awarding bodies, apart from the areas covered, was that BTEC set courses and course specifications but did not set examinations whereas RSA and CGLI were much more like school examination boards. With the advent of the GNVQ (see below) this difference is far less clear.

Although BTEC, RSA and CGLI are the main accrediting bodies there are still a large number of trades which award their own qualifications. For centuries it has been the case that a tradesman (and they were invariably men), once qualified in his trade, would expect to stay in that trade for life. A village blacksmith might send his son to a neighbouring village for his apprenticeship, but the son would expect, and be expected, to return to his native village to take over from his father as he had in turn taken over from *his* father. The trade could become so closely associated with the family concerned that they would be known by the name of their trade. Surnames such as Smith and Thatcher are obvious examples of this.

The situation in the late twentieth century is very different. On the one hand there is a decline in the need for so many of the skilled trades people, partly due to technology and partly due to a fall in demand. On the other hand there is the growth of new needs and skills. Today the blacksmith's children may be graphic designers working with virtual reality – a skill that has only existed for a few years. In all likelihood, those new skills will be superseded by the march of technology in only a few more years.

Society now requires a flexible workforce with people ready and willing to change trade or profession several times during their working lives. This implies a need for some sort of parity across qualifications. In order to ease the chaos of more than 16,000 vocational qualifications – few of which bore any relation to any of the others – the government, in 1986, set up the National Council for Vocational Qualifications (NCVQ) with the brief of bringing all vocational qualifications from bakers to barristers, under one umbrella by the beginning of the new century. All qualifications would be National Vocational Qualifications (NVQs). This was an ambitious project, partly due to the sheer difficulty of comparing very different skills, but also due to the different trades and professions being proud of their history and status. If the highest qualification for barristers was level 5 (see below for an explanation of levels) then other groups demanded that their top certificate should also be at level 5. To complicate matters further, the NCVQ tried to achieve parity not just within vocational qualifications but across the divide into academic qualifications. The situation is summarised in Figure 20.1 where it can be seen that NVQ level 3 is approximately 'equal' to GCE A levels and NVQ level 5 to a Master's degree.

Academic vs vocational

The tradition in schools has been liberal academic rather than vocational. It is only since 1988 that England and Wales have had a national school

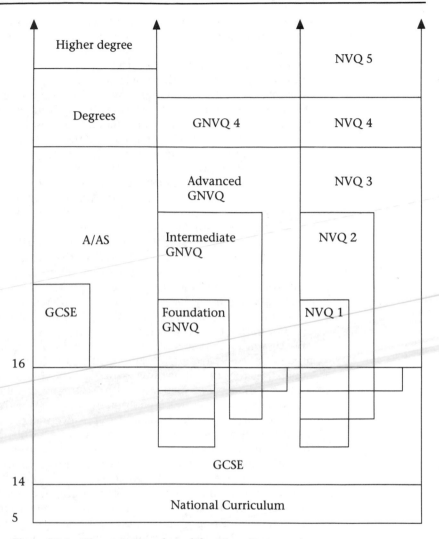

Figure 20.1 The vocational qualifications framework

leaving certificate designed to cover the majority of the population – the GCSE. The GCE O levels that preceded it only catered for the top 20 per cent of the ability range.

The 1944 Education Act aimed to provide more appropriate education for a wider range of pupils; grammar schools to cater for the academic high flyers, technical schools for those with more vocational leanings and modern schools for the rest. This plan did not succeed, very few technical schools ever came into existence and the only qualifications obtainable in schools were the O and A levels designed for the elite. At the end of the 1960s, the Certificate of Secondary Education (CSE) was introduced for the 40 per cent of children below the O-level standard. In fact, the CSE was merely a watered down version of the O level, locally administered. The CSE never gained the status it deserved and perhaps its only lasting effect was to involve a generation of teachers intimately in the examination and assessment business which in turn helped to lead to the compulsory inclusion of teacher assessment in GCSE.

One of the problems of the GCSE and the National Curriculum which followed shortly after, is that the liberal academic tradition is still too obviously apparent, the heavy hand of the old universities still looms large. Many teachers realised that this was still inappropriate for most pupils but attempts to introduce vocational qualifications usually failed because they were simply not designed for schools and the 14–16 age range. Few schoolteachers have the skills and qualifications to teach vocational topics and most schools simply do not have the facilities. An exception to this was the RSA typing qualifications and many pupils (mostly girls) leave school at 16 with RSA certificates in typing and office practice.

During the 1970s there was a growing realisation in industry and commerce that we were not producing a high enough number of school leavers with useful skills and there were several initiatives by the government to try to alter this situation. Most of these initiatives came from the arm of government responsible for employment and training rather than education. This led to several years during which there were very different philosophies fighting for control of the curriculum.

The most significant and successful of the initiatives was the Technical and Vocational Education Initiative (TVEI). In its first manifestation TVEI gave significant amounts of money to a number of schools to design and produce a heavily technologically-oriented curriculum for 14–16-year-old pupils. Much of the money was earmarked for computers and other hardware and the level of spending gave rise to considerable envy in schools which had no access to such equipment. At this stage the TVEI curriculum was only for a small percentage of pupils even in the schools which did get the money and almost inevitably, given the liberal academic tradition referred to above, it was mostly the lower attainers that benefited and the academic-vocational divide remained intact. In the late-1980s, TVEI broadened its remit and offered money to schools that redesigned the curriculum such that *all* pupils received an education that was broadly technologically based. The sums of money were relatively modest but nevertheless welcome. It is interesting to note that aspects of the curriculum model that was being pushed by TVEI, such as core subjects and limited opportunity to specialise, were very similar to what developed as the National Curriculum.

The fight for control of the compulsory school curriculum was won by the traditional liberal academics and the Department for Education, but for 16–19-year-olds the field was wide open. There was little alternative to A levels for those in full-time education post-16. But A levels were designed as university entrance examinations and were taken by only a small percentage of the population. Even after the explosion of numbers of students entering higher education in the early 1990s, the proportion taking what could be called 'vocational' subjects (maths, science and computing) at A level was still well under 10 per cent of the cohort.

There were a number of attempts to bring BTEC and City and Guilds courses into sixth forms. But most of the qualifications were very specifically vocational, related to only one trade or profession, and designed to be taught in FE colleges with their greater range of appropriate facilities. What was needed in schools was something more generalised and for a while there were a number of 'prevocational' courses available. Probably the most successful of these were City and Guilds 365, the RSA Voc. Prep. and the Certificate of Prevocational Education (CPVE) sponsored by the Department of Education and Science. However, these schemes were swept aside as the great NVQ bandwagon gained momentum and in 1991 the government announced that there would be a new prevocational qualification available for full-time students post-16, linked to the NVQ framework and named General National Vocational Qualifications (GNVQ). The level of these qualifications is such that an Advanced GNVQ is equivalent to two GCE A levels and an Intermediate to five GCSEs. Students with very low GCSE grades or who have not taken GCSEs may enrol for Foundation level courses.

Competence-based qualifications

NVQs and GNVQs are examples of competence-based qualifications. Before going into any detail about GNVQs it is important to make clear just what is implied by such a statement. Traditional school qualifications are based on the teaching of material defined in a syllabus the mastery of which is tested by a terminal examination. By contrast, vocational qualifications were mainly about possessing certain skills. The school pupil was expected to have covered the whole syllabus but the examination could only sample part of the area covered, the vocational trainee was being trained for exactly the skills that he or she would be tested in, the driving test is a good example of this sort of thing. If you have read Chapter 16 you will have identified this paragraph as referring to criterion-referenced testing.

NVQs (and GNVQs as a subset) are very clearly criterion-referenced qualifications. In any of their course specifications there are only outcomes. The 'syllabus' defines only what the student should be able to do ('performance criteria'), in how many contexts these criteria should be met ('range statements') and how this competence should be demonstrated ('evidence indicators'). There is no list of material to be covered, no reference to teaching or even if any should take place, and no time limit.

Bringing all existing vocational qualifications into line with this model has been enormously complex and has led to the generation of a whole culture with its own jargon which is barely comprehensible to other practitioners in the field and quite incomprehensible to outsiders, for instance the following comes from the *Competence and Assessment Briefing Series No. 10: The Place of Knowledge and Understanding in the Development of National Vocational Qualifications and Scottish Vocational Qualifications*:

> A range statement defines the scope of an element of competence within a particular NVQ or SVQ. Range statements are made up of a series of dimensions (or categories for SVQ) under each of which there are range classes which are critical for the assessment of competent performance within the occupation. The range classes for each

dimension identify critical differences in application and are mutually exclusive.

(Mitchell and Bartram 1994: 15)

The school examination system had dabbled with criterion referencing both in GCSE and the National Curriculum, but the force of traditional syllabus-led liberal education courses has held sway in those fields. The totally competence-led style of GNVQs is at variance with the traditional school culture and teachers are having problems in coping with both the change in style and the large amount of paperwork involved in any scheme of assessment where the teachers themselves are the leading assessors.

Almost from its inception GNVQ has been embarrassingly successful in terms of the number of students opting to study for it, probably because of antipathy towards the GCSE A-level alternative rather than the inherent attractiveness of the GNVQ. Thus schools wishing to keep up their sixth form numbers are virtually being forced to offer the courses even when the resources (human included) are barely adequate. And it is not just the teachers involved who are finding problems with the culture shift, there are in addition severe problems with the courses themselves. Take for example GNVQ Science. This has just passed through its pilot stage and it has become apparent to some observers that many of the difficulties with running the course are more deeply seated than just teething problems. As I have said, GNVQs are competence based, and where the vocational area is just that, i.e. *vocational* it is relatively easy to come to agreement about what competencies are necessary to perform adequately in that particular field. But what is Science? In some respects, yes, it is a vocation, but not in the sense usually associated with vocational qualifications and anyway all GNVQs are meant to be *pre*vocational. It seems likely that there will continue to be problems of emphasis while GNVQs, grafted onto the NVQ competence model, are taught in schools by teachers brought up in the liberal education tradition.

The structure and assessment of GNVQs

The GNVQ is a modular course. At Advanced level a student will take 12 modules, eight mandatory and four optional. At the Intermediate level there are six modules (four mandatory and two optional). In addition, there are three modules of core skills: Communication; Application of Number; and Information Technology, which are meant to be taught and assessed through the medium of the other subject modules (but see below for recent changes to this pattern). Although there is no time limit for completing modules, the design of GNVQ has been to enable the Advanced level to be completed in two years (as in the Advanced Level GCE). In practice there has been a relatively low completion rate. In 1995 only 47 per cent of students registered two years earlier for Advanced level GNVQ had completed. The figures for the Intermediate and Foundation levels were 58 per cent and 20 per cent respectively. Compare this with a success rate of about 70 per cent for those taking and passing two GCE A levels. On the other hand, those failing A levels come away with nothing for their two years whereas most of those not completing GNVQ still have individual module awards. There is also some evidence that a number of students taking GNVQ actually complete them one term later, i.e. after seven terms rather than six.

Assessment is mainly carried out by the teacher based on the student's work during the course, 'The primary evidence for assessment will be derived from projects and assignments carried out by the student' (NCVQ 1993). In addition, each module (but not the core skills) has a multiple-choice examination paper set by one of the awarding bodies (BTEC, CGLI and RSA). Originally, it was intended that these papers could be taken at any time decided by the teacher and student. The influence of the traditional view of examinations caused the Government to decree that the papers could only be taken on one of a number of specified days during the year. They can, however, be retaken until the student reaches the pass mark.

The assessment of a student's portfolio of work is carried out by reference to the performance criteria, range statements and evidence indicators for the particular module. However, there is scope for a considerable range of interpretation about what work adequately meets the criteria. To help moderate assessment decisions, each school or college offering GNVQs has trained 'internal verifiers'. In addition, each group of schools or colleges will have 'external verifiers' also trained by the awarding bodies. However, there have been many complaints of inconsistency and conflicting advice being given by external verifiers and it seems that there is still a long way to go before we can be sure of consistent standards in assessment of GNVQs.

The multiple-choice papers set for each module have had an even rockier start than the teacher assessment. The papers are meant to cover the entire range of the module in terms of underlying knowledge and the pass mark is set at 70 per cent which may seem high, but of course a competence based scheme actually implies a pass mark of 100 per cent. During their introduction the papers have been dogged by problems of validity and reliability (see Chapter 16 for a discussion of these terms). The latter problem being all the more worrying because multiple-choice papers are, in theory, the easiest to make reliable. The sort of problem encountered can be illustrated by the situation in GNVQ Advanced Science in January 1995. Then, the national pass rate for the physics papers was 6 per cent (compared with 69 per cent for GCE A levels) whereas the pass rate for the biology modules was 87 per cent. On completion of a course, students are awarded a 'Pass', a 'Merit' or a 'Distinction' on the basis of their overall performance.

Both the teaching and the assessment of the core skills has proved problematical. Their integration with the rest of the course material has proved difficult in practice. Sometimes this has been because the core skills include material that is simply not relevant to the subject modules, but there have also been problems with teachers feeling unable to assess their students in unfamiliar areas.

Many schools are finding themselves torn over the issues of the GNVQ. On the one hand, their undoubted popularity with students as a viable alternative to GCE A levels makes it difficult not to offer one or more in the sixth form. On the other hand, the problems described above have caused many schools to reconsider after only one or two years.

In response to suggestions in the Dearing Review of the National Curriculum there have been pilots of what have been named 'Part One GNVQs' designed to be used with pupils in Key Stage 4 as an alternative to, or in addition to, GCSE.

The Dearing 16–19 Review

In the wake of the perceived success of Sir Ron Dearing's review of the National Curriculum (see Chapter 2) he was asked in 1995 to review the qualifications of 16–19 year olds. The Department for Education and the Employment Department had by then been combined into the Department for Education and Employment (DFEE) under one Secretary of State (in England). However, Dearing was not given a free rein and his terms of reference made it clear that A levels were sacrosanct. This is despite the fact that all groups that have been consulted over many years (including industry, commerce and higher education), and have been unanimous in recommending fundamental reforms in the traditional narrow diet of A levels.

As far as schools are concerned, vocational qualifications continue to mean GNVQs. Dearing recommended a number of changes in them, mostly concerned with assessment. As noted above the original GNVQ style of assessment was based on, and indeed lifted from, the competence model adopted for NVQs. However, it is clear that GNVQs are not actually vocational qualifications, prevocational would be more accurate, and the assessment model is simply not appropriate. The report recommends what is effectively something between the competence model and the traditional examination model. There is likely to be more use of externally set tasks both for measuring competence and for grading purposes. In addition, the requirement for competence in *all* performance criteria will change so that poor performance in one area can be compensated for by exceptional performance in another, which is of course what happens in traditional end of course examinations. The fraught area of core skills (renamed in the report as 'Key Skills') is addressed by proposing separate, external, assessment of these. Although this is clearly going to make for more manageable teaching and assessment of those skills it fails to acknowledge the long-standing problem of what used to be called 'transfer of training'. It has long been known that skills learned in one context do not transfer easily (or indeed at all) to other contexts, the original GNVQ model of teaching and learning of core skills tried to address this. The report seems to acknowledge this attempt as a failure.

An attempt to break down the academic-vocational divide and at the same time increase the breadth of study of 16–19 courses is made in the Dearing Review by grouping subjects:

- science, technology, engineering and mathematics
- modern languages
- arts and humanities (including English and Welsh)
- the way the community works (including business, politics and law).

Students who study a range of subjects covering all four groups including either two A levels or a complete GNVQ at Advanced level and who also take the three Key Skills will be eligible for a new award tentatively named the National Advanced Diploma. While this looks to be a good idea at first sight, it is clear that many schools will be unable to offer the range of options necessary because of logistical and timetable difficulties. There have been a number of similar attempts over the years and all have foundered on the rocks of the traditional A level structure and its 'gold standard' status.

As a further attempt at raising the status of GNVQs the report suggests that a full Advanced award of 12 units plus Key Skills should be renamed 'Applied A level (double award)' and a student who gains six units plus Key Skills should be awarded an 'Applied A Level'. It remains to be seen whether this badge engineering will achieve anything in the long run.

Conclusion

Given the liberal academic tradition of schooling in the UK, it is unlikely that vocational or prevocational education will play a significant role for pupils under the age of 16, though the merger of NCVQ and SCAA may change matters. However, for the 16–19-year-olds there is now the possibility of taking combinations of academic A levels with GNVQ or NVQ units. Whether this will take place in school sixth forms or lead to a growth in FE colleges remains to be seen.

Reference

Mitchell, L. and Bartram, D. (1994) The place of knowledge and understanding in the development of national vocational qualifications and Scottish vocational qualifications, in *Competence and Assessment Briefing Series*, 10: 15, Employment Department.

Special educational needs – inclusion, IT and indecision

Chris Abbott

It is important to recognise that this report is based on the belief that special educational needs and handicaps are relative to the contexts in which children and young people are educated ... The aims of education are the same for all and the common human needs of children and young people are of greater significance than individual abilities or difficulties.

(Committee to Review Special Educational Provision 1985: 211)

Introduction

The Fish Report, quoted from above, followed the highly influential Warnock Report (DES 1978), and the 1981 Education Act (DES 1981) both of which came down firmly in favour of integrated education. Many special needs teachers, particularly those in inner London (the focus of the Fish Report) expected that, within a few years, most special schools would be closed, almost all children would be educated together and segregated schooling would become an historical anomaly. That almost none of this has yet happened is explained by several factors particularly the arrival of the National Curriculum and, subsequently, league tables of schools.

At the time the Fish Report was published, the arguments for integrated education seemed compelling and any opposition to them risked being labelled as divisive and inequitable. The authors of the Fish Report were unequivocal:

integration in society is a process not a state. It is not simply a question of placement in the same groups and institutions as others. It is a process which requires continued and planned interaction with contemporaries and freedom to associate in different groups. The potentially adverse effects of isolation and segregation, in whatever context, including comprehensive institutions, are now well-known, including the risks to social competence and to the development of a positive self-identity.

(Committee to Review Special Educational Provision 1985: 5)

Prior to the Fish Report, the 1981 Education Act had led to increasing numbers of young people being considered as having special educational needs at some point during their school career. A figure of 20 per cent quoted in the Warnock Report (DES 1978) was highly influential in changing attitudes, freeing resources and ensuring that serious attention was paid to the issue. Special schools, by comparison, were educating approximately 2 per cent of the school population.

Across London and much of the rest of England and Wales, the mid-1980s was a time of great expectations for those involved in special needs education. The old barriers were to be swept away, young people were to be educated together and mainstream schools would have to become more inclusive. Integration, however, was overtaken by events, more particularly by one event: the publication of the 1988 Education Reform Act and all that followed from it. Suddenly, schools and local education authorities were faced with more fundamental changes than integration; changes that carried the force of law and the insistent voice of a timetable of implementation, neither of which applied to the 1981 Act.

Withdrawal or in-class support?

Prior to the events of the mid-1980s, the fundamental controversy regarding special needs provision in mainstream schools had been the one that has since reappeared in the mid-1990s: is it more desirable to educate young people with special needs by withdrawing them from the lessons where they are experiencing difficulty and educating them elsewhere, or should support teachers be provided to enable such young people to learn alongside their more able peers in ordinary schools? The support system approach has much more in common with the aims and beliefs of the 1981 Act than does the practice, formerly widespread, of withdrawing children and educating them in small groups with specialised resources in the care of a teacher whose only role is to work with those children. This latter approach has its basis in assumptions that children can be categorised.

Categories of need

Teachers entering the profession in the 1970s would have met terms such as 'mentally handicapped', 'maladjusted' and 'physically handicapped'. These terms, stark though they may seem, replaced others that were even more uncompromising. The British education and health systems have a long history of placing people in categories and until the turn of the

century, the categories in general use were terms that would today be
entirely inappropriate:

Idiots
persons so deeply defective in mind from birth . . . (as to be) unable
to guard themselves against common human dangers . . .

Imbeciles
mental defectiveness not amounting to idiocy . . . incapable of managing themselves or their affairs . . .

Feeble-minded
require care, supervision and control for their own protection . . .
. . . permanently incapable of receiving proper benefit from the instruction in ordinary schools . . .

Moral imbeciles
. . . some permanent defect coupled with strong vicious or criminal
propensities on which punishment has had little or no effect . . .

Acute lunacy
. . . has been excluded from the definitions.

(Great Britain 1886)

The categories in use today are based on a belief that special educational need is a product of context rather than an innate state situated
within the child. Teachers still talk about categories of need, however, and
it may be useful to consider these before discussing the concept of need
related to context. The categories of special educational need currently
referred to include:

- learning difficulties
- specific learning difficulties
- emotional and behavioural difficulties
- physical disabilities
- sensory impairment: hearing difficulties
- sensory impairment: visual difficulties
- speech and language difficulties.

Learning difficulties

By far the largest group of children defined as having special educational
needs are those with learning difficulties. These difficulties may be minimal, moderate or severe, depending upon the context in which the young
person is being taught and the task involved. All teachers will have children with learning difficulties in their classrooms, although it is unlikely
that these difficulties will be of a severity that causes the young person
involved to be unable to speak or communicate. Children with such needs
are still most likely to be found in special schools.

Specific learning difficulties (dyslexia)

Some children display a range of difficulties with learning which seem at
odds with what appears to be a high level of intelligence. They are able

to learn in other ways very quickly, but reading, writing and spelling, in particular, appear to give them great difficulty. Many have seen this collection of difficulties as a specific trait and have termed it 'dyslexia'; others resist the notion of one kind of difficulty and prefer to use the general term 'specific learning difficulties'. Whatever the personal perspective on this argument, it is undoubtedly true that some young people do appear to have particular difficulties with language, especially in its non-verbal forms, and teachers need to be adept at dealing with this.

Emotional and behavioural difficulties

Perhaps above all other categories of need, this is the one that is most affected by context. It is also probably the area of need which classroom teachers feel is more difficult to meet within the mainstream classroom than any other. Children can appear to be extremely disruptive, unmotivated or withdrawn, and a whole range of behaviours can be seen as falling within this area.

Physical disabilities

The assumption too easily made about physical disability is that children can be integrated into mainstream schools provided that physical alterations are made to the building. This is too simplistic and fails to take account of the psychological and sociological hurdles that are involved in the successful integration of such young people into mainstream schools.

Sensory impairment: hearing difficulties

It is often those young people who have hearing difficulties or are deaf who have the greatest difficulties with integration into mainstream education. Where children have developed a confident grasp of signing they are likely to feel much more comfortable talking to others who are similarly bilingual. Talking to a hearing person involves learning to lip-read and this can prove very difficult for some young people.

Sensory impairment: visual difficulties

Some children with visual difficulties have been successfully integrated into mainstream schools for many years. In some cases this has been achieved through the sensible use of computers and other specially adapted aids, but in many cases a willing teaching force and a well-prepared group of students are the most important factors. Children with colour vision difficulties may not be able to cope with certain colour combinations when reading; with many computer programs this can be amended, but printed materials present insuperable problems. Science teachers need to be sensitive when dealing with the topic of colour blindness. Other children may suffer from a narrowing of their field of vision; they may not need to sit near to the board but they may need to be directly opposite it, or, in some cases, to one side.

Speech and language difficulties

In recent years, it has become increasingly clear that difficulties with speech and language, if noted early enough in a child's school career, need not be a life-long difficulty. Language units have been set up to provide early intervention during a child's first years at school and these have often been remarkably successful. It is unlikely that many secondary teachers will have to deal with this range of needs.

Attention Deficit Hyperactivity Disorder (ADHD)

Categories of need tend to change regularly and new ones sometimes appear. A recent arrival from the USA is the notion of attention deficit disorder (ADD), sometimes linked to hyperactivity (ADHD). This is an area of controversy in the USA, where many young students have been prescribed drugs to control the disorder. Drug therapy has always been seen as a last resort in the British system where hyperactivity has been recognised for many years and has often been seen as linked to dietary intake of food supplements. ADD and ADHD seem to be gaining acceptance among professionals and are terms which teachers will meet; criticism of their use tends to be similar to that of the notion of dyslexia; that it signifies a model of special educational need as a medical condition for which a cure, or at any rate relief, can be prescribed.

Children and their needs in context

The biggest change, since the 1980s, in the way that teachers think about special educational needs is in the notion of context-related need. This is an important concept that needs to be understood by all who seek to be effective teachers.

It is now generally accepted that special educational needs arise mostly from the contexts in which we place children, rather than from the child itself. A child who exhibits signs of emotional and behavioural disturbance in a mainstream school may be entirely calm and at ease in another setting such as a small special school or an off-site unit. Factors such as the size of a school, the pressure of being one of such a large student body or a bewildering variety of tasks and directives when joining a new school, can cause the special educational need to become noticed, or cause it to become so important that it could not be ignored.

It follows from this argument that an essential requirement is for schools to create contexts that do not aggravate or form special educational needs among the student body. This is a task not only for the senior management of the school but also for all staff (teaching and support) and students.

Differentiation – strategies for support

Tasks given to learners should always be capable of differentiation to meet the different needs and capabilities of those students. Chapter 14 of this book covers differentiation in depth but it is appropriate here to pick out the key points as they apply to the topic of special educational needs. In too many cases teachers use the strategy of differentiation by outcome: at its simplest level this means that one task is given to all students so that some of them produce a range of responses while others struggle to produce anything at all.

A more appropriate strategy involves differentiation by task: a careful teacher will allow for a range of tasks to be offered. There are many ways in which this can be done, and the use of a variety of strategies is likely to be more effective than an over-reliance on the same methodology. Some teachers prepare alternative versions of a task, particularly where an activity is based around the use of worksheets. Others may prepare different tasks for different groups in the classroom, although this has the built-in danger of leading to a permanent setting within the classroom which is unlikely to be appropriate (see, also, Chapter 15). Students who find difficulties with one task will not necessarily react in the same way to another; as with special needs in general, the difficulty will be related to the context – in this case, the learning activity – rather than to the learner. It is unrealistic to expect that teachers will always be able to provide a differentiated range of activities, but it should be the aim of a good teacher to do so whenever possible and as often as possible.

The SEN Code of Practice

Following a consultation exercise, the Special Educational Needs Code of Practice (DFE 1994) came into force and now affects all schools and teachers. The Code of Practice recommends a staged process by which special educational needs should be identified by schools and teachers. Subject teachers have a particular role in Stages 1 and 2:

Stage 1
Class or subject teachers identify or register a child's special educational needs and, consulting the school's SEN co-ordinator (SENCO), take initial action.

Stage 2
The school's SENCO takes lead responsibility for gathering information and for co-ordinating the child's special educational provision, working with the child's teachers.

Stage 3
Teachers and the SENCO are supported by specialists from outside the school.

Stage 4
The local education authority considers the need for a statutory assessment and, if appropriate, make a multidisciplinary assessment.

Stage 5
The local education authority considers the need for a statement of special educational needs and, if appropriate, makes a statement and arranges, monitors and reviews the provision.

There are clear implications here for subject teachers in secondary schools. If a particular student seems to be experiencing difficulties and is not known to have special educational needs, it is the responsibility of that child's subject teachers to spot the difficulty, contact the SENCO and attempt to describe the nature of the needs that have been expressed. Following their consultations with the SENCO, subject teachers then need to take the action agreed. It may be that a move to a different part of the classroom has been suggested, or that the teacher should speak more clearly and face the child concerned. This can lead to a dramatic improvement in communication where a child with a hearing difficulty is concerned. The SENCO may wish to attend a lesson in order to make an informal assessment of the situation prior to any formal process that the school may have developed.

During Stage 2 of the Code, the main responsibility for action lies with the SENCO though it is essential that the subject teacher gives enthusiastic support and co-operation without which there is less hope of improving the situation. The school may decide to provide support in the form of technology, a support teacher or an assistant, if these are available. Extra help may be given by SEN teachers where they exist, and their job is made much easier when subject teachers keep them fully informed about the work in hand and offer to assist them in devising suitable teaching programmes. It may be that, following this process of gathering information, the school decides to seek outside assistance and consider the need for a statement of special educational needs, but this will not always be the case.

Information technology and SEN

The Code of Practice highlights the ways in which information technology (IT) can assist schools and students in the meeting of special educational needs. IT in this case usually means computers and the various pieces of hardware that can be attached to them.

Children with learning difficulties can use overlay keyboards to access an activity which for other students involves the use of a standard keyboard. An overlay keyboard is a flat A4 or A3 device that takes paper sheets containing words or pictures. Pressing on the words or pictures sends commands to the computer, since the overlay has an associated file which contains the instructions devised by the teacher. There are over 100 keys on a normal computer keyboard, and the choice of the correct one can be daunting for children with learning difficulties, even at secondary age. A paper overlay with a choice of eight or ten actions is a much more appropriate tool in this situation. Many teachers also use overlay keyboards to speed up the writing process for learners whose writing is slowly and laboriously produced. In a science lesson, for example, some teachers use overlays which create the phrases and concepts frequently included when writing up an experiment. Pressing on the area concerned will cause these to be written to the screen, and the student can then concentrate on the novel parts of the activity.

Children with visual difficulties may be helped by magnification software, or by the use of other magnification technology to deal with printed material. These devices are easily portable and make it possible for a student with a visual difficulty to be placed on an equal footing with others.

Children with hearing difficulties sometimes communicate using electronic mail, and the rapid increase in the number of schools with Internet access is opening up wonderful possibilities. Children who become very ill and have to spend long periods in hospital can keep in touch with their schools through electronic mail, and be set homework in this way too. Many children in hospital are able to keep up with their coursework in this way, and the ready availability of computers may sometimes result in a vastly improved amount of work being done during a period as an in-patient.

There are some difficulties that arise from the use of a computer itself being a source of stress or frustration. This is often the case when a child has a slight loss of fine motor control and finds that the mouse is very difficult to control. In such cases, it is possible to substitute a trackerball, sometimes described as an upside-down mouse, which enables the two mouse actions of clicking and moving to be separated rather than having to be done simultaneously. More importantly, the trackerball itself remains stationary and movement is controlled by the large ball on its upper surface.

Many other devices can be substituted for a mouse, and children with physical disabilities are then able to use head switches, puff switches (controlled by blowing) or even control the computer with eye movements. Where the degree of difficulty is not so great, the perceptive teacher will use the inbuilt control facilities of the software to alter the mouse tracking speed and rate at which double clicks must be made. This small change, taking only a few seconds and reversible for the next user, can transform a frustrated student into one who is able to become increasingly confident.

Although all these uses of IT, and many others, have always been explored by inventive teachers in enlightened classrooms and schools, the impetus has sometimes come from outside agencies. This can no longer be relied upon, as the major change in this area since the Code of Practice came into being has been the requirement that schools investigate the use of IT for a particular need at Stage 2 before outside experts are called in. This means that all teachers, but SENCOs in particular, must become familiar with the different ways in which IT, which may not only mean computers, can offer support.

Conclusion

The two concepts that teachers should bear in mind with regard to SEN are context and differentiation. Teachers must be able to plan activities that can be offered in a range of different forms to meet the needs of all the students in their classrooms. They need to be perceptive observers of their students, noticing where they have difficulties, and attempting to record and describe those situations so that, in consultation with colleagues, they can attempt to improve the situation. Where difficulties are obvious, they must think not why the student cannot do something, but whether the learning environment provided is appropriate for that student's needs. Some aspects of that environment may be outside the control of the individual teacher; but important factors, teacher attitude, provision of differentiated work and awareness of student reaction, will not be.

References

Committee to Review Special Educational Provision (1985) *Educational Opportunities For All: Report of the Committee Reviewing Provision to Meet Special Educational Needs* (The Fish Report). London: Inner London Education Authority.

Department for Education (DFE) (1994) *Code of Practice on the Identification and Assessment of Special Educational Needs*. London: DFE.

Department of Education and Science (DES) (1978) *Special Educational Needs: Report of the Committee of Enquiry into the Education of Handicapped Children and Young People*. (The Warnock Report). London: HMSO.

Department of Education and Science (DES) (1981) *Education for All*. London: HMSO.

Great Britain (1886) *Classification of Defectives Under the Mental Deficiency, Lunacy, Idiots and Education Acts*. London: HMSO.

22 Beyond the subject curriculum: the form tutor's role

Jane Jones and Christine Harrison

Introduction

Teachers today are not the same as teachers 20 years ago and modelling yourself on good teachers that you had may be problematic. With the advent and spread of comprehensive schools in the 1960s and 1970s, accompanied by a move towards pupil-centred rather than teacher-directed learning, the role of the teacher has changed remarkably. Clive Sutton (1992) stressed the increasing importance in schools of coaching pupils in skills and in particular 'life skills, subject-related skills and vocational skills'. The social aspects of education have grown to be recognised as important factors in ensuring the success of learners: teachers have had more to consider than the knowledge they were required to pass on and the systems they used to check on learning. It is no longer a question of what learners need to learn, but what is the best way to learn it, how can they be supported in their progress and what can be done to motivate and sustain interest in learning. The role of the teacher beyond that of subject specialist has become critically important and is the focus of this chapter.

Tattum (1988) describes the character and ethos of a school as determined by 'decisions about the curriculum, the allocation of resources, the grouping of pupils and the arrangements made for guidance and welfare'. While government policy, particularly through the National Curriculum has determined much of the curricular and resourcing implications, pupil grouping and welfare and guidance, under the guise and auspices of the pastoral system, still remain within the decision-making processes of individual schools and teachers, and it is these factors which may influence the success or failure of learners more than government legislation.

The pastoral system

There are over 4500 secondary schools in England, and within each of these, the headteacher faces the demanding task of organising the pupils, staffing and resources to produce the best learning environment. In the setting up of the comprehensive system in the 1950s and 1960s, considerable thought and effort were given to developing an organisational system in which the individual pupil would feel valued, noticed and encouraged in their learning. Within many schools, a number of subsets ('houses') were established. These varied in number from three up to 10 or more, depending mainly on the size of the school. Within each house, tutors had the responsibility for the welfare, discipline and pastoral care of their groups and became the link between the pupils in the school and the outside community, which included parents, careers services, social services and the courts.

Grouping policy varied in different schools as did the emphasis and importance of the house system. Some schools elected to set up vertical tutor systems, in which three or four pupils from each year group were all placed in the same tutor group. This resulted in a mixed age group somewhat akin to a family, where younger pupils could rely on the help and support of older pupils as well as on their tutor; in return older pupils took on responsibility and care for the younger ones in the tutor group which assisted the development of their social and life skills.

However, while the vertical tutor system provided a strong integrating system to support individual pupils, it also created problems particularly administrative ones. If a particular age group was required for medical examinations or had to select subject options, then messages had to reach the individual pupils concerned. In a school of 1200 pupils, there will be approximately 40 tutor groups each with around four pupils from each year. The logistics of messages reaching the right people at the right time sometimes proved difficult. Another problem involved the role of the form tutor who, at any one time, may have needed to concentrate on Year 11 pupils about to make choices for post-16 education, on Year 9 pupils preparing for the national examinations and on Year 7 pupils anxious about Rubella injections. The difficulties imposed by having a representative sample of the whole school in your tutor group have increased as the administrative demands on teachers have grown since the mid-1980s.

An alternative to vertical systems in which tutor groups consist of a small number of pupils of different ages are horizontal systems in which tutor groups contain pupils from one year group. While the administrative demands on the school and the work demands on the tutor are simpler than with the vertical arrangement, the support systems for pupils fall mainly on the form tutor rather than being shared with older pupils. The system mimics the arrangement pupils witnessed in their primary schools. The form tutor replaces their class teacher and the Head of Year, their primary headteacher. Thus a secondary school organised into a horizontal system of year groups can be treated as five or more primary schools working under one roof to the directives of the headteacher and the senior management team. Such a system, with Heads of Years, Deputy Heads of Years and form tutors creates a management structure on top of the Heads of Department and subject teacher structure that may lead to conflicts of interest and of problems of resource distribution.

As with anything in education there are exceptions and some schools have combined both horizontal and vertical systems with pupils belonging to a house and a year group. In these schools the year group is the main organisational division with the house system 'bolted on' for activities, such as competitive sports.

The daily role of the form tutor

We have already stated that the role of the form tutor has become more and not less important. The form tutor is the one person to have daily contact with the pupils, monitoring their general well-being and possessing an exclusive overview of their progress across all subjects. Just 'being there' is an important factor, providing for the pupils an anchor of security in a large, sometimes impersonal institution.

Your own education, in terms of school studies and degree work will not have prepared you for the variety of routine and not-so-routine tasks that may face you as a form tutor. Reporting the death of a hamster, a dental appointment card, money for the day trip to Boulogne or the skiing trip to Austria, a problem about bullying, a swimming certificate to present and tales of woe concerning an incorrect item of uniform or a suspicious story about the dog chewing up the homework; these might well constitute the daily 'pastoral agenda' of a form tutor and all within a fixed ten-minute slot of registration-cum-AOB time. The range of issues raised in those few minutes may be greater than in the rest of your day in school. Admitting to not knowing the right answer may be your philosophy during lessons and pupils may accept that as a virtue but your responsibility as a tutor makes 'not knowing' unhelpful and possibly harmful for adolescents in your care.

Many of your pupils may come from very different backgrounds to yourself, may hold very different attitudes and may have faced a range of emotional experiences that you will never encounter except through them. The lives of some pupils may be so fraught with problems that you may wonder at how they manage to cope. Trying to empathise when you have no direct experience is challenging and not something that you can learn quickly. Learning to be a good form tutor may be more demanding than learning to be a teacher of your subject.

The role of the form tutor demands a certain amount of administrative competence coupled with the ability to think quickly about and around situations. With schools now obliged to report their attendance rates, filling in the register and 'chasing up' absences have become fundamental issues. A bona fide appointment is an 'authorised absence' and requires the appropriate notation in the register. It is easy to forget that the class register is a legal document which can be used as evidence in a court of law. Do you record someone as 'present' if their friends say the pupil is 'talking to a teacher'? As the attendance register fills up, truancy or other non-attendance related problems are quite easy to spot, especially if absence notes are not forthcoming. Absence notes themselves need monitoring as they are susceptible to forgery. Some pupils intercept letters from school and forge convincing replies. However, some pupils quite legitimately write their own absence notes which are then signed by a parent who is perhaps not a speaker or writer of English. The tutor would need to know this so that appropriate channels of communication can be established. Money is another issue: under what circumstances are you prepared to lend money to pupils? What do you do if you see a pupil carrying £50 in their pocket? The key issue to realise is that schools have policies and that, generally, knowledge of those policies reduces the dilemmas that you may face.

Bullying has become more of an issue over recent years. In the past, many schools would claim that they did not have a bullying problem. The evidence, collected over many years and in many countries, is that bullying is usually a much bigger problem than most teachers realise. A pupil who claims to have been bullied must always be taken seriously. A pupil asking for help needs time and reassurance, even if it is not immediately available. This gives a potent message first to those pupils who are bullied and, even more importantly, to would-be bullies who may be deterred by visible, decisive and speedy action by form tutors. Schools are required to have an anti-bullying policy and the form tutor needs to be familiar with this and with the associated procedures. So long as bullying is endemic to school life, many pupils will experience unhappiness as a result of incidents generated by the school culture. They need to know that the form tutor is the person to whom they can turn. With sensitive issues, counselling skills are needed and the form tutor, who is categorically not a counsellor, may well have to act as counsellor at times. This is an important distinction.

During the 1960s and 1970s, some schools were able to appoint counsellors but their numbers decreased as the recession bit. Counselling individuals will normally be part of the form tutor role but the lack of time and expertise will mean that many issues will, by necessity and perhaps to the benefit of a greater number of pupils, be explored within the tutor group context. The form tutor's role here is to create a supportive environment and to nurture support through activities such as role-play, drama, debate and discussion. One-to-one counselling, with all the time implications involved should still be the right of pupils, particularly those for whom the form tutor is the only caring adult that they encounter on a daily basis.

Tutor entitlement

In order to do the job of tutor effectively, the form tutor needs support and resources. Dolezal (1989) states that every tutor has an entitlement to:

- information on, and time with, individuals
- time with the group
- time with the parents
- time to prepare and access to resources
- support for development via reflection, review and training.

The tutor utilises this entitlement paradigm to describe similar entitlements for pupils, parents, year heads and subject teachers, and, in each case, stresses the importance of contact time, information accessing, appropriate resources and support.

Responsibilities and problems take up a fair share of the tutoring time available, but the picture is not one of unrelieved gloom. We would wish to celebrate the full range of achievements of all pupils, sometimes with due pomp and circumstance if certificates are to be awarded, for example, or a quiet word of praise to an individual pupil in another situation. Interestingly, pupils tend to dislike being praised in public because, it seems, it is embarrassing and because, for some, there is more status to be had in receiving a reprimand. When writing self-assessments, pupils are notoriously poor at identifying their strengths and achievements although these are often considerable. The form tutor needs to coax them out, thereby helping to increase the self-esteem of pupils and the construction of a more positive, more balanced image of self (for a discussion of the importance of self-image, see Chapter 11).

The tutor's role, which up to now may appear reactive and random, becomes coherent within the whole school personal, health and social education (PHSE) structure. In the best systems observed by the inspectorate, teams of tutors work alongside a head of year on a range of issues related to personal development relevant to each age group. This often results in a pastoral curriculum often constructed on the identification of what Hamblin (1993) calls 'critical incidents'. Thus a Year 7 group may undertake an induction programme, Year 9 may focus on 'Options' and Year 11 may look at study skills or careers. While Marland (1974, 1988) sees undeniable logic in this, he argues for a spiralling model whereby themes are constantly revisited but in different degrees and in different ways.

Assessment and communication

Another important function undertaken by the form tutor is that of assessment. Assessment and reports of one kind and another are a regular feature of the school calendar, one which inevitably combines the academic and pastoral roles (for an explanation of reporting and recording, see Chapter 16). The form tutor will, in fact, be the only teacher to have an overview of a pupil's progress across all subjects. Many schools have moved away from the end of year summative report and now build in periods of reviewing progress on a one-to-one basis in tutorial time. Some schools model this on the academic 'tracking' of pupils as happens in schools in the USA. This system is more likely to be targeted at older pupils who may have periodic GCSE support tutorials (Year 10 is a major transition time for pupils who may be launched into a different pace and style of learning and may quickly come to grief without support).

Coupled with this assessment role is that of communicator. The 'record book' or 'homework diary' serves both as a way of checking that homework is set and as a method of communicating with parents and guardians. As with any continuous monitoring, problems can be identified sooner rather than later, solutions negotiated, targets set and, of course, achievements recognised and rewarded. One issue here is the notion that although teachers are meant to be checking that pupils have recorded their homework, they are also checking that their colleagues have been doing their job in setting homework in the first place.

Teacher–pupil interactions

Delamont (1983) investigated the interactions that existed between groups within schools, the most important of which were those between teachers and pupils. She eloquently describes how teachers spend considerable thinking and talking time 'sizing up' pupils. From the body of knowledge that teachers have gained through their professional training and their experience gained within school, a network of systems, strategies and beliefs underpin and direct the way teachers interact with pupils. Pupil behaviour in the lessons, snippets of information gained about pupil's home lives during the lesson and pupil attainment provide the main sources of information from which teachers build a 'picture' of an individual pupil. Within two to three hours a week, in most secondary schools, a classroom teacher is expected to collect, reflect and act on the information gained from each of thirty or so pupils. It is not surprising that some pupils go unnoticed if their behaviour, lifestyle and progress do not immediately attract attention, nor is it surprising that, on occasion, a particular action, piece of information or untypical standard of work can result in individual pupils being misunderstood by their teacher and, as a consequence, stereotyped in future interactions.

Systems and individuals

The pastoral system provides a framework for initiating and sustaining shared perspectives of individual pupils. In secondary school, pupils are frequently taught by ten or more teachers and may be perceived differently by each one. This atomistic approach does little to help them to create a sense of identity as learners and as participants in the school system. The form tutor's role within the system is to mediate between the teachers and the learners. By presenting a more complete picture of the pupils in a class to its teachers, the form tutor may ensure that future interactions take place in an informed and stable environment – neither marred nor exaggerated by uncharacteristic episodes or behaviours.

Handy and Aitken (1988) stress that one of the most important factors in organisational theory is how the organisation is perceived by the individual, which, in the case of schools, must be the pupil. To provide an insight into this, a small piece of action research was undertaken by one of the authors of this chapter (JJ) in a large mixed London comprehensive in 1995. The main focus of the research was to investigate pupils' perceptions of the form tutor role. Forty pupils across years 7–11 were asked:

- What do you think a form tutor is for?
- Who do you think is a good form tutor?

The pupils had very clear ideas and gave responses which were remarkable in their uniformity on both issues.

The responses to the first question focused primarily on the pastoral support role, evidenced by comments such as 'to look after you', 'to see how you're doing' and 'to help you solve your problems'. Some aspects of organisation and administration were identified such as 'to take the register', 'to watch punctuality' and 'to help the kids during fire drills'. Most surprising of all was the fact that almost every response given made reference to what the pupils saw as a central disciplinary function of the tutor role, expressed in a variety of ways: 'to teach you to behave', 'to stop us from talking and getting into trouble' and, more graphically, 'to stop us from getting up and ranging around and stop fights'.

Responses to the second question exemplified and validated these comments, the pupils postulating the following qualities as essential for a 'good' form tutor:

- someone who listens
- having a sense of humour
- being helpful and understanding
- being strict and having the ability to keep order.

Typical responses were: 'She talks to people a lot and listens and she's good fun'; 'He's funny and he helps his tutor group and he's good at keeping order' and 'He's funny, but strict but he makes you laugh when he's strict'.

The usefulness of this small piece of research was a reminder of the expectations that the pupils have of the tutor. These reflect two very basic pupil needs: first, individual care and support, and secondly, the need for the teacher to maintain orderliness within the peer group. This concurs with Delamont's findings (1983) where she states that the 'main strength of a teacher's position is that, in general, pupils want her to teach and keep them in order'. While the demands put on teachers by their pupils seem simple, the means of providing for their needs remains a difficult and diversified task for the form tutor. Sizing-up pupils is a continuous and evolving task for the form tutor who is in a unique position – perceiving pupils in a holistic manner, mapping their strengths and weaknesses and recognising their successes and needs. As such, the form tutor fosters and supports the classroom interactions that can assist pupil learning.

References

Delamont, S. (1983) *Interaction in the Classroom*. London: Metheun.
Dolezal, A. (1989) *Longman Tutorial Resources*. London: Longman.
Hamblin, D. (1993) *Tutor as Counsellor*. Oxford: Basil Blackwell.

Handy, C.B. and Aitken, R. (1988) *Understanding Schools as Organizations*. London: Penguin.
Marland, M. (1974) *Pastoral Care*. London: Heinemann.
Marland, M. (1989) *The Tutor and the Tutor Group*. London: Longman.
Sutton C. (1992) *Words, Science and Learning*. Buckingham: Open University Press.
Tattum, D. (1988) Control and welfare, in R. Dale, R. Fergusson and A. Robinson (eds) *Frameworks for Teaching*. London: Hodder and Stoughton.
Wragg, E.C. (1993). *Class Management*. London: Routledge.

Further reading

Burgess, R.G. (1988) House staff and departmental staff, in R. Dale, R. Fergusson and A. Robinson (eds) *Frameworks for Teaching*. London: Hodder and Stoughton.
Button, L. (1974) *Developmental Group Work with Adolescents*. London: University of London Press.
Collins, N. (1985) *On the Spot: A Counselling and Guidance Handbook*. Oxford: Oxford University Press.
Davies, G. (1986) *A First Year Tutorial Handbook*. Oxford: Blackwell.
Hamblin, D. (1978) *The Tutor and Pastoral Care*. Oxford: Basil Blackwell.
Hargreaves, D.H. (1975) *Interpersonal Relations and Education*. London: Routledge and Kegan Paul.
Jones, A. (1970) *School Counselling in Practice*. London: Ward Lock.
National Curriculum Council (1990) *Curriculum Guidance 5. Health Education*. York: NCC.
Pring, R. (1984) *Personal and Social Education in the Curriculum*. London: Hodder and Stoughton.

Part 5 | Epilogue

Stephen J. Ball

Introduction

In this chapter I intend to reflect upon the role and purpose and thus the education and continuing professional development of the teacher. I have two related starting points for my discussion. First, I want to assert a key role for 'the teacher' as a 'public intellectual' (Aronowitz and Giroux 1991) in late modern society. I shall argue that teachers are important, but not as important as all that. Second, I intend to deplore the use of 'the teacher' as political 'folk devil' and criticise the ongoing attempts by governments in the UK and elsewhere to reduce the role of the teacher to that of classroom technician. From these starting points and in a round about way I will examine recent developments in educational 'research', or more precisely *educational science*, and education policy which contribute very forcefully to the reworking of the teacher as technician.

The politics of education over the past 20 or so years can be interpreted as centring upon a primary concern – the taming of teachers. The major thrust of much of the eruption of education policy during that period has been to control and discipline teachers. The work of teaching has become increasingly over-determined and over-regulated. Policy has been constructed 'in fear and loathing' of the teacher. Four main forms of control are being used in the UK in an attempt to capture, specify and delineate 'the teacher' and to reconstruct and redefine the meaning and purpose of teaching, both as vocational practice and mental labour. They are: the curriculum; the market and management; and most recently, and somewhat paradoxically,[1] *educational science*.

Here I am drawing on Brian Fay's distinction, also used by Gerald Grace, between policy science and policy scholarship (Fay 1975). As Grace (1995: 3) explains:

> Policy scholarship resists the tendency of policy science to abstract problems from their relational settings by insisting that the problem

can only be understood in the complexity of those relations. In particular, it represents a view that a social-historical approach to research can illuminate the cultural and ideological struggles in which schooling is located.

(Grace 1995: 3)

Fay defines policy science as:

that set of procedures which enables one to determine the technically best course of action to adopt in order to implement a decision or achieve a goal. Here the policy scientist doesn't merely clarify the possible outcomes of certain courses of action, he [sic] actually chooses the most efficient course of action in terms of the available scientific information.

(Fay 1975: 14)

This Fay suggests is a type of 'policy engineering': the 'policy engineer . . . is one who seeks the most technically correct answer to political problems in terms of available social scientific knowledge'. Here policy is both de-politicised and thoroughly technicised; the purview of the policy scientist is limited to and by the agenda of social and political problems defined elsewhere and by solutions already embedded in scientific practice, this is what Fay (1975: 27) calls 'the sublimation of politics'. It also produces, I suggest, another effect, that is – by a combination of financial restructuring and Faustian deal-making – 'the taming of the academy'. As a result, research perspectives and research funding are increasingly tightly tied to the policy agendas of government; the already weak autonomy of higher education having been re-defined as part of the cause of the nation's economic problems. Further, this problem-solving technicism rests upon an uncritical acceptance of moral and political consensus and operates within the hegemony of instrumental rationalism, or as Fay (1975: 27) puts it 'man [sic] must plan, and the function of the social sciences is to provide the theoretical foundation that makes this planning possible'. In this scientific and technical project for research the debates and conflicts which link policies to values and morals is displaced by bland rationalist empiricism, and the best we can aspire to is to be 'integrated critics' (Eco 1994). I take school effectiveness research as a case in point of policy engineering (see below).

The curriculum and the classroom

Put in simple terms, here I refer to the imposition of a National Curriculum and national testing and direct and indirect interventions into pedagogical decision-making. The three basic message systems of schooling – curriculum, assessment and pedagogy (Bernstein 1971) – are thus subject to change, and changes in any one system interrelate with and affect the others. In general terms, there is an increase in the technical elements of teachers' work and a reduction in the professional. Significant parts of teachers' practice are now codified in terms of attainment targets, programmes of study, and measured in terms of national tests. The spaces for professional autonomy and judgement are (further) reduced (cf. Dale 1989). A standardisation and normalisation of classroom practice is being attempted. The curriculum provides for standardisation and testing for normalisation – the establishment of measurements, hierarchy and regulation around the idea of a distributionary statistical norm within a given population. This begins with the testing of students, but raises the possibility of monitoring the performance of teachers and schools and making comparisons between them. There is also the possibility of linking these comparisons to appraisal and to performance-related pay awards. Performance-related pay schemes have already been piloted in some UK schools. Furthermore, significant changes in teachers' classroom practice can now be achieved by decisions taken 'at a distance' about assessment regimes or curriculum organisation. Thus, the reduction of coursework elements in GCSE assessment has profound implications for classroom work. And the introduction of separate programmes of study in National Curriculum subjects (most recently English) can 'dictate' the form of student grouping in the school. The possibility of the publication and comparison of examination and test scores may also play a part in teachers' decision-making about how much time to devote to whole class and individual work, or their distribution of attention between different students in the classroom, particularly in Years 10 and 11 when, in some schools, students on the GCSE C/D boundary are targeted for special attention. In all this there is an increasing concern about the quality, character and content of teachers' labour and increasingly direct attempts made by the state to shape the character and content of classroom practice.

Another form of intervention into pedagogy is the campaign among conservative cultural restorationists and some educational researchers to re-establish streaming and class teaching. Concomitantly, methods associated with progressivism are under attack (Alexander *et al.* 1992, *Panorama*, BBC-TV, 10 June 1996). What is important here is not so much what is being asserted in the 'debate' over methods as the 'effect' of these assertions in de-centring the teacher. What is achieved is a redistribution of significant voices. As always it is not just a matter of what is said but who is entitled to speak. The teacher is increasingly an absent presence in the discourses of education policy, an object rather than a subject of discourse.

> We're into a situation now where I think we are definitely not in control, I don't feel in control. I may feel consulted, but the consultations are more or less about what has been discussed and decided . . . even the style of heads of departments is becoming like that too, they're finding their room for manoeuvre is not that great either. So I'm not blaming them so much, they're being told to implement things, therefore they're coming over as being quite, not perhaps dictatorial, that's too harsh a phrase, but perhaps as being determinedly persuasive, 'that's what's going to happen'. And no doubt they're looking over their shoulder, because they're being told, 'look, you are the one that's accountable, so get these things done'. And that's it, the directive is taking shape . . .
>
> ('Experienced teacher, Flightpath
> Comprehensive' quoted in Ball 1994)

One of the worst things about the changes here is that we are not allowed to discuss them properly at staff meetings. If we raise an intelligent question, we are accused of being negative. Critical thinking, logical reasoning, all outlawed. You have to decode everything these days. When they say, 'we had a productive meeting', they mean no real discussion took place. Everyone nodded approval. Another success for the mindless public relations world we are creating.

('Mr Osborne, Brian Baru School',
quoted in Mac an Ghaill 1991: 307)

The market

The second element in the changing matrix of power within which schools are set also has far-reaching implications for the redefinition of teachers' work. The introduction of market forces into the relations between schools means that teachers are now working within a new value context in which 'image' and 'impression management' (the deliberate manipulation of messages and symbols to 'represent' the school 'as it would want to be known') are becoming as important as the educational process. The market is a disciplinary system and within it education is reconstructed as a consumption good. Children and their 'performances' are traded and exchanged as commodities. In relations between schools, the key element of the market is competition. 'The competitive process provides incentives and so evokes effort . . . The essence of the whole process is choice by the consumer; emulation, rivalry and substitution by the producer' (Reekie 1984: 37). Teachers' work is thus increasingly viewed and evaluated solely in terms of output measures (test scores and examination performance) set against cost (subject time, class size, resource requirements). Ofsted (Office for Standards in Education) pursues the calculability of the teacher further by scoring them during school inspections on a seven-point scale, from 'excellent' to 'failing'.

The processes of competition in education are driven by price and by supply and demand, much the same as other markets, except in contrast to most commodity markets prices are fixed in relation to local education authority budgets and a Department for Education and Employment (DFEE) approved formula. Nevertheless, the onus is upon schools to attract clients and maximise income. Marketing and income-generation are presently major priorities in the planning and decision-making activities of senior managers in many schools (Bowe et al. 1992). In some schools the discourses of financial planning and economic rationalism now operate in an antagonistic relation to the discourses of teaching and learning and pupil welfare.

The relationship of schools to 'consumers', the priorities of school organisation and the ethics of impression management are all affected by the market context. Impression management and responsiveness to the consumer re-orientate the values of the institution and subvert and reorder the priorities and purposes through which it presents itself. In crude terms, the important thing is to reflect back to parents their prejudices, setting aside experience and judgement. Traditionalism and academicism are accented, expertise in special needs provision is underplayed, for fear of giving the 'wrong' impression.

Management

The scenario outlined above already begins to point up the intimate relationship between the control exercised over teachers by the National Curriculum, parental choice and competition and the role of management. Management and the market are clearly closely intertwined in UK government thinking. As the Department for Education and Science explained:

> Local management is concerned with far more than budgeting and accounting procedures. Effective schemes of local management will enable governing bodies and headteachers to plan their use of resources – including their most valuable resource, their staff – to maximum effect in accordance with their own need and priorities, and to make schools more responsive to their clients – parents, pupils, the local community and employers.
>
> (DES 1988: 3)

The crucial point about both management and the market is that they are 'no hands' forms of control as far as the relationship between education and the state is concerned. They provide, in Kickert's (1991: 21) terms, 'steering at a distance' – a new paradigm of public governance. Steering at a distance is an alternative to coercive/prescriptive control. Constraints are replaced by incentives. Prescription is replaced by ex-post accountability based upon quality or outcome assessments. Coercion is replaced by self-steering – the appearance of autonomy. Opposition or resistance are side-stepped, displaced. From this perspective acquiring a market awareness and the skills of a self-monitoring and individual accountability within the context of 'normal' school activities, would, at least in theory, consolidate the basic principles of self-management within teachers' individual consciousness – decreasing the need for overt control. The individualisation of consciousness oriented towards performativity, constitutes a more subtle, yet more totalising form of control of teachers than is available in the top-down prescriptive steering of bureaucratic state planning. 'Resistance' in this context threatens the survival of the institution. It sets the dissenters against the interests of colleagues rather than against policies. Values and interests are thoroughly conflated. In the use of discretionary payments, loyalty and commitment become criteria for preferment alongside other aspects of 'performance'.

In all this some decisive shifts are achieved – from public debate to private choice, from collective planning to individual decision-making. Together, management and the market remove education from the public arena of civil society, from collective responsibility, and effectively 'privatise' it. The scope and availability of provision are no longer matters of national or local political debate or decision-making. They rest, on the one hand, with consumer choice and competitive individualism and, on the other, with the responsive, entrepreneurial decision-making of senior managers in schools. We have the closure and atomisation of civil society.

In general terms, at the heart of this reforming thrust, what is being attempted is a breakdown of the distinction between public and private goods and the public and private sectors.

Educational science

Management theories as modes of objectification place human beings as subjects to be managed. This is a 'discourse of right' which legitimates the exercise of authority. Its primary instrument is a hierarchy of continuous and functional surveillance. School effectiveness research can be seen to have played a crucial role in laying the groundwork for the re-conceptualisation of the school within which management discourse operates and has played its part in providing a technology of organisational measurement and surveillance. First, effectiveness studies and school-difference studies re-centred the school as the focus of causation in explanations of student performance and variations in levels of achievement; displacing or rendering silent other explanations related to the embeddedness of education in social and economic contexts. Further, in so far as the gaze of 'effectiveness' provides a scientific basis for the possibility of 'blaming' the school, it fits perfectly into the 'discourses of derision' (Ball 1990a) which target schools as 'causes' of general social and economic problems within society at large. In addition, the focus on measurable outcomes also articulates directly with the political process of the commodification of education involved in the creation of an education market. Second, this research provides a scientific concomitant to the political re-emphasis on excellence, diversity and selection and the attempt to develop methods of appraisal which can be used to identify (and punish) 'weak' and 'inadequate' teachers. Third, the effectiveness studies develop a technology of control which enables the monitoring and 'steering' of schools by applying 'neutral' indicators. In its ambition, as policy engineering, effectiveness research continually attempts to 'tap' and measure more of that which is schooling, including 'the "deep structure" of pupil attitudes and perceptions' (Reynolds 1990: 21). Thus, significant discursive and disciplinary work is done by effectiveness research.

In effect, through such schemes, teachers are entrapped into taking responsibility for their own 'disciplining'. Indeed, teachers are urged to believe that their commitment to such processes will make them more 'professional'. Moreover, effectiveness is a technology of normalisation. Such research both constructs a normative model of the effective school and abnormalises the ineffective or 'sick' school. In relation to the concepts of 'review', 'development' and 'self-evaluation' it then draws upon the 'confessional technique' (an admission of transgressions and a ritual of atonement) as a means of submission and transformation. The secular confession is founded on the notion of normal as against abnormal transposed from the religious opposition of sin and piety. Such a transposition is most clearly evident in the methods of 'appraisal'.

The normalising effects of 'effectiveness' are noted by Laurie Angus. In a recent review of school effectiveness literature, he comments that 'predictability and efficiency are valued to the extent that schools would

surely become dramatically more boring places than they are already'
(Angus 1993: 343). He goes on to suggest that:

> not only is there a lack of engagement with sociological (or other
> theory), but also effectiveness work is largely trapped in a logic of
> common sense which allows it, by and large, to be appropriated into
> the Right's hegemonic project . . . it advocates an isolationist, apolit-
> ical approach to education in which it is assumed that educational
> problems can be fixed by technical means and inequality can be
> managed within the walls of schools and classrooms provided that
> teachers and pupils follow 'correct' effective school procedures'.
>
> (Angus 1993: 343)

By such means 'normalising judgements' are turned upon the whole
school and each school is set in a field of comparison – which again
articulates with other current aspects of educational policy. An 'artificial'
order is laid down, 'an order defined by natural and observable processes'
(Foucault 1979a: 179). The definitions of behaviour and performance
embedded in the order and the norm are arrived at 'on the basis of two
opposed values of good and evil' (Foucault 1979a: 180). The good school
and the bad school, effective and ineffective practice, excellent and failing
teachers. Through 'value-giving' measures the constraint of a conformity
that must be achieved is introduced.

If self-examination fails, the expert, the consultant, the moral disciplin-
arian is at hand to intervene with their models of 'effective practice'. In
all this the scientific and the moral are tightly intertwined. In effect, given
the logic of management, ineffectiveness is seen as a disorder of reason
and as such susceptible to cure by the use of appropriate techniques of
organisation.

It is in this way that epistemological development within the human
sciences, like education, functions politically and is intimately imbricated
in the practical management of social and political problems. The scientific vocabulary may distance the researcher (and the manager) from the
subjects of their action but, at the same time, it also constructs a gaze that
renders the 'landscape of the social' ever more visible. Through method-
ical observation the 'objects of concern' identified in this landscape are
inserted into a network of ameliorative or therapeutic practices. The point
is that the idea that human sciences like educational studies stand outside
or above the political agenda of the management of the population or
somehow have a neutral status embodied in a free-floating progressive
rationalism are dangerous and debilitating conceits.

Theory, intellect and the postmodern teacher

As I have intimated at several points thus far all of the developments
outlined above have been set against, and in part made possible, by the
continuing 'discourse of derision' aimed at the teacher. This discourse,
focused in particular on the practices of comprehensive education and educational 'progressivism', in effect blames teachers for various aspects of
the UKs social and economic problems. The UKs position in international

comparisons of test performance serves as a recurring source of panic and recrimination aimed at teachers in general, their education and training, and particular practices – like group work or mixed-ability teaching. An example comes from the *Daily Mail*; under the headline: 'College crackdown as study highlights Britain's slide – Trainee teachers go back to basics', it was reported that:

> Teacher training will undergo a revolution in a desperate attempt to improve school leavers' skills. Stung by alarming new evidence that Britain is lagging dangerously behind its competitors in literacy and numeracy, the Cabinet has ordered drastic reforms. All trainees will have rigorous instruction in the skills of teaching children the three Rs under a new 'national curriculum' for colleges . . . Government insiders say that the crisis in standards reveals the effect of decades of trendy and politically correct training at colleges.
>
> (*Daily Mail*, 12 June 1996: 2)

There are three significant things to note about such discursive activity. First, there is the issue of what does and does not get 'blamed' in such attacks. That is to say, teachers and their 'training' are the objects of derision, the policies which frame and orient their work rarely are. This displacement also serves to exclude other possibilities for blame; like working conditions, levels of funding, social problems or changes within society generally. It is always and obviously the teacher. Second, these 'attacks' typically rest upon simple but powerful polarities – in this case 'basic skills' as against 'trendy and politically correct training'. The 'effectiveness' of such polarities is related both to the divisions they generate and the unities they conjure up. Thus, basic skills are the one, straightforward solution to the problem identified, all teachers are trained in 'trendy and politically correct' methods (whatever they might be) which are taught in all 'colleges' and these are the cause of all 'the problems'. The problems are 'elsewhere', and can be fixed by a direct intervention which has the effect of even closer specification of teacher preparation and teachers' work (which brings me to the issue of teacher education more generally, see below). Third, within this rhetorical structure those who hold out against change, defenders of 'the trendy and politically correct', can be picked off as both subversive, damaging to the interests of children and the nation, and reactionary, irrationally persisting with the old, disreputable ways. In terms of education policy and practice the sayable and unsayable, doable and undoable, are carefully demarcated. A classic division between madness and reason is enacted.

Teachers and teacher educators are effectively silenced in all this. Their contributions to 'debate', such as it is, are tainted by their positioning within the discourse of derision as 'the problem'. Any response, and counter-arguments are, *a priori*, self-interested or politically motivated – 'they would say that wouldn't they'. Of course, this tactic, which has been used repeatedly over the past 20 years is self-defeating in educational terms but politically expedient. It is self-defeating in that it both undermines the morale and commitments of teachers and steadily weakens parents' and students' respect for and commitment to education and the teacher.

The question begged by the rather sad and depressing account presented here is what kind of teacher do we want or need, or indeed, deserve at this point in our history and, therefore, how should we educate our teachers? In terms of current policies the answer is relatively obvious. Teachers are cast as state technicians whose work is doubly, and contradictorily, determined by government prescriptions on the one hand and the requirements of the education marketplace on the other. Alongside this goes the notion that teachers and teaching are nothing special. That many people could be teachers, as so defined. That teaching involves transmission of a variety of 'basic skills' by the application of simple classroom technologies and management tactics. These can be acquired primarily through an on-the-job apprenticeship. These ideas lay behind various attempts to open-up new routes into teaching – Licensed and Articled teachers and the 'Mums army' (for more details, see Chapter 4) – and the ongoing redefinition and reorientation of teacher education – as teacher training, as specified by the CATE (Council for the Accreditation of Teacher Education) curriculum, as school-based, as basic-skills (see the *Daily Mail* extract above). Again all this is set within a powerful binary. The conception of teaching as constituted, practised and 'taught' as a set of specified skills and competencies is set over and against the role of theory from the education of teachers. One of the intentions embedded in UK government policies for 'teacher training' since the mid 1980s has been to expunge 'theory'. Theory is seen as both irrelevant and dangerous, (I shall return to the issue of theory below.) Thus, writing in *The Times* in 1992, Sheila Lawlor (Education Director of the 'new right' Centre for Policy Studies) accepted the usefulness of Government reforms which intended to put 'more emphasis on subject teaching and classroom work'; and introduced the CATE criteria and the National Curriculum, but believed that they did not go far enough.

> Those reforms may have led to some changes in the broad division of courses and the allocation of time but the heart of the problem remained. Training was in the hands of those whose livelihood rested on the propagation of some educational theory or other.
>
> (*The Times*, 6 January 1992)

There is a second response to the question of the future of 'the teacher'. That is the one which sees teachers as increasingly irrelevant as new technologies take over more and more of the role of schools in 'educating' society. This may be so, who knows? There is some evidence of such developments, but not so much in the UK. It would seem that we will be relying on the older, solid, fixed technologies of classrooms and teachers for some time to come.

So I turn to a third conception of 'the teacher' and, thus teacher education – the teacher as public intellectual or what we might call 'the postmodern teacher'. Aronowitz and Giroux (1991: 109) assert that:

> We believe that teachers need to view themselves as public intellectuals who combine conception and implementation, thinking and practice, with a political project grounded in the struggle for a culture of liberation and justice.

They go on to suggest that, 'Teachers need to provide models of leadership that offer the promise of reforming schools as part of a wider revitalisation of public life.' Clearly, the emphasis on technical-rational goals, prescribed knowledge and teaching competencies has sidelined (to the extent that they were ever present) issues such as the need for critical reflection, the need to focus on learning rather than teaching, issues of social justice, and praxis as opposed to poiesis. All of this attributes significant responsibilities to the teacher for and in society; not simply in teaching subjects or functional skills in traditional classroom contexts and relationships, but in developing intellect and citizenship. As educational leaders, such teachers would 'create programs that allow them and their students to undertake the language of social criticism, to display moral courage' (Aronowitz and Giroux 1991: 109). Here education and the teacher are privileged in the sense that they play a central role, but certainly not an exclusive one, in the re-vitalisation of political culture, civic virtue and intellectual intelligence. Theory is central to this conception of teaching and would have a central place in the initial and continuing education and professional development of the postmodern teacher, and in their practice.

Why is theory regarded with such suspicion? Why go to such lengths to exclude it from the preparation of teachers? The point is that theory can separate us from 'the contingency that has made us what we are, the possibilities of no longer seeing, doing or thinking what we are, do or think' (Mahon 1992: 122). Theory is a vehicle for 'thinking otherwise'; it is a platform for 'outrageous hypotheses' and for 'unleashing criticism'. Theory is destructive, disruptive and violent. It offers a language for challenge, and modes of thought, other than those articulated for us by dominant others. It provides a language of rigour and irony rather than contingency. The purpose of theory is to de-familiarise present practices and categories, to make them seem less self-evident and necessary, and to open up spaces for the invention of new forms of experience.

The point about theory is not that it is simply critical. In order to go beyond the accidents and contingencies which enfold us, it is necessary to start from another position and begin from what is normally excluded. Theory provides this possibility, the possibility of disidentification – the effect of working 'on and against' prevailing practices. The point of theory and of intellectual endeavour in the social sciences should be, in Foucault's words, 'to sap power', to engage in struggle to reveal and undermine what is most invisible and insidious in prevailing practices. Theories offer another language, a language of distance, of imagination. And part of this, as Sheridan puts it is 'a love of hypothesis, of invention', which is also unashamedly 'a love of the beautiful' (Sheridan 1980: 223) – as against the bland, technical and desolate languages of policy science and policy entrepreneurship. However, in taking such a stance public intellectuals (in schools, universities and elsewhere) cannot simply seek to re-inhabit the old redemptive assumptions based upon an unproblematic role for themselves in a perpetual process of progressive, orderly growth or development achieved through scientific and technological 'mastery' or control over events or by the assertive re-cycling of old dogmas and tired utopias. The process of disidentification also involves a transformation of intellectuals and their relationship to the 'business of truth'. What I am groping towards here is a model of the teacher as a cultural critic offering perspective rather than truth; engaged in what Eco calls 'semiotic guerrilla warfare' (Eco 1994). Or to put it another way:

> Criticism is a matter.of flushing out that thought (which animates everyday behaviour) and trying to change it: to show that things are not as self-evident as one believed, to see that what is accepted as self-evident will no longer be accepted as such ... As soon as one can no longer think things as one formerly thought them, transformation becomes both very urgent, very difficult and quite possible.
>
> (Foucault 1988a: 154)

For Foucault, freedom lies in our ability to transform our relationship to the past, to tradition and much less in being able to control the form and direction that the future will take. In the mad scramble of late modernist life we seem to need to latch on to elusive images of who we are and what our existence means. But in the place of such rigid and anterior norms and discourses, we must, as Richard Rorty suggests, locate a playing field on which ideas are toyed with and radical ironies explored. In Rorty's post-epistemological view, edifying conversations, rather than truth-generating epistemological efforts must be the staple of a post-structural social science (Rorty 1979) and by extension, the staple of teacher development and classroom interaction.

Note

1 The paradox is that for the most part the UK Conservative Government regards any kind of social science research will grave suspicion.

References

Alexander, R.J., Rose, A.J. and Woodhead, C. (1992) *Curriculum Organisation and Classroom Practice in Primary Schools: a Discussion Paper*. London: Department of Education and Science.

Angus, L. (1993) The sociology of school effectiveness, *British Journal of the Sociology of Education*, 14(3): 333–45.

Aronowitz, S. and Giroux, H. (1991) *Postmodern Education: Politics, Culture and Social Criticism*. Oxford, Minneapolis: University of Minnesota Press.

Ball, S.J. (1990a) *Politics and Policy Making in Education*. London: Routledge.

Ball, S.J. (1990b) Management as moral technology: a Luddite analysis, in S.J. Ball (ed.) *Foucault and Education: Disciplines and Knowledge*. London: Routledge.

Ball, S.J. (1994) *Education Reform: A Critical and Post-structural Approach*. Buckingham: Open University Press.

Beck, U. (1992) *Risk Society: Towards a New Modernity*. Newbury Park: Sage.

Bernstein, B. (1971) On the classification and framing of educational knowledge, in M.F.D. Young (ed.) *Knowledge and Control*. London: Collier-Macmillan.

Bowe, R. and Ball, S.J. with Gold, A. (1992) *Reforming Education and Changing Schools: Case Studies in Policy Sociology*. London: Routledge.

Dale, R. (1989) *The State and Education Policy*. Milton Keynes: Open University Press.

Dale, R. (1992) Recovering from a Pyrrhic Victory? Quality, relevance and impact in the sociology of education, in M. Arnot and L. Barton (eds) *Voicing Concerns*. Wallingford: Triangle.

Department of Education and Science (DES) (1988) *The Local Management of Schools*, Circular 7/88. London: DES.

Eco, U. (1994) *Apocalypse Postponed*. London: BFI Publishing.

Fay, B. (1975) *Social Theory and Political Practice*. London: Allen and Unwin.

Foucault, M. (1977) *Language, Counter-memory, Practice: Selected Essays and Interviews*. Ithaca: Cornell University Press.

Foucault, M. (1979a) *Discipline and Punish*. Harmondsworth: Peregrine.

Foucault, M. (1979b) 'On Governmentality', *Ideology and Consciousness*, 6(1): 5–22.

Foucault, M. (1988a) *Michel Foucault: Politics, Philosophy and Culture – Interviews and Other Writings, 1977–1984*. New York: Routledge.

Foucault, M. (1988b) Truth, power, self: an interview with Michel Foucault, in L.H. Martin, H. Gutman and P. Hutton (eds) *Technologies of the Self*. Amherst: University of Massachusetts Press.

Foucault, M. (1991) Questions of method, in C. Gordon, P. Miller and G. Burchell (eds) *The Foucault Effect: Studies in Governmentality*. Brighton: Harvester/Wheatsheaf.

Grace, G. (1995) *School Leadership: Beyond Education Management: An Essay in Policy Scholarship*. London: Falmer Press.

Kickert, W. (1991) Steering at a distance: a new paradigm of public governance in Dutch higher education, European Consortium for Political Research: University of Essex.

Mac an Ghaill (1991) State school policy: contradictions, confusions and consternation, *Journal of Educational Policy*, 6(3): 299–314.

Mahon, M. (1992) *Foucault's Nietzscean Genealogy: Truth, Power and the Subject*. Albany: SUNY.

Reekie, W.D. (1984) *Markets, Entrepreneurs and Liberty*. Brighton: Wheatsheaf.

Reynolds, D. (1990) Research on school/organisational effectiveness: the end of the beginning, in R. Saran and V. Trafford (eds) *Management and Policy: Retrospect and Prospect*. London: Falmer Press.

Rorty, R. (1979) *Philosophy and the Mirror of Nature*. New York: Routledge.

Sheridan, A. (1980) *Michel Foucault: The Will to Truth*. London: Tavistock.

Index

BEGINNING TEACHING IN THE SECONDARY SCHOOL

Joan Dean

- What does the work of a newly qualified teacher involve?
- What difficulties are teachers likely to encounter and how can they best be tackled?
- What does research tell us that is relevant to the work of newly qualified teachers?

This book is written mainly for newly qualified teachers but would also be of interest to teachers in training. It deals with all aspects of the teacher's work in the secondary school starting with advice to those about to start in their first post or a teaching practice, and going on to look at the students and the role of the teacher. There are chapters on teaching strategies and class management and the use of time and space. The book also considers special needs, including those of the exceptionally able; the role of the form tutor; evaluation and assessment, and strategies for avoiding stress. The text is illustrated by a number of case studies and each chapter includes suggestions for further reading and a check list for teachers to use in evaluating their work. Each chapter also contains references to relevant research.

Contents
Introduction – Getting started – The students – The teacher – Teaching strategies – Class management – The management of time and space – Students with special needs – The role of the group tutor – Evaluation and assessment – Conclusion – Appendix – References – Index.

192pp   0 335 19619 5 (Paperback)   0 335 19620 9 (Hardback)

RACISM AND ANTIRACISM IN REAL SCHOOLS

David Gillborn

- How are 'race' and racism implicated in education policy and practice?
- What does effective antiracism look like in practice?
- How can teachers and school students be encouraged to think critically about their racialized assumptions and actions?

In exploring these questions David Gillborn makes a vital contribution to the debate on 'race' and racism in education. He focuses on racism in the policy, research, theory and practice of education, and includes the first major study of antiracism at the level of whole-school management and classroom practice. The voices of teachers and school students bring the issues to life, and illustrate the daily problems of life in urban schools. This is a fascinating picture of the key matters facing managers, classroom teachers and their students as schools struggle to develop strong and workable approaches to anti-racist education. It is accompanied by a critical review of current debates and controversies concerning 'race', ethnicity and identity.

Arguing for a critical return to the concept of 'race', *Racism and Antiracism in Real Schools* represents an important addition to the literature on the theory and practice of education in a racist society.

Contents

Racism and schooling – Part I: 'Race', research and policy – Discourse and policy – Racism and research – Theorizing identity and antiracism – Part II: 'Race' and educational practice – The politics of school change – Antiracism and the whole school – Antiracism in the classroom – Student perspectives – Rethinking racism and antiracism – Notes – References – Name Index – Subject index.

240pp   0 335 19092 8 (Paperback)   0 335 19093 6 (Hardback)

MARKETS, CHOICE AND EQUITY IN EDUCATION

Sharon Gewirtz, Stephen J. Ball and Richard Bowe

- What has been the impact of parental choice and competition upon schools?
- How do parents choose schools for their children?
- Who are the winners and losers in the education market?

These important and fundamental questions are discussed in this book which draws upon a three year intensive study of market forces in education. The authors carefully examine the complexities of parental choice and school responses to the introduction of market forces in education. Particular attention is paid to issues of opportunity and equity, and patterns of access and involvement related to gender, ethnicity and social class are identified.

This is the first comprehensive study of market dynamics in education and it highlights the specificity and idiosyncrasies of local education markets. However, the book is not confined to descriptions of these markets but also offers a systematic theorization of the education market, its operation and consequences. It will be of particular interest to students on BEd and Masters courses in education, headteachers and senior managers in schools, and policy analysts.

Contents
Researching education markets – Choice and class: parents in the marketplace – An analysis of local market relations – Managers and markets: school organization in transition – Schooling in the marketplace: a semiological analysis – Internal practices: institutional responses to competition – Choice, equity and control – Glossary of terms – References – Index.

224pp   0 335 19369 2 (Paperback)   0 335 19370 6 (Hardback)